Nonprofit Mergers and Alliances

A Strategic Planning Guide

NONPROFIT LAW, FINANCE, AND MANAGEMENT SERIES

The Art of Planned Giving: Understanding Donors and the Culture of Giving by Douglas E. White

Beyond Fund Raising: New Strategies for Nonprofit Investment and Innovation by Kay Grace

Charity, Advocacy, and the Law by Bruce R. Hopkins

The Complete Guide to Nonprofit Management by Smith, Bucklin & Associates

Critical Issues in Fund Raising edited by Dwight Burlingame

Developing Affordable Housing: A Practical Guide for Nonprofit Organizations by Bennett L. Hecht

Financial and Accounting Guide for Not-for-Profit Organizations, Fifth Edition by Malvern J. Gross, Jr., Richard F. Larkin, Roger S. Bruttomesso, John J. McNally, and Price Waterhouse LLP

Financial Planning for Nonprofit Organizations by Jody Blazek

Fund-Raising: Evaluating and Managing the Fund Development Process by James M. Greenfield

Fund-Raising Fundamentals: A Guide to Annual Giving for Professionals and Volunteers by James M. Greenfield

Fund-Raising Regulation: A State-by-State Handbook of Registration Forms, Requirements, and Procedures by Seth Perlman and Betsy Hills Bush

Intermediate Sanctions: Curbing Nonprofit Abuse by Bruce R. Hopkins and D. Benson Tesdahl

The Law of Fund-Raising, Second Edition by Bruce R. Hopkins

The Law of Tax-Exempt Healthcare Organizations by Thomas K. Hyatt and Bruce R. Hopkins

The Law of Tax-Exempt Organizations, Sixth Edition by Bruce R. Hopkins

The Legal Answer Book for Nonprofit Organizations by Bruce R. Hopkins

A Legal Guide to Starting and Managing a Nonprofit Organization, Second Edition by Bruce R. Hopkins

Managing Affordable Housing: A Practical Guide to Creating Stable Communities by Bennett L. Hecht, Local Initiatives Support Corporation, and James Stockard

Nonprofit Boards: Roles, Responsibilities, and Performance by Diane J. Duca

The Nonprofit Counsel by Bruce R. Hopkins

The Nonprofit Guide to the Internet by Robbit Zeff

The Nonprofit Law Dictionary by Bruce R. Hopkins

Nonprofit Litigation: A Practical Guide with Forms and Checklists by Steve Bachmann

The Nonprofit Handbook, Second Edition: Volume I—Management by Tracy Daniel Connors

The Nonprofit Handbook, Second Edition: Volume II—Fund Raising by Jim Greenfield

The Nonprofit Manager's Resource Dictionary by Ronald A. Landskroner

Nonprofit Organizations' Business Forms: Disk Edition by John Wiley & Sons, Inc.

Partnerships and Joint Ventures Involving Tax-Exempt Organizations by Michael I. Sanders

Planned Giving: Management, Marketing, and Law by Ronald R. Jordan and Katelyn L. Quynn

Program Related Investments: A Technical Manual for Foundations by Christie I. Baxter

Reengineering Your Nonprofit Organization: A Guide to Strategic Transformation by Alceste T. Pappas

Reinventing the University: Managing and Financing Institutions of Higher Education by Sandra L. Johnson and Sean C. Rush, Coopers & Lybrand, L.L.P.

Strategic Planning for Nonprofit Organizations: A Practical Guide and Workbook by Michael Allison and Jude Kaye, Support Center for Nonprofit Management

Streetsmart Financial Basics for Nonprofit Managers by Thomas A. McLaughlin

Successful Marketing Strategies for Nonprofit Organizations by Barry J. McLeish

The Tax Law of Charitable Giving by Bruce R. Hopkins

The Tax Law of Colleges and Universities by Bertrand M. Harding

Tax Planning and Compliance for Tax-Exempt Organizations: Forms, Checklists, Procedures, Second Edition by Jody Blazek

The Volunteer Management Handbook by Tracy Daniel Connors

International Guide to Nonprofit Law by Lester A. Salamon and Stefan Toepler & Associates

Private Foundations: Tax Law and Compliance by Bruce R. Hopkins and Jody Blazek

Financial Management for Nonprofit Organizations by Jo Ann Hankin, Alan Seidner, and John Zeitlow

The Universal Benefits of Volunteering: A Practical Workbook for Nonprofit Organizations, Volunteers and Corporations by Walter P. Pidgeon, Jr.

Nonprofit Mergers and Alliances

A Strategic Planning Guide

Thomas A. McLaughlin

John Wiley & Sons, Inc.

New York • Chichester • Weinheim • Brisbane • Singapore • Toronto

This text is printed on acid-free paper. ♾

Published simultaneously in Canada.

Library of Congress Cataloging in Publication Data:

McLaughlin, Thomas A.

Nonprofit mergers and alliances : a strategic planning guide / Thomas A. McLaughlin.

p. cm. — (Nonprofit law, finance, and management series)

Includes index.

ISBN 0-471-18088-2 (cloth/disk : alk. paper)

1. Nonprofit organizations. 2. Consolidation and merger of corporations. 3. Strategic alliances (Business) I. Title. II. Series.

HD2769.15.M34 1998

658.1'6—DC21 97-13384

CIP

Printed in the United States of America

10 9 8 7 6 5 4 3 2

To Gail, Paul, and Emily

About the Author

Thomas A. McLaughlin is a Senior Associate in the division of tax-exempt and governmental services of the accounting and consulting firm BDO Seidman, L.L.P. Having served as an executive of two social service agencies and a trade association, he has more than 23 years of nonprofit management experience. He is also an adjunct professor at the Boston University School of Social Work and a contributing editor for the Nonproft Times. He is the author of *Streetsmart Financial Basics for Nonprofit Managers,* also published by Wiley.

Contents

Preface

We are right on schedule. Historically, the American health and human services system, of which nonprofits are a significant part, seems to re-invent itself approximately every 30 years. In the 1930s there was the New Deal, which gave rise to many of the laws and programs that still exist today. In the early 1960s we had the Great Society and the beginning of such programs as Medicare, Medicaid, the Community Mental Health Centers Act, and other groundbreaking programs.

Today, we are in the very beginning stages of what promises to be the single largest restructuring of our system of service delivery in history. It is reaching across sectors, from hospitals and social service agencies to associations and cultural groups. But unlike those two previous landmark periods, this restructuring is not federally initiated. It is not a top-down program filled with mandates and laws and regulations that must be allowed.

Rather, this restructuring is privately initiated and privately managed. It goes by code names such as managed care, capitated payments, block grants, and program-related investments. While the impetus is economic in nature and more or less actively encouraged by all levels of government, the details of the transition are largely left up to the private nonprofit sector itself.

This situation has two results. First, it is enormously disorienting for everyone involved. There are few templates and fewer certainties. Ambiguity abounds. The old rules are changing and it is far from clear what the new rules look like.

The second result is that the focus of innovation in the nonprofit sector has shifted. In the last two or three decades, innovation occurred in the delivery of services. Terms such as community residences, outreach programs and supported employment that are commonplace today were revolutionary program innovations as recently as the 1960s.

The bulk of innovation today will take place not in programs and services but in management. And the thrust of that innovation will be toward greater collaboration between nonprofit organizations and all others carrying out similar missions. What we call mergers and alliances are really just a part of the innovation that the nonprofit sector must deliver over the next two or three decades.

This is why, for nonprofit organizations of all kinds, considering mergers and alliances will be the new strategic planning for the 21st century. Nonprofit service systems in areas ranging from the arts and health care to social services and advocacy are on the verge of significant change. Nonprofits in some parts of the country have already entered into a period of rapid change in the way they are structured and managed. Most others will follow. This book attempts to explore the choice that many of them will be making.

To some in the nonprofit field, the idea of mergers is scandalous and distasteful. Decades of media coverage of Wall Street mergers has permanently linked the idea to images of human suffering caused by heartless downsizers whose designer suits are worth more than their ethics. To inflict the same fate on nonprofits seems cruel and unnecessary.

Yet this restructuring is occurring in banking, financial services, retailing, bookselling, and many other fields. There is no reason to think that nonprofits will—or should—be immune from it simply because of their tax status. The reality is that mergers among nonprofits are necessary. In many parts of the country today, there are simply too many nonprofits. This situation is caused by many factors, including the best of intentions, but the plain fact is that having an excessive number of nonprofit organizations actually weakens the collective power of the entire field. Organizations that should be serving a mission must instead spend disproportionate amounts of resources worrying about how they are going to fund it, manage it, and perpetuate it.

Nevertheless, nonprofit mergers are different from those in the for-profit sector. A fair amount has been written about the latter. Very little has been written about nonprofit mergers, probably because the widespread adoption of the technique is relatively recent. Consequently, board members and nonprofit executives considering a merger or some form of strategic alliance often can find little specific guidance. More insidiously, transposing the for-profit merger experience and related techniques to the nonprofit sector is often frustrating and ineffective. Nonprofit collaboration of this kind requires different expectations, processes, and techniques. We hope that this book will help fill that gap.

Happily, nonprofits have many structural advantages that can allow them to enter into mergers without repeating the same behaviors as some of their Wall Street counterparts. We will cover these in some depth, because managers and board members who understand these dynamics will be able to make the process work for their missions and their consumers, and it is to them among others that this book is addressed.

We have two goals for this book. The first is to describe a context for nonprofit mergers, including a discussion of the forces helping to shape nonprofits' use of mergers and alliances. It is important that nonprofit managers and board leaders be aware of both the similarities and the differences in their sector's merger patterns and techniques. Ultimately, a nonprofit sector that knows well how to collaborate will be far more effective in the pursuit of its public-spirited mission.

The second goal is to provide concrete guidance based on actual nonprofit mergers. Ultimately, the information presented here will become common knowledge among some nonprofit managers and the inevitable cadre of merger specialists that the trend will create. Some of it will likely be proved wrong, while undoubtedly a few strategies and tactics that no one has even thought about yet will become routine. For the present, it is hoped that this material will be a creditable start.

The book is divided into five sections: a discussion of reasons to merge; a description of the C.O.R.E. model, a merger/alliance analysis framework; structure choice analyses; and a section each on the processes of mergers and alliances. The book tends to present specific material on the how-to of mergers in the last two sections. The computer disk included with the book offers many practical forms and templates for carrying out a merger or developing an alliance. Whenever possible, passages in the text that relate to a computer file are marked with a disk icon and the name or names of the corresponding file.

Different readers will treat this book differently. Most readers can be expected to gain something from the first two sections. Board members, executives, funders, government officials, nonprofit advisors, and academics can profit from all sections, while managers may wish to concentrate primarily on the last two sections. Staff members of nonprofit organizations may focus largely on one of the last two sections, as their situation permits.

As prevalent as they are likely to become, mergers are not a panacea for all the challenges facing the nonprofit sector. Carried out poorly, they can create as many problems as they solve. Nor do they always work. There is much we all must learn about both the process of merger and alliance development and how to manage the new entities that they create. But there is no doubt that it is time to begin this grand restructuring of society's most underrecognized and underappreciated sector. Let the rebirth begin.

THOMAS A. MCLAUGHLIN

January 1998

Acknowledgments

As always, many people assisted in the development of this book in some way. I have been fortunate enough to have worked on dozens of nonprofit mergers during the last several years, and virtually every one provided an important insight or a fresh perspective on some aspect of nonprofit mergers. These insights were just as likely to come from a casual conversation as an intense board meeting, and I am sure that I am unaware of the origins of some of the ideas in this book.

I owe a special acknowledgment to many clients. I carried out my first mergers while working for Dr. Yitzhak Bakal, though I would not have said that that is what I was doing at the time. Later, I applied some of my early methodologies on behalf of Punky Pleten-Cross, Kathy Wilson, Dianne McCarthy, Geri Dorr, and Deb Ekstrom. Along the way, some individuals have made valuable suggestions, challenged my concepts, or helped clarify parts of my thinking. Ginny Purcell, Jim Boles, Kitty Small, Bill Taylor, Jim Heller, Rob Hallister and Sue Stubbs are among these. Dave Eaves and the A & F merger subcommittee at Partners for Community developed the prototype for one of the computer files, and Dennis Rice suggested the idea for another one.

Many association executives have helped develop the content of this book by giving me the opportunity to speak to their members. Betty Beene, Geri Ratcliff, Bob Hatheway, Michael Ford, Michael Morris, Michael Parker, Gordon Allen, Drew Hastings, Ann Stern, and Dave Garvey are just a few of the people to have extended me this opportunity.

Rick Moyers at the National Center for Nonprofit Boards was kind enough to commission a booklet in 1996 that helped me crystallize my framework, which until that time had been lying in pieces in the workshop of my mind.

At John Wiley & Sons, editor Marla Bobowick first signed on to this book project at a time when for many people the terms "merger" and "nonprofit" didn't belong in the same sentence. Martha Cooley succeeded her and has been very supportive.

Most important of all, I want to thank Gail, Paul, and Emily for the time and attention from me that they sacrificed to help make this book a reality.

PART ONE

Decide to Merge

CHAPTER ONE

The Preferred Strategic Option of the Future

The best time to consider a merger is *before* it is necessary, when coming together with another organization will mean combining strength with strength, and when the collective energies and creativity of the two entities can be used proactively instead of being sapped by the demands of crisis management. Old-fashioned thinking about mergers is that they should occur when one organization is too weak financially to continue and needs a merger in order to survive. When the time comes to choose between merging or going out of business, it's too late. Decisions made in the haste and desperation of near bankruptcy are not likely to be good ones, nor will the mission be adequately served.

The single most compelling reason to merge nonprofits or to consider developing an alliance is to tap into complementary strengths. Many times two different organizations come together and in the process discover unexpected sources of strength in the other: the ballet company with excellent administrative systems merges with a dance troupe with high public recognition; a small clinic that owns its own building merges with a larger set of clinics that needs to diversify its asset base; an executive director with good "outside" skills brings her organization together with another whose executive director is excellent at overseeing operations, and so forth.

Good leaders read the signals of their environment, and nonprofit leaders are no exception. For many decades, nonprofit board members and senior managers have been astutely reading the

Note: Why Mergers Have a Bad Name

One of the reasons why mergers may have a bad connotation for nonprofit board members and managers, aside from the botched for-profit mergers the media has covered so thoroughly, is because of when they occur. In any industry experiencing consolidation, weaker players will always be the first to merge or go out of business. What the casual observer doesn't realize is that whatever bad things may happen to such an organization after a merger, such as services being shut down or people losing jobs, would almost certainly have happened without a merger, and probably worse.

messages sent by funding sources, government regulators, and social leaders. Universally, these signals said *grow.* Expand your services. Create more organizations. Innovate.

Nonprofits responded. Beginning in the mid-19th century with child welfare and mental health organizations and continuing throughout this century with the modern hospital, symphony orchestras, economic development groups, museums, civic leagues, associations, and acquired immunodeficiency syndrome (AIDS) service providers, the nonprofit form of organization has witnessed a tremendous growth in scope and application.

Along the way, something subtle but very important occurred. Nonprofits by nature are intermediary organizations, serving as private buffers between the individual and government. While acting as an instrument for a particular part of society, they serve as the proving grounds for social values and as vehicles for interpreting potential changes in those values. Consequently, nonprofits as a class invariably reflect the times in which they were created. On a practical level, this happens because they must solve most of the same economic challenges that any business must solve: ensuring a demand for their service or product, selecting and hiring staff, and overseeing operations. At a higher level, it happens because nonprofits represent one way in which society attempts to prevent or manage what could be a major dysfunction in the way it operates at a given time.

Thus, the mayor of an early 20th century mill town invited an order of nuns to create an orphanage for children whose parents were killed or maimed by unsafe production processes and poor public health practice; a major national advocacy organization mobilized an unprecedented campaign of fundraising and research to eradicate polio; and governments at all levels encouraged the creation of shelters for people left homeless by trauma ranging from poverty to domestic violence. What all of these and countless other programs had in common is that they were the product of a unique mix of social, economic, cultural, political, legal, and other forces.

The people who lead these programs must negotiate an individualized balance of all these forces in order to be successful. It is an underlying theme of this book that there is about to be a dramatic change in the way that balance is achieved. Put simply, the way to be successful as a nonprofit organization will be very different in the early 21st century than it was in the past fifty years. Like all business organizations, nonprofits must learn to do more with less. This means not just that costs must be cut, but that there needs to be a real change in the way nonprofits deliver their services. In short, they must improve their productivity. Mergers and networks are simply one of the logical ways of doing so.

THE INDUSTRIAL AGE

As the nature of the larger society and the economy changes, so does the nature of accomplishment. Exhibit 1.1 shows the changes in key aspects of success in any business organization. To derive a word portrait of successful companies of the 20th century until about 1980, read down the first column. Starting in the beginning of the 20th century, Henry Ford pioneered mass production of

From The Industrial Age . . .	*To The Information Age*
Hierarchy	Network
Command and control	Shape and influence
Square footage	Megabytes
Vertical integration	Virtual integration
Employee	Consultant
Growth	Productivity
Innovation through programming	Innovation through management

Exhibit 1.1 Patterns of Change in Nonprofit Strategic Accomplishment

such unprecedented high volume that his company set records it would take others decades to reach. The Western industrialized countries fought and won two wars using principles of what was known as scientific management. Manufacturers of all kinds invested in huge manufacturing facilities designed to produce goods faster, cheaper, and more efficiently than ever before.

To manage this enormous production engine, companies erected large office buildings comparable to their factories and filled them with employees assigned ever smaller pieces of larger tasks; not surprisingly, this was the same method by which the workers themselves were managed. The company was seen essentially as the sum of a number of slots into which people with the requisite skills were placed. Management, whether on the shop floor or in the executive suite, became essentially a matter of manipulating occupants of slots. Personal growth was defined as climbing up a ladder, the better to scale the pyramid-like hierarchical organization. Enormous companies spanning many different industries and even countries were put together, and company growth was defined as increases in revenue.

NONPROFITS REFLECT FOR-PROFITS

Like successful companies in for-profit business, nonprofits of the Industrial Age tended to be hierarchical command-and-control organizations too. To deliver their chosen services, they needed to invest extensively in bricks and mortar—orphanages, residential schools for developmentally disabled, hospitals, and museums. If they came together at all, it was to expand services, such as when hospitals attempted to open nursing homes in order to capture a downstream share of the market.

Employees were needed to make these service enterprises work. Often, great quantities of employees were required, which is one of the unacknowledged reasons why community-based programming in the social services spread so rapidly during the 1970s when the idealistic first wave of the baby boom generation was entering the workforce. Government funding became widely available to support this style of programming, spurred on at least indirectly by Great Society programs and the evolution of the welfare state. Growth was the priority. Foundations experimented with a variety of grant making initiatives, and government encouraged innovation in programming either directly through contracting and grant making or indirectly through tentative direction giving or loose oversight. Like their for-profit counterparts, managers in the nonprofit world thought in terms of slotting commodity-like employees, secure in the knowledge that there would always be more of everything next year.

THE INFORMATION AGE

Now to the right hand column. No longer is our production capability likely to be organized around traditional pyramid-like hierarchies emphasizing militaristic command-and-control techniques. Today, organizations are less hierarchical and more like a network. Management must rely on shaping and influencing instead of issuing outright orders (although issuing orders is usually quicker and easier, social and economic conditions simply prohibit it). The predominant volume measurement is not the square footage of a manufacturing plant but the power of its information system (and the latter is not necessarily even operated from the plant but possibly from a different country altogether).

Traditional ownership linkages are being replaced with complicated relationships called such things as alliances, outsourcing agreements, and privatization. Employee-style relationships of the middle part of the century have been replaced with what are effectively multiyear consulting engagements, meaning that the average employee's reason for existence lies not in the way they fill a slot, but in the economic value they bring to the company. Highly visible management initiatives ranging from downsizing to corporate spinoffs to total quality management (TQM) all have in common a striving to improve productivity.

As always, nonprofit organizations of all kinds are reflecting the same changes seen in the for-profit sector as they too adapt to the unique demands of the Information Age. The drivers of change for nonprofits may appear to be reduced government funding and more intense competition for the philanthropic dollar, but those are only symptoms of the same changes sweeping their for-profit counterparts. Although nonprofit organizations rarely were able to afford the size and richness of management that the for-profit sector favored, the underlying models of organization and style of management were always the same.

So are the changes taking place now. Nonprofit organizations adapting their existing services today operate more like networks. They invest in information processing capability and consider forming strategic alliances with each other and even with for-profit organizations. They too embrace TQM, or something like it, and find that they must be even more vigilant about unnecessary spending than ever before. It is no accident that characteristics of new nonprofits founded in the 1990s resemble the right hand column far more than the left. From associations and international relief organizations to hospices and software foundations, nonprofit accomplishment of the late 20th century and beyond bears a distinctive stamp.

What this all means is that existing nonprofit organizations, as instruments of society, must change their ways of doing things. A big part of that change is to embrace mergers and integrated service delivery as the preferred strategic option of the next decade, rather than as something one must be forced to consider.

THE FREESTANDING NONPROFIT AND OTHER RUGGED INDIVIDUALISTS

It may not have seemed it at the time, but IBM symbolized the beginning of the Information Age in the mid-1980s with a simple change in its advertising. For the first few years of its existence, the IBM PC had used the lovable tramp created by silent movie star Charlie Chaplin as its logo. In many ways this was a good choice. Charming and funny, the little tramp was designed to be as engaging in print and television advertising as the company wanted its personal computers to be.

But with the introduction of newer and more powerful versions of the PC designed to be linked together in networks, the company had a problem. The lovable tramp, for all his endearing and non-threatening qualities, was the ultimate individualist. If the future was in networking, as IBM correctly foresaw, they needed a completely different theme. And what better way to bring alive the idea of computers in a team than to feature in advertisements the single best known team in America at the time—the soldiers of M*A*S*H, the wildly popular movie and television series.

Did IBM make this switch with as much deliberation and foresight as we have implied? Maybe, maybe not. It really doesn't matter. The point is that the changeover from standalone to team has been planted in our collective public consciousness for longer than we realize.

WHY NONPROFIT SERVICES ARE FRAGMENTED: A STORY

The practice of maintaining heroin addicts on methadone is not an easy business. The clients are a notoriously fickle lot with multiple physical and psychological problems and a tendency to operate outside of the law or to associate with people who do. Governmental authorities impose rigid controls and pay as little as possible to groups providing the service. Many professionals scorn the whole idea of methadone treatment and their colleagues who work in the field, and absolutely no one would choose a methadone clinic as a neighbor.

Most providers of methadone services are single site providers, often connected in some way with a hospital or a larger substance abuse treatment organization. In one state, however, an individual for-profit entrepreneur opened a methadone clinic in the late 1980s. Initially, the clinic took only private paying clients, of which there are a surprising number in urban settings. Later, methadone became a Medicaid reimbursable service.

When that single for-profit clinic began, the only other methadone providers were traditional single-site nonprofits. After two years, the original clinic added a second site in a major underserved city. A year later, it added a third. Within five years, the for-profit clinic had captured 50 percent of the market.

Why did this happen? Two separate organizations' stories will serve to explain. One of the other nonprofit methadone providers was a large city medical center. Their mandate to serve the urban poor was clear, but the institution's market was hemmed in on all sides by larger suburban and national teaching hospitals and it had little choice anyway. They had opened one of the first methadone clinics in the state, but not without internal controversy. The clinic's location off campus near a large municipal parking garage was a reliable indicator of the service's place in the hospital's social and political pecking order. Even if they had wanted to expand to other geographic locations—and there was no indication that they did—it was politically inconceivable.

Another methadone treatment provider was located halfway across the state in a small city that was, politically, economically, and literally, an island. Under the leadership of a charismatic executive director, they would have perhaps been ready to take on other methadone services but based on the fact that the cultural identification with their city was enormously strong among both board and staff. Acquiring the necessary capital for expansion would also have been a problem.

These two situations illustrate why it was easy for a for-profit firm to dominate the market. First, the entrepreneur chose to go into business. He had worked for another methadone service provider and felt that there were opportunities to provide better services and to make money in the process. By contrast, all the nonprofits either had been effectively asked to begin providing methadone services by funding sources or health officials, or did so only incidentally to their fundamental mission. Second, all the nonprofit providers were constrained—at least in their own institutional psychologies—by geographic ties. Once the need for methadone or any other service was fulfilled in their area there was little incentive to try filling a similar need elsewhere. Finally, expansion of any kind in nonprofit organizations is limited by lack of access to capital.

This story of market development illustrates the barriers that must be overcome among nonprofit board members and their executives if they are to position their organizations for maximum effectiveness in the 21st century. The natural tendency to focus services in a narrowly defined geographic area, the lack of an inherent motive to spur growth, and the inability to raise large amounts of capital are powerful elements that tend to keep nonprofits isolated from each other and fragmented in their delivery of services.

Part of what mergers and strategic alliances will do is to lower some of those externally imposed barriers that tend to make services fragmented and inefficient. The ideal of integrated services will likely occupy managers in all sectors of the economy for the next few decades, whether in nonprofit services or retailing or warehouse storage and delivery. Much of the practical structure of this idea we cannot even begin to glimpse yet. One thing that we can understand, however, is that organizations must be economically sized in order to participate in this new level of integration.

Note: The Third Health Care Revolution Is about to Begin

All the talk about the revolution in health care is becoming predictable, widely understood, and, well, a teeny bit boring, so let's skip directly to the third revolution. This is where we'll find something highly unpredictable, virtually unconsidered by the public at large, and packed with enormous potential for positive change.

First, a sentence for each revolution. The first revolution is the nation-wide realignment in our health care system propelled by managed care organizations, changing public funding policies, and universal demand for lower cost and higher efficiency. The second revolution, a bit more focused than the first, is the far-reaching changes that the first one will cause in the nation's nonprofit hospitals.

The third revolution is the impending takeover of large parts of the health and human services system by for-profit, publicly held companies. When a for-profit company buys a nonprofit hospital, the proceeds from the sale typically create a grant-making foundation. Put simply, the third revolution will consist of how we answer this question: what are we going to do with all that money?

Each of these conversions will result in the transfer of millions of dollars to newly created foundations. For example, some conversion plans call for the creation of a nonprofit community health foundation with the proceeds from the sale of a hospital.

Why are these conversions occurring? In a word—*capital.* To compete in tomorrow's acute care world will require massive infusions of capital to create state of the art information processing systems and to upgrade aging plant and equipment. Nonprofit organizations, without the ability to sell shares to raise investment capital, must rely on governmental assistance, internal profitability, or borrowing to raise their capital. Governmental assistance is not forthcoming, profitability is constrained by regulation and increasingly shrewd purchasers, and borrowing is inherently limited, so the logical next step is to consider a buyout.

To put the amount of money these transactions could produce into context, consider the following. In one state, the largest domestic foundation gives a total of annual discretionary grants in the $8 to $9 million range. All the United Way organizations in the entire state account for roughly $50 million in yearly contributions. The amount of investment in even a medium size conversion, if invested very conservatively and the proceeds used strictly to fund programs, would equal the size of both the largest foundation and all United Ways put together.

Clearly the influence of foundations created by hospital conversions is potentially huge. Which brings us back to the question: what will be done with all that money?

The answer is of more than casual interest. On a moral level, that capital is the product of many years worth of different payers and funders, many different managers, and a massive number of economic trends and developments. In short, it comes from the public at large, and that means it must be used for solving some of the most pressing health and welfare issues of today.

The problem is that the task of overseeing grant making is much different than the task of managing a hospital, and trustees that do not appreciate the difference risk squandering a major public asset. They will have the responsibility, ethical if nothing else, to see that the funds are not used for narrowly provincial purposes. They will have a legal responsibility to be accountable in their decisions, and they will need to carry out their philanthropic activities with a long term vision.

Along with this infusion of new capital into the health and social welfare system will come new laws, new regulations, and perhaps even new organizations. Most states will be hard-pressed to envision the specifics of each until the first conversion or two occurs, but by then it may be too late. The time to start preparing for the third revolution is now.

CHAPTER TWO

Achieving Economic Size

Nonprofits generally are forced to spend a lot of time focusing on their revenues and expenses, and virtually no time on their economics. Funding sources give money as though it were a stack of wood, which they insist on being burned in a stove of their own specifications. The result is that a growing nonprofit is like a multistory building heated entirely by a basement filled with stoves, each capable of warming no more than a room or two, instead of a single centralized heating system.

AN ILLUSTRATION

Foreign Neighbors Institute (FNI) is a $1.9 million nonprofit organization dedicated for many years to helping its city's recent immigrants. Its revenues come from a variety of sources, including state and city government, the Legal Services Corporation, the United Way, and a small amount of special event fundraising. By far, its single largest revenue source is the United Way.

Immigrants typically require a variety of types of assistance, including language instruction, job search, housing support, legal advice, adjustment counseling, and so forth. Most immigrants need at least one of these services over a period of time, and many need more than one. Predictably, FNI's smorgasbord of services is paid for by a comparable smorgasbord of funding sources. City and state education monies pay for language instruction, legal funding sources pay for legal advice, mental health and social service funders pay for adjustment counseling, and so on. United Way money, however, is unrestricted.

Note: The Nature of Nonprofit Competition

More and more, nonprofit managers speak easily of competition between their organizations. Externally, the media and the general public are beginning to realize, that the absence of a profit motive does not mean the absence of competition. And since competition is the bedrock of our economic system, the increased sense of competitiveness among nonprofits is generally applauded. Yet it still confuses and annoys many people who equate competition with wastefulness or unsavory business practices.

Part of the answer lies in the nature of competition in the nonprofit sector. When Ford and General Motors compete, it is as two major suppliers for millions of buyers. When forty nonprofit social service agencies of all sizes and sophistication levels compete in the same geographic area for program funding, which comes largely from one or two government agencies, it is very different. Ford and General Motors compete in the consumer market, where a small number of suppliers are all that are needed for millions of buyers. In the social service example, the agencies represent a large number of suppliers to a very small number of buyers.

Competition in this type of setting—which is typical of most social service systems around the country—is not true competition as in a consumer setting. Rather, it is more like competition between different departments of the same large company: possibly intense, but ultimately having more in common interests than differences.

In the traditional view, FNI presides over a dizzying array of programs and services, or stovepipes. But immigrants using these services do not compartmentalize their needs in the same way. Usually FNI staff act as de facto case managers to insure that the immigrant in need gets the appropriate services. In effect, FNI's real value is as a general contractor—a party hired not for specific expertise but rather to plan, design, and coordinate the efforts of others.

Looking at FNI's yearly revenue from a traditional revenue-and-expense perspective clearly suggests that United Way funding is a major part of operations, and that if the agency ever lost that money it would have to make serious budget cuts. An economic analysis takes this obvious conclusion one step further. Not only is the United Way money a big part of its revenue stream, it funds the agency's only rationale for existence. Language instruction can be obtained elsewhere, for example, and the agency is actually a rather small provider of job training and of legal and mental health services. What United Way funding does is provide enough money to cover all of those cross-disciplinary activities that no other funding source even recognizes but which are its single most compelling claim to public support.

Should the United Way ever decide to reduce or transfer its funding to other populations in need, FNI would have to define itself as little more than a menu of services, hoping that it could survive by skimming a bit of administrative funding from each. More positively, however, FNI may actually have a unique model which could be extended to other immigrant service providers. Should it choose to define its underlying economics in this way, FNI's logical strategic direction would be to prove that its model works well both for users of the service and for society. If they could do this, it could mean tremendous growth and recognition for the agency, and potentially even the beginnings of an entirely new way of providing services to immigrants.

In FNI's case, ignoring economics would have led to the right conclusion—to protect United Way funding at all costs—for the wrong reason (because without it we'll have to cut the budget). More important, it would completely miss the entrepreneurial opportunities inherent in the very services that United Way funds make possible. In practical terms, FNI has made a bet either that United Way will never reduce its funding or that they have a model that works and can be replicated elsewhere.

ECONOMICS ARE A PART OF STRATEGY

Board members, nonprofit managers, and advocates all must begin making nonprofit economics part of their strategic planning processes, and one of the simplest ways of doing that is to consider the role of economic size in its field. Let's begin with a statement of a goal:

> *An organization has achieved its economic size when it can operate over a period of years without substantially reducing its net assets (fund balance).*

Net assets—which used to be called fund balances—are simply the nonprofit organization's equivalent of net worth or accumulated surplus. When an organization incurs a deficit in any given year, it reduces its net assets by the amount of the deficit. Over time, a string of deficits will reduce net assets to zero or below, and the agency will face bankruptcy. As with a for-profit company, successive yearly deficits in a nonprofit mean that current management is using the built-up net assets of previous managers to stay alive. In other words, it is mortgaging its future.

At base, economic size has to do with the ability of the organization to cover its fixed costs. These are expenses that will be incurred regardless of the volume of service the nonprofit provides. Fixed costs typically are things such as occupancy costs, depreciation on assets, and interest payments. For labor-intensive operations like nonprofits, compensation and benefits also act very much like fixed costs, since labor is such an essential element in providing services.

Put all these costs in a budget and there isn't much room left—most of the remaining costs that will go up or down, depending on the volume of service, are small amounts. Fixed costs simply limit a manager's discretionary spending, and when they get to an insupportable level the agency either finds outside funders to pick up the difference or eventually goes out of business. As the demands on nonprofits continue to increase and funding continues to be cut or restricted, more and more agencies will experience a financial crunch. In fact, a failure to achieve economic size will be one of the primary reasons for nonprofits merging or restructuring in the early part of the 21st century.

There will probably never be a statistically reliable way of predicting economic size for any given organization because the factors that determine it are so variable and not usually under the nonprofit's direct control. Still, it is possible to identify some of the elements that combine to determine the economic size. Some of the more common ones follow.

Industry

Predictably, the nature of the nonprofit's field determines a great deal about its economic size. The economic size for a museum is considerably different from the economic size of an independent living facility for elders. Furthermore, the distinctions between certain types of organizations can blur over time, thereby altering the nature of the economic size. For instance, most hospitals were stand-alone facilities until at least the 1980s. By the beginning of the 21st century, in most industrialized states, the definition of a hospital will be virtually synonymous with an integrated system of acute care hospitals, physicians' practices, clinics, nursing homes, and support services. Even then, some of the smaller networks—in objective terms much larger than a stand-alone facility used to be—will falter because they will not have achieved the new economic size.

Government Regulation

Next to industry type, the single greatest determinant of economic size of most nonprofits is the degree and nature of its governmental regulatory environment. The formula is simple: the greater the degree of governmental regulation, the lower the economic size. This phenomenon has occurred in industries as diverse as airlines and public utilities.

In the nonprofit field, a classic example of the effects of governmental policy is the history of associations of retarded citizens (or ARCs). Until the 1960s, ARCs were largely advocacy organizations. But with the retreat of government from a provider of services role, these formerly advocacy-oriented organizations were called upon to begin providing services. Fairly quickly in states where this transition occurred, ARCs found themselves having to grow larger organizations quickly in order to have the infrastructure necessary to administer these newfound responsibilities.

Labor Markets

Labor in most nonprofits is a fixed cost over short spans of time. Any service that is open 24 hours a day or that must meet minimum staffing standards of some kind has to deal with costs that are predetermined within a relatively narrow range.

Another aspect of labor that cements it as a fixed cost is collective bargaining. Labor cost is particularly intractable because of the nature of the collective bargaining process, but also because the "political" characteristics of nonprofits can easily become political in the electoral politics sense of the term. One major nonprofit institution trying to merge with a public entity needed more than two years to make the idea work because neither labor nor management could agree on terms for a very long time.

The changing nature of labor markets also complicates this aspect of economic size. Not only do segments of nonprofit service delivery have natural life cycles—mental health clinics are a mature type of entity, for example, while homeless shelters are still very young in their cycle—but local labor markets can fluctuate widely too. During recessions, nonprofits typically face soft labor markets (i.e., it's easy to hire employees), while prosperity brings hard labor markets because the labor force has other options. Hard labor markets can force employers to pay proportionately more for staff, which can increase the pressure on agencies' fixed costs. This is what happened during the late 1980s in parts of the country during the recession.

Geography

Geography shapes economic size. When an organization must cover the entire nation, a physically large state or just a sizable rural area, travel costs are inescapable. Rural agencies that must do any kind of outreach inevitably find that it takes longer and is therefore costlier than the same service in an urban area. In some instances, it simply may not be feasible to deliver a service. Health clinics that depend on a certain volume or cultural organizations that need a concentrated market are examples here.

Use of Capital

Any time a nonprofit has to invest in capital assets to provide a service—typically buildings and equipment—it increases its fixed costs. Not only does it commit to paying back loans it may have obtained to buy the asset in the first place—a classic fixed cost—but large assets always require upkeep and specialized staff to make them work properly. All these things raise the minimum economic size for the acquiring organization.

Capital requirements are one of the most important forces determining economic size for nonprofits. Especially because nonprofit corporations cannot raise capital through selling shares, an in-

Note: The Life Cycles of Nonprofit Organizations

Nonprofit organizations can be said to have distinct life stages just like any type of business organization, and the place where each type of nonprofit finds itself says a lot about the possible readiness to merge of a particular organization. Here is one framework for analyzing the "life stage" of groups of nonprofits:

- *Formless.* In this stage there are not enough comparable nonprofits to constitute a recognizable type. Different groups respond to similar social needs and economic realities in similar ways without necessarily understanding why or even communicating with each other. Affiliations of any kind are virtually out of the question. Nonprofits associated with telecommunication issues or innovative urban youth services are good examples of this category.
- *Growing.* There is at least a general recognition that the particular nonprofit service is needed, but most of the energies are devoted to building organizations and solving operational problems.
- *Consolidating.* At this stage the general type of agency is recognized and accepted by society and the nonprofit sector itself. Some organizations take on a leadership role while others struggle to come into being in order to cover geographic gaps left by the early types. The groups create formal associations and other support entities, and a recognizable national identity begins to emerge. Battered women's shelters are just beginning to enter this stage.
- *Peaking.* As a field and as individuals, these nonprofits enjoy newfound acceptance and growing influence. The pace of new entrants slows, but those already in existence experience previously unimagined success in areas such as operations and public relations. Mergers occur for strategic purposes when strong players take over the few weak ones which falter. Health maintenance organizations began to peak during the 1990s.
- *Maturing.* Maturing nonprofits have long ago hit their peak and are beginning to lose some of the strategic momentum

they had earlier. The services they offer are now being offered at least in part by others or are no longer perceived to be as necessary. No one can doubt their collective influence, but some are beginning to doubt their future. Hospitals are at this stage of development.

- *Refocusing.* Once past maturity, some nonprofits find they must reinvent themselves in order to survive. Some do, others fade gradually away or merge what's left of their services with compatible groups at an earlier stage. Many orphanages refocused themselves to become special needs service providers.

crease in the need to make massive investments in new buildings and major pieces of equipment puts greater pressure on management. If the minimum investment level rises high enough, some nonprofits are forced to fold. This is the scenario playing out currently among hospitals. It is also the reason why at extreme points (likely to be seen only in the health care field), for-profit companies with their far greater access to low-cost capital may have a distinct advantage.

Typically, economic size increases more rapidly than the rate of inflation. As a consequence, nonprofits may have to grow a bit

Tip: How to Know if You're Keeping Up Your Capital Investment

To find out if your nonprofit is keeping up its capital investment level, try this test. Find the agency's total accumulated depreciation and divide it by the depreciation charge for that year. The result will give you an "accounting age" of all property plant and equipment measured in units called "accounting years." The higher this number, the lower your investment in replacing old assets. See whether the number of years makes sense in the context of your overall strategic direction. Better yet, calculate the same ratio for a handful of nonprofits comparable to yours and see where you stand versus others doing the same thing.

fintools.xls

Note: Need More Benefits?

Sometimes it's helpful to be able to cite other potential benefits of a merger or alliance. Here's a laundry list—some may apply in your circumstances, others won't. Take the ones that fit.

- Acquire intangible assets (e.g., a prized board member)
- Acquire tangible assets (e.g., a building)
- Change staff compensation patterns
- Create more varied career options for employees
- Create operational efficiencies
- Gain greater visibility in the community
- Gain market share
- Improve fundraising
- Improve prospects for a new service
- Increase political clout
- Rejuvenate the organization
- Reorganize more easily

attques.doc
attques.xls

faster than the rate of inflation just to stay ahead. With governmental and many private sources of funding either plateaued or declining in many service sectors, growth is no longer just a matter of hiring the right proposal writer or making contact with a good foundation or two. In fact, significant growth in most mature or near-mature nonprofit sectors will be virtually impossible for the foreseeable future *except* through mergers.

A word about growth. There is a prevailing sentiment against bigness in much of the nonprofit community, and for good reason. A great deal of what nonprofits have done well in the past has been firmly rooted in local areas with all the responsiveness and grass roots characteristics that that entails. Many nonprofit leaders reject growth itself, arguing that it will dilute the nature of the organization. For some types of nonprofits they are undoubtedly right. But for the majority there is no intrinsic reason why they could not grow significantly larger and still maintain faithfulness to their mission and their roots. Moreover, the absence of growth can lead to the kind of stagnation and tiredness that society cannot afford in its mediating organizations. A component of achieving economic size is therefore learning how to grow strategically, and not simply quantitatively.

APPENDIX 2A

Low on Cash and Options (Case Study with Responses)*

A few national publications dedicated to nonprofits have begun considering various aspects of mergers and alliances. Here's a case study with three responses reprinted with permission from the September/October 1996 issue of "Board Member," a publication of the National Center for Nonprofit Boards.

Alex Joyner shifted nervously on the overstuffed couch as he waited for his appointment with Susanna Ridge, a program officer at the Aaron and Elizabeth Wolfe Family Foundation. While he always enjoyed his visits with Susanna and appreciated her consistent support and valuable advice over the years, Alex had good reason to be nervous. For the fourth time in three years, he was about to ask for "emergency" funding to help the Metropolitan Arts Project (MAP) through a financial crisis.

The Wolfe Family Foundation was one of the few community grantmakers with an interest in promoting innovative and avant-garde art forms. Five years ago, when Alex had taken over as executive director, the foundation was one of a dozen corporate and foundation supporters of MAP—now it was one of four. Contributions from the Wolfe Foundation comprised nearly 40 percent of MAP's current annual budget.

---

*Reprinted with permission from *Board Member* (September/October 1996), a publication of the National Center for Nonprofit Boards, Washington, DC.

Several factors had precipitated the current crisis. MAP had lost one major funder when two local banks merged; another had withdrawn its support after a controversial exhibit featuring the American flag. A major cut in appropriations from the state arts agency had been the last straw. With no reserves and thousands of dollars in unpaid bills, the future of the Metropolitan Arts Project had never looked bleaker.

Alex heard a conference room door open and stood to greet Susanna Ridge, who was cordial but serious as they walked to her office. After getting Alex a cup of coffee, Susanna sat down across from him at the small conference table. "I've discussed your proposal with Mrs. Wolfe and with several other members of our board," she began. "We'll do what we can to help, but we're becoming more and more uncomfortable with this crisis mode of operation. We don't feel it's a strategic use of resources to bail you out every year."

"I know we've asked a lot recently," Alex replied. "It seems like every time we come up with a plan to get back on track, we get hit with something else."

Susanna nodded her understanding, then continued. "It goes without saying that we enthusiastically support MAP's work. You're a unique resource to our community. However, given your recent experiences, we're no longer confident that MAP is viable as a stand-alone organization. Next week, our board plans to approve the emergency grant you requested. We'd also like to give you an additional $5,000 to study a possible merger with another arts organization. As a program operating within another nonprofit, you'd have more financial security and would be able to concentrate on what you do best."

"Of course, we don't want to dictate to you; we're just trying to give you the resources to take a serious look at the possibility of merger. It's up to you how to proceed."

THE BOARD'S RESPONSE

Charlotte D'Arcy, chairperson of MAP's 15-member board of directors, stood at the end of the board table, magic marker in hand, next to a large easel. The board's discussion of Susanna's suggestion had been long and inconclusive. She and Alex studied the list of discussion points that were summarized on the easel pad.

"The board seemed evenly divided about the pros and cons of a merger," Charlotte said. "Board members recognize that a merger could bring increased stability and perhaps save money on administration, but they fear loss of visibility and freedom to pursue our mission. I'm also worried that we won't be very attractive as a merger partner. We have no money and a controversial reputation. I want to take advantage of this opportunity, but I'm not sure how we should proceed."

Alex nodded. "Susanna wants a report next month on how we plan to use the grant, so we need to do something."

What should Charlotte and Alex do?

—Some Solutions From:

Marta Sotomayor, Executive Director, The National Hispanic Council on Aging, Washington, D.C.

Unfortunately, MAP's situation is not unique; financial difficulties are becoming more the rule than the exception. In the present environment, many organizations in the private and public sectors are struggling to balance dwindling financial resources, increased demands, and changing priorities. Every nonprofit organization must be cognizant of this new reality and prepare itself to make different types of plans and decisions if it is to survive.

Resolving MAP's crisis requires more than confronting the interrelated issues of this new environment, but in this situation the merger is given as the only possible option. Mergers are not always the best option, particularly when done under pressure or crisis.

Also, I am troubled that this is the fourth time in three years that MAP has made an appeal to the foundation because of a financial crisis. Was the board aware of these changes in financial status? Were they dealing with these issues *before* they became a crisis?

The decision to merge must be made under different circumstances, requiring examination of every possible option in the context of the new environment, considering possible partnerships and collaborative relationships, and examining the availability or deployment of resources. The outcome of this potential merger could well be more innovative responses to the community's needs, but the board must make this decision in a much broader context.

This situation clearly points out the tremendous need for nonprofit boards to stop and assess an environment that inevitably will bring drastic and sudden changes. For certain, there is a need to identify and discuss the roles and responsibilities of all the sectors so that the nonprofits' ability to address critical societal problems improves.

Lynette M. Montoya, Board Vice President, Youth Shelters and Family Services, Santa Fe, New Mexico

As a funder, the Wolfe Family Foundation is in a good position to suggest a merger, or any contingencies they deem appropriate. It is much more desirable to consolidate services and see a merger succeed than to see a single nonprofit fail. And a failure is reflective of the funder as well as the defunct nonprofit.

The board of MAP should use the money to hire a trained facilitator. The board is responsible for a final decision about merging, and a facilitator can help the group gather information so that the board members reach agreement—and it's important that the board reach a consensus because it will create a forum for quick implementation of their final decision.

A merger would likely be the best decision. One of the many challenges faced by MAP is finding a nonprofit that is similar in vision while allowing for some autonomy. But the weak position of MAP could be attractive to another nonprofit because the more stable nonprofit would benefit by becoming the surviving entity of the two organizations.

Once a potential partner is found, the boards of both organizations should attend a joint retreat and once again use a trained facilitator to determine the pros and cons of the potential merger, with a final commitment in place to continue the efforts. A paid consultant can review budgeting, programming, and personnel policies—and help the board work out a plan of action. The $5,000 grant from the foundation could be a worthy investment, ultimately creating a new entity that would greatly benefit the community.

Thomas A. McLaughlin, Senior Associate, BDO Seidman, LLP, Boston, Massachusetts

Charlotte, forget about studying mergers, just do one. MAP needs action, not contemplation. Take the money and run to a merger facilitator. Worried that the foundation will object? Don't. Susanna was just being nice. What she was really saying is that she's tired of the aggravation and she wants you folks to do something. She likes Alex, but lately he's been like a little brother, constantly annoying, and you can't shake him.

Let's talk facts here. As a corporation, MAP is history. You say the board is evenly divided? That's code for lacking leadership. Take charge, Charlotte. Tell them that there's a difference between MAP the legal entity and MAP the mission. Ask them to make two lists. For the first one, ask them to tell you sincerely what they would hope to gain from a merger. For the second, ask them to worry out loud about a merger. Now take the second list and flip it around. If a merger will gain you the first list while finding ways to avoid the second, why not do it?

Next step: clarify your mission. Is it to present art? Foster controversy? Make people think? Maybe MAP knows, but the rest of us can't tell. Your facilitator can be helpful here, too.

And why would you be such a sorry merger partner? Money isn't everything in nonprofit mergers. You're in a metropolitan area—I'll bet there are a few arts or related groups that would love to have a thought-provoking program as part of their offerings. Do pay attention to compatibility between MAP's and a merger partner's cultures, however.

The first duty of this board is to preserve the mission. Let somebody else deal with the bank and negotiate leases. You've got art shows to run.

CHAPTER THREE

The Logic of Integrated Service Delivery

Consider the following scenario: A child is taken to a hospital emergency room with clear signs of abuse and neglect. He is treated and transferred to the medical/surgical floor while the state department handling child abuse cases is notified. The state agency assesses the child, confirms the abuse, then assigns him to a private organization for case management. A publicly funded attorney is brought in to deal with the implications of removing the child from his natural family and after a day or two the child is referred to a provider of foster care. To help him cope with the trauma the child is assigned to a psychologist with a local mental health center. Follow-up for the physical abuse is to be provided by the child's previously assigned physician at a local health center.

Look closely at this progression of events. Within a few days of the incident, the child has been seen or in some way touched by seven different entities. This pattern is not unusual. In fact, something like it is far more likely to be the norm than virtually any other scenario.

Fragmented service delivery is so common that we barely even think about it. Yet it doesn't have to be that way any more. Services don't need to be broken up into artificial segments called departments or bureaus or divisions they way the used to be. New information management technology and our refined knowledge of how systems work allow us to integrate services to a degree never before possible. Moreover, we can't afford fragmented service delivery anyway. Breaking down a process or flow into small packages always costs more than keeping it all together. Most important of all, fragmentation impairs quality.

APPLICATIONS OF INTEGRATED SERVICE DELIVERY

Integrated service delivery will be the central goal of the next generation of nonprofit managers. The drive toward integrated care is most advanced in health care as acute care hospitals move toward what are being called integrated service delivery networks (or something similar—significantly, there's no universal agreement on terminology). But other fields are experimenting with the concept as well, and more will follow.

Take public libraries, for example. The traditional library essentially represents a way to use public capital to secure assets (books) for the public good. No one individual or family could possibly afford to keep a copy of all books easily accessible for their use, nor would they want to. By pooling resources through government, a municipality drastically lowers this obstacle, changing the nature of the barrier from capital to one of traveling physical distance.

Still, even individual libraries face very real limits on the size of their collections, and there's no guarantee, especially in small towns or rural settings, that any one library will have all the books that patrons may seek. The first solution was an interlibrary loan program, which many libraries established earlier in this century. But even an interlibrary loan program is cumbersome and inefficient—until the system is computerized. Today, computerized in-

Note: Of Slide Rulers, Rotary Phones, and Hospitals

It looks like the hospital is about to join the rotary phone and the slide ruler as a treasured momento of the past. In 1995 the American Hospital Association (note the name for future reference) issued its multiyear strategic plan. The executive summary used the word "hospital" *once.* Everywhere else it spoke of "health systems" and "communities of health" and the like.

Note: Cyber Fog Settles over Library

A few years ago the Boston Public Library found itself in the middle of a public relations crisis when media outlets and politicians began demanding that it control Internet access by children using its computers. The expressed fear was that children were easily able to gain access to pornography. While there was ultimately a political solution to the problem, a more subtle and enduring message to the public was missed: the venerable institution had begun to transform itself from a place where people got information from books and magazines to one where they got access to information via computers as well.

terlibrary loan programs are growing rapidly. Many even offer remote access from users' home computers, and some offer internet access as well.

Nevertheless, computerized interlibrary loan programs beg the fundamental question of what a library should be in the next century. If easier physical access to a capital asset was the governing principle in previous years, Internet access undermines the rationale for public libraries themselves—as long as people can afford to purchase and operate the smaller capital assets of a home computer and a car. Moreover, in a fully computerized system, we would approach the point where the underlying organizational principle of a library for every governmental subdivision is essentially arbitrary and irrelevant to access. These are some of the surprisingly difficult questions that librarians and governmental officials are wrestling with today, and it is safe to predict that the eventual outcome will include more intensive and innovative versions of today's interlibrary loan networks.

The drive to integrate services will affect most other fields too, even those which today seem impervious to it. Education is riddled with fragmented service; the fact that so much of it is provided by public entities under enormous constraints will only slow the pace of change, not stop it. Public television is undergoing dramatic change. Public security, once the exclusive domain of government, will need to network more and more with private security initiatives and the courts themselves. Environmental nonprofits, currently a wide mix of advocacy, operational and land preservation initiatives, are fairly crying out for service integration.

THE ELEMENTS OF INTEGRATION

Integrated service delivery has its own special logic. When a variety of services are put together in an integrated fashion, things happen differently. Crude analogies with the physical world are instructive. City planners, for instance, have long known that less is more when it comes to street design. In certain instances, adding more roads to a congested traffic pattern can worsen the flow. Fiberoptic cable networks can add a fourth city to a planned three-city network and actually need fewer miles of cable to do it.

Integrated service planners are just beginning to consider how to increase nonprofits' productivity by putting them together in alliances. As suggested, it will be a long and slow process lasting a generation or more. At the same time, it is possible to see the roughest of outlines appearing to guide us in the journey. Some of the elements that will be present are as follows.

Trust

Trust is probably the least appreciated engine of economic success in the world, yet it has had a profound impact on the way all organizations conduct their business. For quick evidence of its role, look no further than the difference between industrialized countries and nonindustrialized societies. What is the rational response to the demands of doing business when trust is generally absent from the larger society? Make the family the prime business unit, not the corporation. Unfortunately, as an economic unit, the family is severely limited. There are a limited number of members, there's no good basis for ensuring their fitness for employment (let alone their ability to get along), and the amount of capital it can raise is constrained. A society that can't figure out how to trust nonfamily members is doomed to second rate industrialism at best.

Our appetite for litigation notwithstanding, the United States is actually a high trust economy. Nonprofits in particular benefit from this dynamic as fundraisers and as recipients of tax exempt status for presumed publicly beneficial activities. No one, the IRS included, plays a widespread and systematically proactive enforcement role with public charities. Boards and their management are simply expected to adhere to high standards of accountability, and in the vast majority of instances they do just that. Contrast the United States with the recent history of the former Soviet Union, where years of political leadership purposefully attempted to wipe out intermediary organizations between the individual and the state such as organized religion and voluntary associations. Now that the Communist party has lost power, the resulting vacuum is being partly filled by organized crime.

Of course, it is one thing to have public policies built on trust, and it is another to run systems based on trust. The latter is much harder. One of the reasons why one health care entity never accepts a referral from another without doing its own intake is because on some level they don't trust the referral source, a posture supported by a rich body of convention, regulation and laws. As a consequence, each clinical organization spends a certain percentage of its professional resources doing steps that have already been done.

While all mergers require an operative degree of trust early in the process, as of this writing, few alliances of nonprofits around the country appear to have approached the point where one or more members will have to give up something substantive in order to remain in the network. On the other hand, especially in health care groups facing managed care, it is not difficult to foresee a time when that will be commonplace.

This is why the first few weeks and months in any merger or alliances development initiative must be spent in developing trust among participants. It's also why the best partners are often the ones an organization already knows and has worked with in some small way in the past. After all, mergers and integrated service networks are still new as a widespread phenomenon in nonprofit fields. Ultimately there are no guarantees that any individual project will work, so it makes sense to be comfortable with those with whom one is taking a leap of faith—even if the leap is a small one.

Information as a Strategic Tool

Think about the roles most employees of a nonprofit organization play. Teachers transmit information and create settings in which learning can occur. Therapists learn about their patients and use a variety of languages and other tools to help them get better or learn to cope with their illness. Social workers take in large amounts of information about their client and one or more environments in which he or she operates and then they attempt to influence that client or the environment in some way. Physicians diagnose, artists interpret, and researchers gather information and analyze. In one way or another, all of them, as typical employees of nonprofit organizations, work with information.

Now think about the obstacles in the way of each of these professionals as they try to use knowledge to add value and meaning to others' lives. To do a proper job, teachers must spend inordinate amounts of time preparing and evaluating students and maintaining order in the learning environment. Therapists, social workers, and physicians are typically limited to single sessions for getting and sharing information, and it is very hard to achieve any kind of consistency from one session to the next and virtually impossible to achieve it between the professionals themselves. Artists and researchers often have to put in nonproductive time before being in a position to carry out their crafts.

What if it didn't have to be this way? What if students could do 'pre-learning' before formal classes in order to make the best use of teachers' time? What if other nonprofit employees had a way to eliminate or minimize their nonproductive time so that, for example, physicians and social workers could concentrate on the important things without being hindered by minor obstacles and inefficiencies? What if they could stay in touch with their clients not just 1 hour per week but 24 hours per day?

Naive and unrealistic musings? Not at all. In fact, all of these professions have at least the possibility of information currently being available to them which would make their time more efficient and more satisfying to them and their clients or patients. The exact details will vary with the field, of course, and some fields can use more information faster and better than others, but it is within reach of all.

Dramatic and continuing advances in computer technology are putting comparable advances in productivity within reach of the average nonprofit. The first use of information technology is usually to do existing tasks faster. Frequently this happens by clearing away needless work steps or by doing by computer what formerly could only be done by hand. The next step is to integrate those tasks with each other, and the third step is to automate entire processes. Nonprofits are just beginning to get comfortable with the first step and to explore the second. Within a decade many will be automating entire processes which in turn will position them to use information strategically, not just as an operating tool.

Massive Investments in Information Technology

Integrating all those services is going to require a lot of computing hardware, and this will be a change in many nonprofits' management style for two reasons. First, nonprofit managers are not accustomed to using technology very much. They can even be technology averse on a personal level, though less so than in the past. Second, technology investments will be continual. For the foreseeable future, information technology represents our single best hope for leveraging productivity gains. Older systems will be replaced, not so much because they are worn out or broken (as has

Pitfall: Integration is Harder than it Sounds

Just as revenue sources operate through stovepipes, so do most administrative systems. Take a small example in fiscal operations, typically one of the first areas to computerize in any nonprofit. A new employee in a large nonprofit must give his or her name to the human resource person upon being hired. Payroll will ask for it a second time, and it is not out of the question for that same employee to have to furnish that same information at least one or two more times to others ranging from the pension plan to the dental benefits administrator and even the parking garage manager. Why can't the employee give it once and expect all pertinent information to be transferred automatically to appropriate others? There's no particularly good reason, except that it's never been done that way. What would it take to make it happen? In truth, it would take much more powerful and sophisticated software than presently exists, plus some managerial commitment to use it. The commitment to use it must come first.

been the case with equipment in the past) but because the next generation of technology offers proportionately greater gains in productivity.

The other non-inconsiderable fact about the need for information technology is that it will take capital, and probably lots of it. Many agencies are already on their second or third cycle of technology and can expect their future systems to have shorter useful lives. The anticipated increase in integrated services will be paralleled by—in fact, be facilitated by—an increased degree of integration in information technology.

The need for investment in information technology will have two effects. First, it will boost the minimum economic size in virtually all fields, which in turn will put more pressure on agencies to merge and find new ways of working together. Second, it will make it likely that for-profits will enter or expand their positions in fields where nonprofits have traditionally been active. For reasons discussed earlier, nonprofits cannot raise significant amounts of capital for administrative purposes, and this will handicap their ability to respond to the demand for integrated services.

Networks of nonprofits may offer the best hope in this regard. It is significant that networks of long term care providers in California and one or two other states have listed as one of their main objectives the development of some aspect of financial information applications. Cost accounting in particular will be more and more necessary in most fields, but the expense of developing a system from scratch is prohibitive for most organizations. Voluntary groupings, either as alliances formed for that purpose or as part of a more ambitious attempt to integrate services, offer a way to spread the cost and the risk that a single organization usually could not afford.

More Standardized Services

Many nonprofit organizations are fiercely dedicated to their local communities, which is appropriate and helps fundraising. Many also encourage innovation in service delivery. But those same characteristics break up service delivery into thousands of little groupings, between which there is usually little or no sharing of information or accomplishment. Consequently, there are no heroes in the world of nonprofit management, and word of successful practices tends to leak out only slowly.

Some management advisors advocate the benefits of benchmarking in both private industry and in government. At its most complex, benchmarking is a rigorous process of identifying comparable organizations and then studying their techniques and practices in order to incorporate them. Alliances development can have the same rejuvenating effect. Once an alliance's program managers begin working on ways to standardize their services (the Organizational level in the C.O.R.E. model), the collegiality of the work can be infectious. We have often heard of program staff returning from an alliance development meeting brimming with ideas and enthusiasm generated by the give-and-take with other professionals.

One of the best ways to get program personnel working together is to give them a real problem to solve. One of our alliance's individual members realized after several months of working together that virtually all the participants were planning to pursue a certain type of certification during the next year. This certification was a long and complicated process and typically involved individual organizations studying the requirements, hiring a consultant, doing self-studies, gathering data, and writing policies. Why not, they reasoned, approach the certification process as their first big program-related joint venture? It took less than two months for them to develop a strategy and solicit and hire a consultant, and at that point they had not only saved a few dollars over what it would have cost them individually but they had gone through an enormously important confidence-building exercise.

Still, the primary purpose of integrating services is not for the internal benefits it brings but because users of the services will demand it. And, to be frank, it should help compete against large for-profit chains in health care (and eventually in other fields) whose sheer size and scope give them a certain level of de facto integration. From the vantage point of the latter half of the decade of the 1990s, it is reasonable to assume that just about every type of health and human service will ultimately be managed more tightly than it is today, whether the mechanism is called managed care or something else.

Nonprofit managers and board members who believe otherwise should look at modern economic history. Standardization alone is enough of a service to handsomely reward whatever groups can achieve it. Entrepreneurs who could produce large quantities of reliably high-quality commodities like heating oil, soap, or hamburgers not only survived in their industries but dominated them. Why should we expect it to be any different in fields traditionally served by nonprofits? Networks of related nonprofit service providers are the best hope for achieving the economic benefits of greater size while preserving the localized character of nonprofit services.

Fewer Employees

Without a doubt, this is going to be the toughest part of integrated services to swallow. Nonprofits traditionally have used—and, in some cases, have even prided themselves on using—a lot of human labor to deliver services. Tightened funding will continue to ratchet down personnel complements in most sectors, but greater use of information technology will play a major role too. Although this trend will grow out of greater service integration in the nonprofit sector, it has already touched most for-profit industries. Many professional service organizations in areas such as law and accounting saw their total head count drop during the early 1990s while their revenues stayed stable or even increased. The same will happen in nonprofits.

Those employees who remain, especially in professional positions, will be of a different type than their predecessors. Of necessity, they will tend to be more flexible in the way they do their jobs, and more oriented to results and roles than to inputs and job titles. They will instinctively understand the need to refocus and rethink the way services are delivered, and in many cases they will have special talents to help the organization accomplish those things. Often they will have gone through at least one merger, so the concept itself won't scare them.

Most important, they will have witnessed the value of collaborative skills and the value of genuine teamwork. To be sure, a good part of all this will be making a virtue out of necessity. We will build more collaborative capacities into our nonprofits because we will have no choice. Even the limited management structures of

Pitfall: Collegiality Can Fade in Mergers

Generally speaking, we have found much more enthusiastic sharing of ideas and practices in alliances than in mergers. The reason is probably obvious. When corporate-level merger is not the ultimate goal, where participants are simply trying to create new ways of working together, there is little overt competition for jobs. In a merger, the fear that a peer from "the other side" may be a competitor for a job is distracting. No matter how slight the threat may be, job security hormones flow at top volume during preparation for merger.

the past will no longer be possible in many cases because the available funding will not support them.

One agency we know has carried the spirit of this change further than most. Recognizing the inevitability of many of the factors cited above, they began experimenting with self-managed teams early in the 1990s. The transition was rough at first, and many of the most basic aspects are still being worked out several years later. Most profound was the need to reorient program staff from asking "what do we do next?" to saying "here's what we need in order to accomplish the results being asked of us."

An experiment with self-managing teams represents in a small way the kind of transformation that many nonprofits will undergo in tomorrow's world of mergers, alliances, and collaborations. So do the countless other ideas, small and large, currently being explored by nonprofits of all kinds to better integrate, standardize, and make seamless many services first offered in a previous era of stovepipe funding and structural fragmentation.

CHAPTER FOUR

Deciding to Collaborate

Many people correctly observe that nonprofit organizations take a lot of time to make a decision. Some, especially those in the for-profit sector who have had little or no contact with nonprofits, think that this is because the people who work in and manage nonprofits are more prone to procrastination, disorganization, and indecisiveness than their for-profit counterparts.

It is a dubious proposition to suggest that there is some sort of inherent relationship between managers' personalities and the tax status of their employers, but at any rate it completely misses the point: people act as they do because of the systems in which they operate. It is not financial matters where one sees the greatest differences between nonprofits and for-profits, but in the area we might call institutional imperatives—things the organization must do in order to survive. We call this the difference between *stewardship* and *profitability.*

The pursuit of profit is one of the easiest organizing principles available to managers. It is measurable, concrete, and immensely practical. It can be communicated to a wide range of people both inside and outside the unit, and it is the subject of a rich body of analyses and recommendations. Most important, it can be attained in any number of ways. One of the enduring myths of the for-profit world is that profit can be achieved through skilled management of a quality product or service. This is certainly true, but it is just as likely to be attained through ownership of a valuable patent, domination of a distribution network, market inertia, or any one of dozens of other routes having little to do with quality.

Note: The Fallacy of the "Bottom Line"

A common measure of good management is spoken of as the "bottom line," which is intended to connote a no-nonsense measurement of effectiveness. But in reality the bottom line, in the sense of a point beyond which an organization cannot go, is really the inability to bring in new money. If a company cannot make a profit, convince investors to buy new stocks at a high enough price, or borrow money, it hits the real bottom line. But nonprofits that are not profitable and have reached the limits of their borrowing capacity can almost always convince new donors to donate money or can sometimes convince funding sources to contribute new revenue precisely *because* they are in financial trouble. So nonprofits don't face the same penalties inherent in violating the "bottom line" that for-profits do.

Pursuing profit has another subtle but very significant impact on a firm or individual. It develops the discipline of focusing attention outside the company or the immediate unit of production. Terms such as "the customer" or "Wall Street" are shorthand for this outward-focusing effect, the intensity of which will rise or fall depending on competitive and regulatory realities.

Nonprofit corporations have no such pressures. As intermediary organizations, they are not even particularly expected to play an explicit economic role (which explains why their actual economic clout is often overlooked). Instead, they are expected to be fiduciaries, entities set up to receive, hold, and manage assets intended to be used for some type of public purpose. In a very real sense their single most important mission is a stewardship of public assets and trust.

A major impact of the nonprofit structure is that accountability has to be raised to the highest level. This is why most nonprofit public charities must have full-blown financial audits every year when for-profit corporations engaged in similar work may need the less rigorous financial review. It is also why so much of nonprofits' business must be conducted in the open via things like public financial reports and rigorous disclosure laws.

However, all this emphasis on accountability is focused on inputs, such as money and in-kind donations. The overriding question to be answered at all times is "how did you handle the money we gave you?" not "did you get the job done?" Consequently, nonprofit managers' and board members' focus often gets turned inward in the same way. Proving that one spent one's funds prudently tends to become the highest goal of operations, and this blunts nonprofit managers' ability and incentive to read signals from the environment.

There is another effect of nonprofit structure that planners of a merger must recognize and incorporate in their strategy. For all its obvious and well-documented flaws, the profit motive can have an intensely unifying effect. Business partners in a profitable enterprise can usually put aside personal differences enough to capitalize on their success. Moreover, they have every incentive for doing so, even if considerations of ego cloud their business judgment.

On the other hand, in nonprofit organizations ideas and values are far more important than financial performance. When egos on

Tip: The Importance of Outside Experts

Typically, nonprofit boards are reluctant to take what they may perceive as pioneering action without a great deal of examination and discussion. In a decade or so the notion of nonprofit mergers and integrated services will probably be comfortable for most board members but for now it may be necessary to legitimize the concept before any serious discussion can take place.

In cases like this it is usually true that an expert is someone from out of state. In the absence of a presumed expert, a credible local figure will do nicely. A recently resigned government or foundation official, or someone with easily-understood responsibility in a similar but somewhat distant service area can work very nicely. Arrange for the individual to speak to the board. Often, this is as simple as a speech to the annual meeting, a special segment of a board meeting, or just distributing a short piece of writing. At this point, no serious discussion need take place. The idea is simply to get the concept introduced and then let it percolate.

slideshow.ppt

both sides of a question are equally strong, there is no appeal to reason that can be counted on to be strong enough to offset the divisive effects of the conflict. In these cases, resolution is essentially a matter of internal politics.

Deciding to merge or to seek to build integrated services is difficult enough as it is, but until the decision becomes commonplace (certainly within five years in most areas), those seeking these choices will have to sell the idea as an idea before they can sell the particular merger they have in mind. This is why it is wise to begin discussing the concept months or even years before it may become a real option. Especially for boards of directors, much of the reason for delay in considering a merger comes from lack of familiarity with the idea itself as opposed to something about a specific proposal.

Ironically, the best way to counter the natural tendency to go slow or reject the idea of merging is to focus first on inputs. Board members, senior managers, people who work in nonprofits and even consumers of the services can understand strategies based on achieving savings. It has also been shown on numerous occasions that, short of a full merger, one of the easier ways of getting agencies to work together is to take on an economic project together. We will present a more formal framework for thinking about economics as a starting point in the following chapter.

Most discussions about merging today start at the executive level and move quickly to the board of directors. The best way to begin serious discussions about merging is at the board level with

Tip: Financial Indicators

The worst time to consider merging is when an agency is on the brink of disaster. The hobbled nonprofit offers little value as an attractive merger partner. Fortunately, there are some financial indicators of impending disaster that are fairly reliable. Here's one: pull out your most recent IRS Form 990, the nonprofit tax return. Look on line, "Fund Balances or Net Assets." This is the nonprofit equivalent of net worth. If the number on that line is negative (enclosed in parentheses), financial disaster is probably not far ahead.

Tip: Conduct a Ministrategic Planning Process

To get a merger process started with a board of directors, try this simple exercise. Ask all members present at a meeting scheduled for the purpose to write down a handful of ideas about why they might want to merge with another nonprofit. Take one idea from each director and write it out on a single piece of poster paper on the wall. Do the same with reasons why they might fear or be concerned about a merger. Summarize and synthesize the ideas listed (chances are there will be about 15–25 raw ideas of each type). These are now your interests in a merger—if the positives can be achieved and the negatives either avoided or mitigated, the board should feel confident about approving a merger.

the kind of general discussion, preferably well before any specific step is contemplated, as described earlier.

BOARD CONCERNS

Once they have worked through the notion of a merger as a strategic option rather than a sign of failure, boards of directors of nonprofit organizations tend to exhibit predictable concerns. We have found that they generally accept most of the projected benefits of mergers, if only because on an intellectual level they are hard to deny. Most of the concerns will be stated in rational terms but will often be more emotional in nature. Some will seem identical to issues raised by staff—these are covered in detail in a later section—but the dynamics of board deliberations are different enough to warrant some specific mention here.

Concern for Mission

Most board members believe in their organization's mission. This is only natural, since mission is one of the most appealing characteristics of a nonprofit. Concern for the way the mission may change, positively or negatively, is typically one of the first reactions a board will have to the suggestion of a merger. Curiously, this concern tends to be microscopic. That is, it is always expressed in terms of *this agency* and *these clients,* even if other comparable groups have identical missions. For example, if a homeless shelter's board were to consider merging, the expressed concern would likely be for *its* group of homeless clients, not for the problem of homelessness in general.

This tendency is related to the difficulty many groups encounter as they attempt to create an overarching vision within which their individual mission will make sense. If, for example, an urban gardening group's mission is to beautify its neighborhood, it should presumably do so within a larger vision such as the desire to bring the benefits of natural spaces to urban dwellers. It is the vision that is the larger force here, to the extent that if there were ever a choice between beautifying the neighborhood or serving the larger vision, the vision should prevail. This is a fundamental difference between nonprofits and for-profits, since the latter are expected and even encouraged to act in their own narrow, short-term interests. It's also extremely hard to do, and is as good a recommendation for board training in strategy and public accountability as there could be.

In any event, the fear of loss of institutional mission is often surprisingly easy to allay. Sometimes it is based on misinformation or just plain lack of information. In one network we helped initiate, the matter was handled in an exemplary way. Several faith-based organizations had come together for preliminary talks but were worried about the compatibility of their missions. At an early meeting before any outsiders were brought in, the chief executives literally laid the respective mission statements side by side on a table. What they found was that the thrust of each mission statement was surprisingly close. Words and style varied, but in some instances they had independently used some of the same words and phrases to describe their missions.

We have found this to be more common than not. The drive to provide services that creates a nonprofit organization often seems to be so strong and universal that there are more similarities than differences, and often all it takes to uncover them is some dialog and mutual respect.

What can make the concern for mission so difficult to answer is when it obscures a more fundamental discomfort that isn't or can't be expressed. There is a general unspoken contract between board members to avoid sharp disagreements if possible—after all, these are unpaid positions and who really needs that kind of aggravation?—so an expressed concern for the organization's mission could really be a roundabout way of saying something else more controversial. Again, there is no substitute for honest dialog and careful listening.

Loss of Identity

A second concern frequently expressed by boards of directors is the potential loss of identity they expect from a merger or alliance. This one deserves some gentle probing. Identity in the marketplace is a fragile thing that derives from a number of factors such as the name, specific staff people, services delivered, and community history. From a purely rational, self-interested point of view, why would the newly merged entity necessarily want to change *any* of these things? Assuming the reputation is positive there is actually more incentive to keep the name since it will bring good will and a greater expectation of continuity. The new entity will also probably want to retain the people and, for some period of time at least, the portfolio of services they offer. So most of the elements of an identity in a market sense are not likely to change. Boards of directors can find this kind of analysis comfortably reassuring.

Still, what many boards of directors mean by identity is often more complex than identity in the market. It is better understood as the complex product of *internal* factors that have little to do with market conditions. This kind of identity is often expressed as institutional history, legends, apocryphal stories, and so forth. Typically, it is the smaller agency in a merger, fearful of being "swallowed up," that has these concerns. Larger agencies in this type of merger need to be aware of this dynamic and to be sure to honor that internal identity.

Loss of Services

A third significant concern of many boards is the possibility of losing services. It can be handled in many ways, but the first step is recognizing that this is really a control issue. The service delivery area of so many nonprofits is extremely local and a merger can at least seem to threaten resources or services formerly dedicated to a

Tip: Confront the Reality of Service Loss

While boards and even executives may be concerned that a merger could threaten the existence of services to a certain neighborhood, town or county, be clear about the nature of that threat. In many areas of health and human services today, areas may be poised to lose services anyway, irrespective of governance questions after a merger. In fact, it may be that a merger is the best hope of keeping those services in the area.

particular geographic region. Typically, the concern is that, in a new entity with a wider geographic focus, there could be a dilution of services or outright neglect of an area that formerly got exclusive attention from one of the partners. Concerns of this sort can be dealt with by such things as governance structure, restricted fundraising, and premerger conversations with funding sources.

OTHER BOARD BEHAVIORS

Once a decision has been made to at least seriously consider a merger or some form of alliance development, most boards of directors will demonstrate a deep concern for doing it "the right way." Some of this desire stems from a predictable focus on compliance issues, which usually serves boards well in matters of fundraising and reimbursement, and some comes from an unconscious assumption that creating mergers and developing alliances must be like baking a cake whose recipe they've never seen. Early on they need to embrace the idea that every merger or alliance is unique, and that most of the work lies in figuring out how to put a particular group of two or more agencies together.

Closely related to this behavior is a frequent lack of institutional self-confidence. Often, this comes out as an expressed need for more education on the topic; until nonprofit mergers in the local area are as commonplace as for-profit mergers, this will be a fairly predictable response and is easily handled through conventional means of board education.

The reverse situation is the board that believes itself to be highly sophisticated (and is, at least in the sense of having members who are sophisticated individuals) and concludes that for this reason it needs to do nothing now (the option for later action is usually left open). This typically happens with boards of large and prestigious organizations such as universities and hospitals. In reality, truly sophisticated leadership is actually more humble and less apt to close off options on the basis of insular judgment. A hybrid of this posture occurs when a small board has one or two genuinely high-powered members whose sheer energy can dominate the others and preclude contrary opinions from ever forming.

UNCORKING THE BOTTLE

A final, usually positive, aspect of the merger process is worth mentioning here. Simply starting to talk internally about merging or joining a network tends to unleash tremendous psychic energy which, when handled carefully and constructively, can be a source of creativity and one of the most satisfying by-products of the process. One management team we know deliberately opened up its ranks to a midlevel manager as a kind of "wild card" participant on the Merger Committee. Well-regarded beforehand, she played such a crucial leadership role during the early stages of the merger that she ended up being recruited for a high level management position by the local hospital (where she may yet figure in a more complex and far-reaching merger).

Pitfall: Weak Leadership

No matter how collegial and trusting the relationship with a potential merger partner may be, board members and staff must have confidence in those negotiating the details of the merger. If they do not, they will resist the process for reasons that may not always seem obvious. One solution is to add members to the merger team to complement the missing strengths and/or to add consultants to the team just for the purposes of the merger.

Of course, it can work in the other direction too. The prospect of imminent change uncorks a lot of sentiments that might otherwise have gone unexpressed. Paranoia is perhaps the most common response to the pressures of a merger. It doesn't take much to see confirmation of one's worst fears in what may have been an entirely innocent action, especially when keeping internal communications flowing freely is so difficult. Ways to lessen the inevitable paranoia among staff are discussed in Chapter 7. Experience in separating what's real from what's simply feared is a big help here, as is the ability to set up and maintain honest dialogs between the boards of directors.

PART TWO

The C.O.R.E. of Nonprofit Collaboration

CHAPTER FIVE

Toward Common Definitions

Merger is a dirty word for most nonprofit managers and their boards of directors. Corporate America's excesses of the 1980s combined with various structural disincentives for merging except as a last resort have given the term a sour taste for many managers and their boards. Because the strategy of merging and integrating services is so new to most, there is an understandable neglect of even basic terminology. Finally, as with any emerging field, a few participants are doing genuinely new things for which there is as yet no well-worn path, let alone words to describe it.

Consider the words *merger* and *alliance,* which are emerging as two of the favorite descriptors of this kind of activity. Attorneys and finance professionals use the term merger all the time, as in the phrase *mergers and acquisitions.* Right away there are obvious problems translating the concept to the nonprofit field, for exactly how does one go about acquiring a nonprofit entity which, by definition, no one owns? Technically, the best one can do is to control it, which gives the same results as an acquisition but for different reasons. Emotional connotations aside, there is not a good fit.

Alliance suffers a different fate. Unlike other terms, there is no such legal entity. A partnership, for example, is accepted as a form of business operation. How does one create a partnership? Describe it in writing, sign it and, subject to a few regulatory requirements, one has created a partnership. But what is an alliance? Is it two groups acting together for a specific purpose? Is it dozens of groups deciding to cooperate in a general way? Is it a way to avoid the dreaded "M" word? Judging by what we have seen to date, it is all of the above and more. The word is in danger of being stretched to the point of meaninglessness.

OUR MODEL

This book takes a different approach. In order to give our terminology specific meaning, a conceptual model is laid out against which terms can be measured. Our model is based on the premise that different forms of collaboration affect different aspects of the nonprofit organization. The four aspects affected are:

Corporate
Operations
Responsibility
Economics

It's worth a few words to clarify exactly what each of these terms mean. By corporate, we mean the legal entity of the nonprofit corporation. This is the business structure that has an official purpose, a board of directors, officers, bylaws, and all those other things generally recognized to be part of overseeing a corporate body. The corporate level is where the Internal Revenue Service (IRS) lodges responsibility for financial accountability. It is typically headed up by the president or chairman at the board level and by the executive director as part of management. It may be freestanding, or it may be controlled by another group; for our current analytical purposes, it doesn't matter. More concretely, the corporate level includes actions of the board and agency-wide management that shape matters of substance involving the organization as a whole.

Many alliances will also affect the program or operations level of the nonprofit organization. Operations are the heart of the nonprofit's unique reason for being, whether those operations carry out research into molecular structure, care for preschool age children, or develop the economy of a neighborhood. Sometimes this level of activity is called programming. Whatever the terminology, the operations level is where the nonprofit delivers on its promise of serving the public good.

All of this corporate oversight and program activity requires someone to be responsible from day to day. Paychecks need to be generated, bills sent out, expenses paid, and a myriad of other tasks need to be performed if any nonprofit of any size is to keep the doors open. We call this the responsibility level.

Finally, almost all collaborations affect the economics of participating nonprofits somehow. The outcome of collaborating to affect economics could be as simple as bartering free office rent in return for certain services or as complicated as establishing a jointly owned for-profit support services company.

DEFINING THE C.O.R.E.

Exhibit 5.1 shows the C.O.R.E. concept visually. In this display, the areas of greatest impact on participating organizations are shown as four horizontal bars. Vertically, the graph represents a continuum from the earliest and easiest area of impact (economics) to the highest level (corporate). Human nature and organizational realities being what they are, most alliances start with economics and work up to corporate restructuring.

The vast majority of discussions around forming strategic alliances today are prompted by economic considerations—cutbacks in revenue, insupportable expenses, or simply a desire to do things more efficiently. This is why we said earlier that it is usually easier to get a board of directors to focus on the economic benefits of an alliance before any other type of benefit. Even if the discussion proceeds quickly to a full blown merger, the chances are that it started with economics.

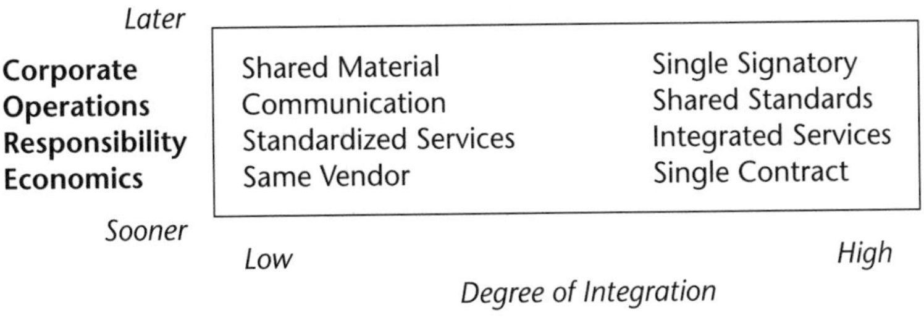

Exhibit 5.1 Continuums of Collaboration

There is another reason why economics usually come first; they're easier to grasp. We can measure and communicate the impact of a dramatically lower out-of-pocket cost for copier paper much more readily than we can quantify the virtues of a new multiple-corporate structure. It doesn't make the benefits of the latter any less real, of course, just harder to demonstrate.

Exhibit 5.1 also displays these concepts visually. On each of the four levels, there are a range of possible choices starting with the easiest and least powerful on the left and ranging up to the most

Miniglossary

The following miniglossary eliminates doubt about the terminology:

Affiliation: the lowest level of collaboration. Requires little more than meetings and good faith.

Alliance: collaborations that entail change on any one or all three of the O.R.E. levels. In alliances the participants keep their corporate vehicles intact and under their own control and simply collaborate in other ways.

Collaboration: our generic term for what happens any time two or more nonprofits work together in some formalized way.

Integrated service network: a slightly more focused version of an alliance. Participants will keep their corporate identities, but there is typically an element of common control. In practice, the fact of separate corporate vehicles may be nothing more than a concession to complex legal and financial imperatives.

Merger: a collaboration that entails change on all four C.O.R.E. levels and which ultimately results in consolidation on the corporate level.

Network: another name for an alliance, or a shortened reference to integrated service network.

Partnership: a legally binding agreement between two or more entities that is intended to produce economic benefit for both that is to be shared in some predetermined fashion.

potent options on the right. Therefore, the quickest and least binding of the possibilities are economic initiatives involving things as simple as sharing information on common vendors as shown in the southwest corner of the graph. The highest and most powerful choice that takes the longest to achieve is for the participants in the alliance to act as a single entity in their marketplace, as represented in the northeast corner. This can happen either as the result of a complete merger or through the creation of an integrated service system or some form of alliances of nonprofits.

Alliances operating at one level will also probably affect levels below, but rarely above. Also, there is no implied push up the C.O.R.E. Alliances can form at any one level and stay there just as easily as they can expand to a higher level. One of the inescapable practicalities of alliance development is that over time they will only go as far as the members want them to go.

The model can also help sort through common terminology describing various types of alliances. Exhibit 5.2 shows where various terms describing types of alliances might fit. Note that some of these terms could apply to more than one level of alliance.

Much about the art of nonprofit alliance building has yet to be documented and agreed upon, but Exhibit 5.2 may help add some definitiveness for the purposes of this book. The remaining chapters will take up the four levels of organizational impact, how they work and what they look like, starting from economics and working up the continuum.

Corporate	Merger Management company LLP Network Joint venture Collaborative LLC
Operations	Network Alliance
Responsibility	Affiliation Subcontracting Alliance Shared services corporation
Economics	Shared services corporation Collaboration Joint purchasing Alliance

Exhibit 5.2 The Terminology of Collaboration

CHAPTER SIX

Applying C.O.R.E.

CHANGING ECONOMICS

Chances are, few nonprofit organizations would seriously consider any type of alliance if there were not economic pressures to do so. No matter how compelling the strategic, public-interest, and moral arguments for nonprofit alliances might be, economic considerations are what move people. Organizations resist change for the simple reason that it causes pain, and usually it is only when the present or anticipated pain of economic stress outweighs the pain of having to change that the process of alliance building gathers momentum.

Given the typical origins of alliances in economics, it is perfectly understandable that the details of day-to-day operations are usually the first area of focus. There is often plenty to do. Unlike for-profit organizations in which the owner or owners have a real interest in minimizing expenses so as to maximize profits, nonprofits do not have an inherent incentive to keep expenses low.

For example, providers of various types of residential human services in the 1960s and 1970s often began as a single program. Each one had its own director, its own financial person, its own chief clinical person, and so on. Eventually, since providing good service essentially required a limit on the maximum number of clients per site—lest operators risk returning to the warehouses they were trying to replace—the only way to operate these programs economically was to downgrade on-site management and string several together under the control of a smaller management team.

A similar thing is happening to the organizations themselves now. Managers are being forced to become more productive in the sense of the scope of their responsibilities, and in many cases the programs themselves are being redesigned. This trend lays the groundwork for capturing efficiencies at a level beyond that which is normally available to smaller standalone programs.

Alliances created solely for the purpose of changing participants' economics are the loosest and least demanding kind. Since most of the simpler economic gains involve more efficient dealings with outside suppliers, it is easier to get unity against an external economic focus. This is helpful because, as all political leaders know, it is much easier to unite groups in opposition to a common enemy than any other way. By contrast, all the other levels on the continuum deal primarily with those inside the member organizations, so a certain discomfort can always be present.

There are many ways to achieve greater efficiencies in nonprofit organizations. Happily, few of them truly risk interfering with the accomplishment of the mission, which is what many people understandably worry about when attention turns to economics. In fact, anecdotal evidence suggests that in some cases, it is entirely possible to save money and provide higher quality services at the same time. The rest of this chapter will be dedicated to the description of a few distinct strategies for deriving economic gains from collaboration. Most examples will be keyed to alliances, since it is presumed that merged entities can accomplish the same results simply by taking advantage of their newly increased size, whereas alliances will have to work harder at the same thing.

Sharing Information

One of the quickest, least expensive, and most potent ways of making economic progress is sharing information. Although information can be shared about any number of economic areas in a nonprofit, in this section and the following sections, we will draw heavily on the area of supplies purchasing practices for our examples. We do this largely because vendor-provided services are so easy to quantify and so familiar to most people. Be aware, however, that other areas such as benefits and professional services may be equally promising candidates for comparative analysis.

There are many different levels of sharing economic information. The easiest is to compare recent invoices or purchase orders from vendors of the same sort of product or service. A deeper approach would be to share copies of contracts and purchasing agreements along with accounting records. A yet more sophisticated technique would be to select one or more comparable items and track their price history side-by-side over a period of months.

The advantage to information sharing as an economic strategy is that it is quick, easy, and inexpensive. The disadvantages flow from the same facts. There are no guarantees that any participant in the process will gain from the effort, since it is left to them as individual purchasers to act on the information they gained. Second, there is no structured means of following up on any gains, so suppliers could eventually revert back to their old pricing structures without notice. Finally, any gains are elusive and hard to document. Opportunities for building momentum for collaboration and proving success slip away.

Bidding Jointly

Bidding jointly is a step up from the simple sharing of information. In this approach the participants go through a purchasing process together. They might design and issue a joint Request for

Pitfall: The Potato Chip Bag Trap

Purchasing analyses aren't as easy as they sound. Sloppy analyses will lead to bad conclusions and may even result in spending more money. The key is to arrive at the same unit of measure for each item being compared and then to rigorously extract the price per unit from the inevitable jumble of vendor-related records. Vendors don't want you to do this sort of thing so they try to make it difficult. Ever notice the measurements on snack size bags of potato chips, pretzels, and other junk foods? Vendors need to sell their bags at the same price as the competition's, so their size varies wildly. Making comparisons between them is tedious and time-consuming, which is precisely what the higher-priced manufacturers want.

Proposals (RFP), research the responses together, and interview bidders jointly. In the end, however, they negotiate separate deals.

This method has the advantage of reducing overhead slightly by sharing the costs of purchasing administration, and it may also encourage suppliers to be a bit more aggressive in their pricing, but there are no guarantees. Again, the risk is that unmonitored and independently structured arrangements can easily fall apart.

Joint Purchasing

Joint purchasing is a favored strategy of alliances of all kinds, and for good reason. It can take many forms. In some cases the alliance—frequently an association—simply researches and endorses a particular vendor. In this case the association is effectively turned into one of the vendor's sales representatives, and can often get paid the same commission that a single human being might get paid if he or she were to have brought in all that business.

bidsuma.xls

In other cases, the alliance will create a business entity expressly to carry out purchasing activities. The hospital industry has a handful of major national purchasing alliances designed for that purpose. These organizations can grow to be quite sophisticated.

Most joint purchasing initiatives operate on the same principle: create savings for members and/or make money for the alliance by cutting out the last distribution point for the end user. The office supply superstores that have sprung up in the last decade illustrate the principle nicely. Office supplies used to be distributed to the consumer largely through small "mom and pop" stationery stores, who were in turn supplied by larger wholesalers. Office supply superstores effectively turn the wholesaler into the last stop for the consumer, thereby cutting out those smaller and less efficient retailers.

The more the alliance can act like a wholesaler, the higher the savings it will produce for its members. For example, if an alliance can buy huge quantities of some commodity such as paper it can offer substantial savings for members in addition to some profit for itself. But this strategy requires an investment in appropriate storage capacity, a distribution system, security provisions, and so forth; in short, it requires the alliance to act like a true wholesaler. That's a responsibility only the very largest and most sophisticated

Tip: Respect the Economics of Purchasing

Different products and services respond differently when purchased in quantity. Commodity products such as paper or computers behave predictably when purchased in bulk; the more you purchase, the lower the unit price is likely to be. Other things such as insurance are so complex and individually tailored that they defeat efforts to rationalize and bulk purchase them; in these cases the primary advantage of joint purchasing is likely to be access to the product or perhaps a higher-quality product (for having been designed expressly for the purchasing group).

alliances are likely to take on, so most efforts will probably stop considerably short of this level.

Management Services Companies

Management services companies, also known by such names as management services organizations and shared services corporations, are one of the more sophisticated forms of economics-based alliances. As such, they will also appear at other levels in our hierarchy of collaboration. We mention them here chiefly because they get much of their staying power from economic efficiencies.

Tip: Strategic Planning is Built into the Process

For managers considering joining a network or merging organizations but feeling wary of the price tag of outside consultants, note that much of the planning process for either choice amounts to a mini-strategic planning project. Furthermore, the act of hiring a facilitator jointly may itself produce the first piece of savings since the facilitator may charge less for both groups combined than for each group separately. It's just another illustration of the power of joint purchasing.

SHARING RESPONSIBILITY FOR MANAGEMENT TASKS

The next step up the continuum is sharing responsibility for basic management and administrative chores. Although obviously related to changes in economics, this area is considerably broader and less susceptible to quantification. Changing the locus of management responsibility happens automatically in a merger, but typically only after a great deal of trust has been established and some economic groundwork laid in a network of service providers. Also, unlike economic changes, shared management responsibility can be hard to see, not necessarily measurable, and subject to rapid changes.

This level of collaboration is qualitatively different from the others in that it tends to be coupled with one or both of the two higher levels. Nonprofits may want to stay indefinitely at the level of economic collaboration and could actually do so, but sharing management responsibilities makes most sense as a prelude to greater collaboration in the future. Shared responsibility is a way station toward a more comprehensive form of working together.

Sharing at the management level does not come easily to most organizations. Unlike, say, education where teachers have the benefit of planned curricula or behavioral health where psychologists broadly agree on what constitutes a proper battery of tests, management in nonprofits is still largely a do-it-yourself proposition. Organizations and their managers develop ways of doing things that reflect their values and beliefs and that fit with their cultures, and these things are hard to share.

In this chapter we will identify three types of shared responsibility arrangements and suggest how each type might fit with different strategies for collaboration. Each option requires a different degree of rigor and commitment, but each can be used separately from the others.

Adopting the Same Standards

One of the biggest barriers to more efficient management of a network of services is that the participants usually have different standards. This means a total lack of predictability, which in turn means that the market for most routine services is not as developed as it could be. True, certain situations such as the performing arts demand innovation and creativity, but these are in the minority. And, as foundations inevitably begin to rethink their pilot funding-only strategies—a product of the days when some governmental agency could reasonably be counted on to pick up a good idea when its first three years of funding ran out—the overall level of innovativeness in mainstream social agencies will decline as well.

Standards, of course, is an all-encompassing concept. We will narrow it a bit by focusing on the area of information processing to show how nonprofits can begin to set the stage for greater collaboration simply by handling their information systems similarly. But standardization is ultimately an agency-wide concern of management. Nonprofits of all types will have to get better at providing and describing standardized levels of care in program management.

Sharing Managers

A simple, natural, and cost-effective way of integrating nonprofits at the management level is to share staff. Most often this occurs at higher professional levels such as the chief financial person or chief program director because these are the positions that tend to be more expensive and yet effective even in part time roles. In fact, in the majority of mergers in which we have participated there has been some sort of staff sharing during the merger process.

Sometimes this sharing has been deliberate and long standing. One nonprofit we know jointly employs a CFO with a for-profit property management company down the hall; neither could afford such a high caliber person on their own, but together they can get most of the advantage of having him on their full time staff at a fraction of the cost.

More often, the sharing is just a convenient thing that happens in varying degrees of formality in the course of a full merger. Especially in medium to large organizations, there is enough turnover in senior management ranks that at least one or more positions are likely to be vacated during the merger process. Alert management or a sharp Merger Committee can take advantage of this natural phenomenon to install a bit of responsibility sharing before the official date of merger.

Compatible Information Systems

In the days of IBM's lovable tramp, when computerization meant having one or two pieces of moderately expensive beige iron on a desk, software compatibility had little meaning. As the need to connect previously disparate internal banks of information becomes critical to the operations of most nonprofits, that is changing. Later, as many become part of a larger system in some way, the ability to link different information—processing operations will be critical.

Let's take a small but important example. Many nonprofits provide some sort of service and then charge for it, often sending a bill. The bill eventually gets paid, one hopes, and that results in a series of events in the accounting system. It sounds simple enough, but the brief process described can almost never be done with the same piece of software. Here's why.

Not surprisingly, accounting applications were among the first business practices to be computerized. At this point, there are some very good generic accounting packages available; many nonprofit packages lag their generic counterparts, but nonetheless are more powerful and efficient compared to the paper methods of yesterday. It is important to note that accounting standards and practices are highly national in character—deliberately so, in order to facilitate commerce.

Billing, on the other hand, especially in the fields in which nonprofits are active, tends to be extremely local in nature. Certain government agencies want their bills to be delivered in a certain way, often on a certain form. Foundations can be demanding as well, plus the requirements change frequently. Consequently, the same people who develop software for accounting can't afford to develop it for highly variable billing purposes. Either it doesn't get developed, or it gets put out by local experts who couldn't possibly afford to integrate it with all the accounting packages out there.

All of this goes on in parallel with the other major area of data management that most nonprofits must accommodate: program services. Even more so than billing, managing programs is a highly individualized affair. Even if there were agreement on exactly what constitutes a service—and there usually isn't—there would be a wide disparity in the way that individual agencies identify and keep track of the information about that service and its recipients. Consequently, the nonprofit service field, like most others, is still stuck in the starting blocks over how to integrate such basic functions as accounting, billing, and program management.

There are some technological solutions to this dilemma for budding alliances. The simplest is to identify information technology compatibility as a priority of members. This can be done by agreeing to adhere to standards such as using the same in-house applications and by insisting on minimum standards for computer equipment purchases.

Groupware is a common way of insuring compatibility at least in external communications. Applications such as Lotus Notes allow users in different sites with different architecture to work collaboratively. We once used Notes successfully to link innovative job training centers in different areas of the same state not only with each other but with potential users of their information. Wide area networks (WANs) can shrink cross country distances to nanoseconds, and of course the Internet holds enormous promise for aiding collaborative efforts.

Other emerging technologies hold equally great promise. Ron Marinella and Chris Williams, colleagues on the West Coast, have developed something called a data warehouse for a group of hospitals that allows managers to "drill down" into a database to the level of an image of the original case notes. With this approach, a network of hospitals using different information systems can "deposit" their data in a centralized database. Managers can then identify the hospitals with the best records for a procedure such as hip replacement among dozens of hospitals, then identify the best of their physicians' best practices, and go on to use that knowledge to train and educate other hospitals and other physicians in the group. This innovation allows managers to manage an entire system the way they might have managed a single hospital twenty years ago, and with less time necessary.

On the East Coast, Maxine Rockoff brought together five New York City settlement houses to design and implement a shared computer network that will eventually be the groundwork for a leading-edge information system. Similar efforts are going on in other areas as well, and the next several years promise to bring breakthroughs in both the technology and the way nonprofits use it for greater integration.

Pitfall: The Part-Time CEO

Ironically, sharing management staff may be healthy for nonprofits, but sharing the executive director is not. No statistics to back this up—just lots of anecdotes—but nonprofits with part-time executive directors tend to suffer for it. The reason seems to be that the part-time CEO always has at least one other focus for his or her professional energies, and this tends to dilute their impact on the organization. The real damage comes from the fact that it's an insidious effect, hard to detect from day to day and most often discernible over the long term as lost opportunities.

Sharing Administrative Tasks

Administrative tasks can be divided into two types: those that are repetitive, such as maintaining a payroll and handling accounting functions; and those that are one-time projects. Collaboration on repetitive tasks is still relatively rare. Those instances when it does occur often are temporary stops on a path to full merger, such as when one agency takes over one or more back room functions of a smaller agency with whom they later merge. Other nonprofits have set up what might be called shared services corporations to carry out a defined set of management tasks. In yet other instances, nonprofits get together in a single building and share some level of copying, receptionist, and other services: this is happening in California, Michigan, Massachusetts, New Hampshire, and Texas among other states, and it seems to be growing in popularity.

Like the man who spoke prose and didn't know it, some nonprofits may already be sharing management responsibility. Some auditing, legal services, billing, and other professional service firms specialize to such a high degree in a particular area of nonprofit activity that the simple act of engaging one of them is like getting instant help from peers. Formal seminars and training sessions further cement the alliance-like nature of these relationships. As things like specialized software combining financial and programmatic functions become more vital—and more available—we can expect to see more sophisticated collaborations combining features of all of the above become popular. It is not even out of the question for specialized software companies or other financial advisors to be at the center of future networks put together around a common application, in much the same way that Japanese banks anchor many of the entities that Americans would call strategic alliances.

Another form of management sharing is called *benchmarking*. At its lowest level, benchmarking can be little more than sharing compatible and otherwise private data with a select group of peer organizations. At the high end, it can involve an intensive institutional relationship in which one party spends considerable person hours identifying and studying a set of practices in another with the intention of adopting the best features of those practices. Although we have not heard of any nonprofits actively pursuing this type of relationship, it is common among some noncompetitive for-profit companies and is fairly well developed among a group of municipalities in California, Arizona, and Utah. On the face of it, there is no reason why nonprofits could not do the same.

INTEGRATING OPERATIONAL STRUCTURE

In the end, nonprofits provide services, and any kind of meaningful integration must include program services. Although health care services are somewhat more advanced than other types of nonprofits in this area, the demands of public service in the 21st century will soon cause others to catch up. In many ways this is the level of integration that ultimately means the most for any merger or alliance of nonprofits because without success here nothing else matters.

It is also the most difficult level at which to create alliances because so little has been widely accepted as successful and because program personnel tend to be indifferent or even overtly hostile to working together unless doing so is perceived as compatible with their mission. Conversely, because opportunities for professional interaction are hard to provide in settings with a limited number of each type of professional, programmatic integration can be a very appealing process. One of the least recognized disadvantages of working in small nonprofit settings is that they can be tremendously isolating. Mergers and alliances can help provide a bigger pool of peers with whom to interact.

As with the previous levels, this level on the continuum of collaboration is itself a continuum. We have identified three different ways of increasingly more complex and effective programmatic collaboration. As before, there are undoubtedly other options possible, but these should suffice as representative.

Shared Training

Good managers of service providers know that over time the key to producing consistently high quality service is training. In the American economy we rely on undergraduate programs to provide future employees with an education; training is what their employers must give them. An unfortunate reality of budgetary politics in most organizations is that training budgets are the first to get cut. Like skimping on capital expenditures, the results of slashing training take a while to show up and are hard to quantify anyway so they are usually irresistible targets.

Still, training gets done. Often it is informal, ad hoc, and self-initiated, but it happens. Conferences are one way to get key employees trained, as are specialty meetings and orientation sessions. In merger situations training policies tend to be driven by the merger partner with the strongest philosophy about training (for or against), but in alliances there is room for different approaches.

The simplest approach is to coordinate training programs. Similar to the low end economic strategy of sharing information about vendors, this tactic is largely one of comparing calendars and attempting to coordinate efforts so that both parties get maximum coverage out of whatever training does take place. Participants might even try appointing a staff member to attend a class and then teach an in-house session for all agencies' staff that did not attend (although this is one of those ideas that always sounds like it ought to work much better than it does). More formal attempts would involve the active commitment of all parties to invite the other's staff members to ongoing in-house training.

Joint Programming

The easiest way to integrate programming is through mergers, when the control and accountability structures are reworked and the services that were formerly independent come under the same roof. But nonprofits are going to have to find ways of integrating programming short of full mergers and that promises to be no easy chore, as the Western Alliance of Arts Administrators (WAAA) Foundation found out in a novel experiment funded by the James Irvine Foundation in 1993.

Noting that there was a fundamental split in the performing arts community between the well-endowed mainstream presenters and community-based, often ethnically oriented groups, WAAA Executive Director Evan Kavanagh called for an experiment in seeking equity in collaborative relationships. Mainstream, largely Euro-American presenting arts groups viewed community-based presenters of color as essentially convenient doorways to diversification of audiences for their existing presentations, while the latter viewed more well-established agencies suspiciously but with great envy of their first rate facilities and resources.

Eight partnerships between these two types of groups were funded in order to facilitate a collaborative process that could be replicated and improved upon in the arts community, and to broaden the appeal of the WAAA's annual conferences. The results were mixed, and in the WAAA's study of the project, they drew some important conclusions:

- *Successful programmatic collaboration takes time:* One of the unfortunate aspects of the project was that the funding came with deadlines that were not always practical to the participants. Larger presenting organizations tend to be hierarchical and layered with management, and their representatives needed time to accept the collaboration.
- *Trust underlies collaboration:* We have made this point before, but it is worth repeating that participants need to develop understanding and respect for each other, and this cannot be willed into existence simply because a funding source requires it.
- *Knowledge of your partner is essential:* Related to the above points, when the two collaborating organizations knew each other at least minimally, the relationship tended to work better.

- *Flexibility is mandatory:* It was not uncommon for one or both organizations to lose key staff people midway through the process. For different reasons, each type of presenting arts organization often had difficulty delivering on its commitments to the other, and a last minute patch was necessary. Always there were completely unforeseen events, but the successful collaborations were somehow able to adapt to them.

These simple lessons can be summed up with the following thought: *good programmatic collaboration requires excellent planning and lots of time.* Participants need to develop mutual trust and respect over an extended period, understand a great deal about the other, and be willing to be flexible. Only then can the technical skills such as those involved in staging a concert or caring for elders get the clear field they need.

Joint Quality Standards

For an alliance in which members retain their independent corporate identities, the logic is to be so integrated programmatically that any one participant's services reliably meets the same minimum standards of quality. Theoretically, if one guarantees a minimum level of quality no matter which provider is chosen, then the choice of provider will be made on less dramatic grounds such as geography, name recognition, etc.

This is the same principle that has made everything from McDonald's hamburgers to an Ivy League education so successful. The consumer is guaranteed a minimum level of quality and a predictable experience, whether it's the consumption of a meal or the completion of a four-year educational program. What the deans of Yale, Princeton, and Hamburger University understand is that the single strongest factor in consumer motivation is the desire to avoid risk. Risk in this context means everything from the risk of an unpleasant dining experience to inadequate preparation for adult social and economic life. By delivering services which effectively remove the risk of a bad "purchase," they can dominate whatever segment of the market they choose. To be sure, most consumer motivation rests on other factors too. But the integration of a large group of services around a single standard of quality will always be an extremely strong force.

And a frightening one. Because the truth is that shared standards of quality is a very threatening prospect for most organizations right now. The story of a proposal for a quality modification factor is instructive both as a sample of how service providers could work together and as a metaphor for the resistance to change that quality standards represents.

For many years, nursing homes in many states have been reimbursed on a cost-reimbursement basis. This means, within limits, that any dollar spent in the course of providing services to elders is fully reimbursed. It also means that individual facilities' reimbursement rates are produced by a blend of history, coincidence, and management gamesmanship. In other words, they have little or no statistically valid relationship to the quality of services provided.

Working with a group of nursing homes, we proposed that they adopt a state-wide program we dubbed the Quality Modification Factor (QMF). The effort would have left in place the existing cost-based reimbursement system, with all its flaws. However, each rate issued by the rate making body would be modified up or down according to a measure of quality calculated each year, or the QMF. This factor would be derived from a panel of evaluators composed of consumer representatives, funders, and provider representatives. Each facility would receive a yearly visit by a panel of at least three evaluators, some of them peers, and each evaluator would give the facility a single whole number rating on a scale of 1 to 7.

Each year's raw score would be added to the raw scores of the two previous years. The average of these three years would become the QMF for the next year. The next year the oldest year's set of scores would be dropped in favor of the new year's scores, and that average would become the new QMF. Thus, the cost-provocative disincentives of a cost-reimbursement system would be muted by the incentives of a system that rewarded the provision of quality services. Further, no single organization could afford to be complacent, since they would always be judged in the context of the entire industry. The QMF would be calculated so as to modify each rate by a relatively small amount—say, no more than three percentage points plus or minus—so that both success and failure would be rewarded or punished slowly over time. Eventually, underperformers would be forced to drop out, achievers rewarded, and the entire minimum standard of the industry lifted.

Those familiar with meaningful reform efforts in any industry will not be surprised that the QMF was never implemented. Partly this was because the idea was not actively "sold." Partly it was because the idea was first introduced by a group of nonprofit providers which lacked political clout and which the general public nevertheless would not readily identify with a sincere reform effort; it would have been more credible coming from a consumer group. Unfortunately, there was no appropriate consumer group willing and able to take that role.

This is the heart of why service standards will be difficult in the nonprofit sector. In the absence of popular pressure, no industry will voluntarily subject itself to such action. The movie industry instituted a rating system only when pressured to do so. Japanese auto companies agreed to "voluntary" quotas only after the federal government appeared ready to impose import tariffs. Physicians steadfastly refuse to allow public disclosure of even the most rudimentary of performance data.

It's not that every participant within an industry fears accountability for standards of some kind. In fact, as individual organizations many probably hope for such standards, or at least would be confident about working with them. But they are acting in their own best interests as individual entities to resist them initially, so pressures for quality standards have to come from a much more persuasive and reliable source, and that source can only be found in joint action of some kind. For health, social service, and educational organizations, that source eventually is going to be payers, and those payers will likely be facilitated somehow by laws and regulations. Better to begin the process of standard-setting voluntarily than to have it mandated later on.

INTEGRATING MARKETING

We arrive now at the highest level of nonprofit collaboration, the level of corporate change. No value judgments to be made here. We refer to corporate as the highest level not as tribute but rather as the point on the collaboration continuum that is the most profound arena of change. The corporate vehicle is the legal fiction that we overlay on programs, administrative tasks, and support services and, for better or worse, it carries the identity that our programs use in their interaction with the outside world. It is also the basis of accountability and the reconciler of conflicting demands on resources.

Mergers create change at all levels of the participating nonprofits, which is why we say that mergers fulfill all the C.O.R.E. requirements of a collaboration. However, an alliance—or network or integrated service system—can stop short of corporate change, which may be why alliances appear to be growing in popularity more than outright mergers. To illustrate the difference between this level and the previous three, we repeat Exhibit 6.1, but with a twist.

Up to this point, the levels and examples of collaboration we have discussed had this one thing in common: *no one other than the participants cared.* This may sound blunt, but it's true. The reason is because economic collaboration at its most successful will yield savings for all participants, which they can use however they see fit. Participants can and will use savings for different purposes. The same is true of collaboration at the management or responsibility level. Administrative and financial matters are invisible to most users of a service—as they should be. Collaboration in programming is likely to be ad hoc and ever-changing, and its effects are usually hard to track. All of these changes occur below the line in Exhibit 6.1. In truth, the market has every right to be indifferent to them.

Above the line is a different question. When nonprofits act in concert on the economic, management, programmatic, as well as corporate levels, they achieve their maximum power together. The reason for this is a concept we call alignment. Look critically at the three lower levels of collaboration in the C.O.R.E. model. Eco-

Later		
Corporate	Shared Material	Single Signatory
Operations	Communication	Shared Standards
Responsibility	Standardized Services	Integrated Services
Economics	Same Vendor	Single Contract
Sooner	*Low*	*High*
	Degree of Integration	

Exhibit 6.1 Continuums of Collaboration

nomic change is desirable and helpful, but changing the way nonprofits buy their copier paper has no effect whatsoever on the agency mission. Nor does a change in administrative procedures. Changing programs through collaboration will directly affect only the programs involved.

It is only when those responsible for the overall direction and oversight of the organization commit it as an entity to some shared external goal that there exists the possibility of action at the lower levels that is consistent with the larger direction. To put it in different terms, it is always easier to unite a group of people behind an external goal than an internal one.

In a merger, the groundwork for alignment is laid as soon as two or more corporate structures become one. In a strategic alliance, the participating corporate entities need some type of common goal around which to organize themselves. This is the purpose of presenting the market with a united front. The work required to present that front is what aligns the participants.

Shared Marketing

The easiest way of effecting change on the corporate level and therefore of aligning collaboration at all other levels in an alliance is to share marketing responsibilities. Art schools aligning explicitly with art museums, or medical schools with hospitals are two good examples of how this can work. Practically, this kind of sharing can be done by using the same marketing material, or at least marketing material with the same recognizable logo and style. Simply presenting one's organization in collaboration with another to potential users of the service can be a kind of shared marketing.

For a more profound type of shared marketing, consider a word not commonly associated with nonprofits: *franchise.* The word evokes connotations of classic American businesses from Coca Cola to Mary Kay Cosmetics. At its simplest, franchising is a way of spreading a product or service across a wider market area in a shorter time than could be achieved through the resources and efforts of a single company. Franchising is a staple of the business landscape both for large national firms and for the smaller local franchise holders. Too bad nonprofits don't franchise.

Or do they? Think about the YMCA. Does the name Goodwill Industries sound familiar? Make a Wish Foundation? United Cerebral Palsy Associations? United Way? If some of the names sound familiar it's because the nonprofit field's own version of franchising has been successful. Some nonprofits have been doing a form of franchising all along. What all these names have in common is that in some way they are examples of what we might call nonprofit franchises.

Let's look at the idea of nonprofit franchises more closely. One thing that all these names share, at least within their own fields, is instant recognizability. Another thing they share is predictability. People know generally what to expect when they enter a YMCA or when they deal with a United Way. The local embodiment of the national concept may vary to one degree or another, but users have been educated as to what they'll find. Often the source of that education is hard to pinpoint because it's so much a part of everyday culture.

Push a bit harder on the analysis and you'll find that the reason for predictability is that the national body has taken steps to insure that local groups using their name meet certain standards. This is a matter of communicating exactly what it means to be a member of that particular franchise and then requiring adherence. It's not unlike the way the IRS works with nonprofits: prove that you meet specific criteria for being considered a tax exempt public charity and you're admitted into the circle. Deviate from those criteria and you're out.

Without question it is difficult to create a national name for a nonprofit enterprise, though perhaps it should be easier (see Idea box). It is even harder to make that name truly mean something that the market values. However, the broad outlines of what others have accomplished should serve as a useful guide to concerted action at the corporate level.

Shared Contracting

The most powerful form of alliance at the corporate level, other than what happens in a merger, is when two or more groups bind themselves contractually to provide a given service. In one sense it is little more than an extension of other types of alliances, but the

Idea: Foundations as Nonprofit Venture Capitalists

What is it that usually stands in the way of a new (or contemplated) nonprofit and widespread advancement of a good idea? And what is it that foundations have in abundance? The answer to both questions, of course, is money. How long will it be before a few national foundations reverse course on allocation policies and act as venture capitalists for the purpose of spreading good new ideas? Foundations typically fund operating costs and actively avoid capital investments. But what if a national foundation were to discover a proven idea in one of their grantees that others could use? And what if they were to act as venture capitalists to franchise those ideas, awarding grants measured in the hundreds of thousands of dollars to many different groups for the purpose of creating new, well, franchises? And what if they were to treat their grants the way a venture capitalist sans profit motive would treat them? What if they were to sit on the board, offer intangible assistance and advice, and work their networks on behalf of the new entity? What might happen is that we would create powerful alliances of nonprofits around the country with the strategic position, resources, and talent to serve the public good.

element of legal enforceability adds a completely new dimension. Shared contracting inherently provides the kind of alignment we spoke of earlier throughout the participating agencies.

To some extent this is the Holy Grail of nonprofit alliances, having been attempted by few agencies so far. Still, it is clear that present trends in nonprofit funding will force more and more groups to enter into some form of legally enforceable joint contracting. This direction is most obvious in the health care field where managed care is at the heart of many reform efforts. A form of payment called capitation is a good example of what payers of all kinds will be demanding and that will eventually lead to joint contracting.

A program originating in San Francisco is an example of how capitated payment will force joint risk taking and contracting. The On Lok program, so named for the area in San Francisco where it first began, targets elders who have been recognized as being eligible for nursing home placement. Through a novel blending of the

Medicare and Medicaid streams of payment that would otherwise have been available separately to pay for an elder in a nursing home, funds are given in a luinp sum each month to the On Lok-style provider (as of the mid-1990s, there were about a dozen such demonstration projects around the country). Each such provider handles a predetermined number of at-risk elders—often one or two hundred at a time.

Out of the monthly allotment of money that each provider receives for all of its elder clients, it must arrange, procure, and pay for all services ranging from hospitalization to nursing home stays to home care to hospice. This is what it means to receive capitated payments. Each provider must become skilled at determining the least costly and most efficient course of treatment for every elder. The key is that the risk for misjudging care needs or over-providing services lies entirely with the provider.

Although most of the On Lok (also known as PACE) pilot programs are based in a single entity such as a health center, if the program model is adopted around the country it will almost certainly require future providers to develop integrated service delivery systems. Consequently, independent entities will have to find ways of jointly contracting and of sharing risk under capitated systems.

Pitfall: Your Market is Watching

Don't outrun your market. Strategic alliances like the ones we have been describing here are so powerful that in some instances they can actually backfire. One physicians' group, for example, tried to put together its own network to contract with managed care organizations. It was a good idea, except for one thing the managed care organizations weren't interested. As payers, they can be expected to fear alliances and will usually prefer to deal with members one at a time in order to maximize their own negotiating leverage. The problem with this network was that they had nothing that the managed care organizations wanted. Had they possessed natural advantages such as an undisputed regional reputation for quality *as a group* or perhaps if they controlled a big enough pool of patients the outcome might have been different.

The equivalent of managed care can be expected to be used in other areas as well. Some government corrections officials are already rethinking their traditional style of prison-based services in favor of a continuum of services. Behavioral health providers in many areas are already under some form of managed care, and it is not out of the question for the methodology to be adapted to education in some way. All these trends eventually will create new ways in which nonprofits contract jointly and share on all four C.O.R.E. levels. The result will be powerful incentives to integrate services, and the development of new models of collaboration.

Postscript: Competition versus Collaboration

One of the quiet results of the trends described in the first section and the collaborations being considered as a result of them is that many nonprofits will find themselves simultaneously collaborating and competing with their peers. For instance, two different major nonprofits in the same geographic area providing similar services may compete for grants and contracts on the one hand at the same time that they collaborate to establish quality of service standards and purchase goods and services together.

The C.O.R.E. model explains how this can be possible (note: it's been happening for a long time in the for-profit sector, in areas such as computer manufacturing and airline reservations). That doesn't make it any easier to cope with, of course, since it contradicts everything we think we know about how organizations get work done in this society. Part of the answer lies in understanding how it is possible and even advisable for the same organization to operate in two different ways on two different levels of the C.O.R.E. model.

The other part of the answer is to reorient ourselves to the fact that competition means something different among nonprofits than it does in the for-profit sector. When Ford and General Motors compete, they are two suppliers reaching for millions of consumers. But for most nonprofits in the health, social services, and related fields, the situation is different. Instead of millions of buyers there are only a handful such as government, insurance companies, private consumers, and philanthropies. And instead of a handful of suppliers, there are usually a relatively large number in a geographic area.

In the absence of a profit motive, therefore, competition in the latter arena becomes less like the competition between Ford and GM and more like the competition that frequently exists between two different departments in a large bureaucracy. It can become heated at times, but ultimately the competitors have more interests in common than they have differences. The only time that competition is likely to resemble consumer market competition is when survival is at stake.

Ironically, those who fear or disapprove of competition between nonprofits are really just the photo negative of the rabid capitalist who believes that competition is the answer for everything. Many practicing nonprofit managers recognize already—or will begin to do so soon—that implementing a mission in the future will require an ability to compete and collaborate at the same time.

PART THREE

Structuring the Collaboration

CHAPTER SEVEN

Selecting a Partner and Building Trust

FIRST STEPS

Most nonprofit organizations, especially public charities, are very local in character and have extensive ties to a geographically defined community. Even large national nonprofits usually have local chapters. Fundraising efforts and visible services reinforce that local identity, regardless of where the corporation is chartered. Many boards of directors maintain a fierce commitment to their community. In the past, health care and social service organizations even received governmental funding according to carefully drawn boundaries. Terms like *catchment area* and *health systems area* are relics of those days that have little or no operating significance today, but that linger in the self-identities of many organizations.

These characteristics of the nonprofit service delivery system mean there is an excellent chance that you already know of at least one potential merger or alliance partner. For many groups there are several potential partners operating nearby. Sometimes in a merger situation there was even a previous attempt at discussing merger within the past few years. Participants on both sides may describe the attempt with phrases like "it never went anywhere" or "I don't know exactly what happened." In these cases the factor which seems to catalyze a second attempt is a change in the leadership of one or both parties.

Other relationships can predispose certain nonprofits toward allying with each other. In one situation a three-way merger was actually a kind of 20-year attempt at organizational closure. Three different behavioral health clinics, each concentrating on a particular population or funding source, had been part of the same smaller agency many years earlier. Funding source pressure and philosophies of the time had led them to split into three different groups, each operating program sites no more than four miles from each other and in one case actually maintaining headquarters three blocks apart. Although almost none of the original personnel or board members remained, the merger represented a closing of the loop as three distinctly different agencies melded their identities to create a new large service provider.

Not all relationships are built at the top levels. In many instances program staff or managers used to work at a logical merger or alliance partner. More significantly, their daily responsibilities may bring them into contact with each other. In some instances there may have even been explicit attempts at collaboration that were never particularly well-publicized because they were informal or temporary.

Whatever the origins of the relationships between the organizations seeking to collaborate, managers and boards of directors need to make maximum use of them. Generally, this is done on an informal basis, since there is rarely an opportunity for the person

Tip: Look for Relationships Everywhere

Even in small nonprofit agencies it's easy for managers to live an insular existence, talking only to peers and outsiders about weighty matters such as mergers and alliances. For some organizations there may actually be an active history of collaboration about which the leaders know little. In the course of solving daily problems, program staff have to make countless little alliances to get the job done. School personnel need access to a huge range of social welfare, health care, and educational institutions. Many social service workers must make it their business to know about the range of services available to their clients, and this inevitably brings them into contact with the agencies providing those services. All these forces can produce exactly the kind of experience needed to instill institutional trust.

or persons involved to stand up and testify to the overall trustworthiness of the prospective partner.

CHARACTERISTICS OF A COMPATIBLE PARTNER

Several distinct characteristics suggest a compatible partner agency. They do not all need to be present for a merger or alliance to work, nor does the absence of all of them predict trouble. However, they can help paint a reliable portrait of a good partner in a successful collaboration. Keep in mind that these characteristics are described from the perspective of an outsider. Further investigation may reveal a much different reality from that first perceived, but that would become clear during the due diligence phase of the process.

Absence of a Permanent Executive Director

A good catalyst to a nonprofit merger is the absence of a permanent executive director. In a nonprofit organization the executive director, or chief executive officer, has almost unparalleled power. In fact, with the possible exception of a self-financed sole proprietor, no other managerial position in the American economy carries the potential for power to such a degree as the nonprofit executive director.

The reasons are complex. Board members serve without pay and cannot hold a stake in the organization. Their chief source of industry-related information will almost always be the executive director who, they are fully aware, spends many more hours each week pondering strategic issues than they can. Bankers rarely assert themselves in leadership matters and there are no stockholders to face. Funding sources tend to be more interested in accountability for funds than for performance, and external watchdog agencies are few in number and concentrate mainly on extreme cases. Within these very broad limits the executive director has virtually unassailable power to set and maintain strategic direction.

Take that person away, and what does the average agency have left? The answer will vary according to each situation, but, owing to the very personal nature of nonprofit leadership, there will at least be a period of transition before the next leader is comfortably in place. It is during this period that the nonprofit is likely to be most open to new ideas.

At present, there is little precedent in most areas for nonprofit boards to consider merging instead of replacing their chief executive officer (CEO). That will change in time as more and more organizations opt for an alliance or merger of some sort. In fact, it is entirely conceivable that an empty CEO's chair will automatically prompt consideration of merger at some point in the future.

Note that the situation is reversed for developing an alliance or integrated service network. Since these types of collaboration typically require intact corporate leadership, a CEO transition is the hardest time to initiate an alliance.

Nonoverlapping Markets

A second aspect of a potentially compatible partner is nonoverlapping markets. Although not essential, it is helpful if the partners do not routinely compete with each other. When the competitive hormones have been stimulated regularly over a period of years, it is easy for misunderstandings and hard feelings to develop in one or both parties. The obvious way that markets can be nonoverlapping is through geography (see the section "Geographic Compatibility" in this chapter for a detailed discussion of this method), but the more sophisticated segmentation is through services offered.

The three-way behavioral health services merger described earlier is a classic example of how nonoverlapping markets can help the process. With one clinic focused on children, another on adults, and the third on chronically ill residents of government-funded residential programs, there was little opportunity for the three to collide. In fact, the child-oriented clinic often referred its aging clients to the adult program, while the residential programs often dealt with the adult clinic.

Certain characteristics of the market can help determine the degree of competitiveness any two groups feel. The smaller or more controlled the market, the more likely that groups will feel competitive with each other. Government funding through a formalized Request for Proposals (RFP) process deliberately reinforces an ethic of competitiveness, while a largely foundation-funded sector tends to segment organizations along economic and cultural lines. Long established services such as nursing homes or museums are likely to be quite starkly segmented, while newer services will have more blurred boundaries.

Geographic Compatibility

Few things have changed more quickly in nonprofit service delivery in recent years than the role of geography in determining the scope of a nonprofit's market. Until fairly recently, geography was a source of both limits and a guideline to the proper structure of a nonprofit. One could reliably know that a nonprofit operating in a major city was unlikely to have offices in a nearby suburb, and a non-national nonprofit operating in more than one state was unheard of. Similarly, a wide range of geography was usually handled by branch offices, which were essentially miniaturized pieces of the main office broken off and planted in the field.

Today, information technology has obliterated the former truisms. Fax machines, modems, wide area networks (WANs), e-mail, groupware, and now even videoconferencing have made physical location much less of a concern in managing a far-flung enterprise of any sort. Along the way, the pertinent geographic question about expansion has subtly changed. Implicitly it used to be "can you control it?" Today, the pertinent geographic question about a merger or alliance tends to be "does it expand your market?" In fact, increasing geographic scope is often a very attractive reason for merging or forming an alliance.

At the same time, let us acknowledge that this aspect of mergers and alliances is a grand experiment. Geographic expansion pushes the envelope of nonprofit management in a way that it has never been pushed before. Many, especially those closer to program services than financial management or the executive ranks, worry that increasing nonprofits' size will wipe out innovation, motivation, and community identification. There is no reason to think that they are right. Managing a $50 million a year nonprofit is not inherently different than managing a $1 million one; the differences are more in style and degree than in size. What geographic expansion can do is to help agencies and systems climb over the minimum economic size required for their sector.

Tip: Use Zips

One of the quickest ways of determining market and geographic compatibility is to get a list of the Zip Codes of all current service users from all partners as of the same point in time. Plot the numbers of users from each Zip Code on a map (there are inexpensive computer mapping programs for this purpose, though a plain old map from under the driver's seat will work too). As a rule of thumb, consider the primary market to be the area encompassing approximately 65–70 percent of all the zip codes. Put the two primary markets together on the same map. Is there overlap? Is it substantial? Does it represent direct competition or just different ways of serving the same population? The answers to these questions will help determine how compatible the partners will be in these two categories.

Compatibility of Services

A sensible way to evaluate a potential partner is how compatible the two sets of services seem. Nonprofit agencies are organized around the delivery of services. Staff are hired and trained in a certain way, sites are acquired and managed according to particular needs, and the whole administrative and programmatic infrastructure is organized to support those services. None of these things change easily, and sometimes they don't mix well with another version of the same elements. If you're considering a merger it is particularly helpful to know ahead of time whether the parties' services are compatible or not.

One useful way of analyzing services is the idea of core competencies. First articulated by management theorists Gary Hamel and C. K. Prahalad, the notion of core competence is a powerful management tool. Briefly, a core competence is a blend of institutional knowledge and structure that accomplishes a generic task for a market in a unique way. For example, a core competence of a foster care program is the ability to broker. The fundamental core competence of a residential school is hospitality services—food, room, and safety. One of the core competencies of a trade association is information management, and so on.

The difficult part about core competencies is that certain major ones can only exist in the same entity with a great deal of effort and managerial self-awareness. Social clubs for the mentally ill or developmentally disabled have an inclusionary ethic that is at odds with the more rehabilitation-oriented get-them-into-the-workforce philosophy of supported work programs. Associations for Retarded Citizens (ARCs) often find it difficult to maintain their advocacy role when they also provide services. Hospice programs are part service, part social movement, and it can be difficult to integrate them into traditional home health care providers.

In the end, there is no substitute for getting inside an organization and seeing its various competencies from the inside out. Until you get a chance to do that, everything else is just informed speculation.

A second way to assess a possible partner's services is by the degree to which a merger or alliance would create a fuller continuum of services. Although the notion of a continuum of care started in the health and human services field, where it was hastened by the coming of managed care organizations, the principle of a continuum of services is so economically sound and programmatically attractive that it will almost certainly spread to other fields such as corrections, education, and arts. Payers and users alike are going to insist on seamless integration and a full range of services, and when that happens the only strategic response is to begin putting together groupings of services with natural pathways in between them.

Pitfall: Premature Disclosure

Though it may seem unnecessarily cloak-and-daggerish, it's usually better to conduct the type of research described here with discretion. Why? One reason is that it's highly premature: there will be plenty of time for complete disclosure later if affiliating seems to make sense. Another is that it can easily be misinterpreted. Once two parties are identified in the context of seeking a partner, both are likely to be stamped with that perception no matter how accurate or inaccurate. Premature full disclosure loses more than it gains.

Tip: Public Information Resources

As publicly approved and monitored entities, nonprofits must make key types of information readily available. Most often the information is financially based, but it still can be useful for general research, especially by someone who knows how to read and interpret it. Thanks to a 1996 law, nonprofits must give copies of their IRS Form 990, the nonprofit tax return, to anyone who asks for one. As this is being written, there are plans to put the forms on the Internet. And don't overlook the organization's own marketing material for some insight into how a nonprofit partner presents itself.

In this context, we introduce the concept of vertical alliances versus horizontal alliances. Briefly, the difference is whether participants align themselves with others doing the same kind of thing (i.e., a group of nursing homes) or whether they join a group representing the full spectrum of services in their field (i.e., a hospital, nursing home, home health provider, and neighborhood clinics). Neither choice is automatically right or wrong, because the advantages and disadvantages of each stem from the complex interactions of a number of facts and circumstances, but potential partners need to consider at least broadly which choice the objectives of their collaboration would require.

Special Assets

Sometimes the characteristics of a good partner don't fit neatly into one of the above categories. Sometimes the attractiveness of another nonprofit isn't easy to quantify or even to describe. We put these situations into the general category of special assets. These can range from things as common as real estate ownership and endowments to features as abstract as good political connections or a strong entrepreneurial culture. One merger we know of occurred in part because one executive director tired of the day-to-day management demands of the agency he had created and wanted instead to concentrate on his first love, making political connections, and doing neighborhood development. For his part, the other executive director was more than happy to take over the executive director role since he had long cherished the notion of using a complex and powerful social service delivery system to deliver a high volume of quality services.

Making the Approach

Not surprisingly, the simple act of suggesting that another nonprofit organization consider merging can be a difficult proposition. Since in many areas of the country the idea of merger is still synonymous with failure (old ideas die hard), it's possible that the comment might be seen as insulting. The bearer of the suggestion has a lot to do with how it is taken. For this reason, it is usually best to use an intermediary. Finding the right intermediary is the challenge.

The board is a good place to start. One of the bits of homework that can often be done through publicly available sources (tax forms and the agency's own letterhead, for example) is to obtain the list of a potential partner's board of directors. Particularly in towns, suburbs, and small urban areas, there is a good possibility that one of your board members will know someone on the other board. In that case, initiating a discussion about aligning in some way might be done over a casual cup of coffee between old friends.

Employment Tip: Your Next Boss Could Be an Alliance

All these alliances, once they get formed, are going to need staff. One of the most intriguing boomlets in the nonprofit field is—and will continue to be—the jobs created by alliances themselves. Obviously there is a great temptation to simply slip excess staff from one of the alliance partners into newly created alliance jobs, but the need for people who can facilitate and get groups working together is so different from the operations-oriented jobs that most employees currently have that this may not work. No hard facts and figures available on this trend yet, but it's such a logical one that it'll pay the future job seeker to keep an eye on it.

If board-to-board contact doesn't work, there are always built-in intermediaries such as auditors and attorneys. Professional advisors often specialize in industries, so there is a good chance that these individuals will know people in the potential partner. One of these professionals might be willing to help out. Funding source representatives may also be able to initiate a contact, although there are enough inherent tensions in the funding source's relationship with its recipients that this can be risky.

Finally, paid intermediaries can serve a useful purpose. These are individuals the need for which will be obvious once large numbers of organizations start to merge and create alliances. Chances are that they will be management consultants of one sort or another. Like all consultant populations, they will probably fit one of two descriptions. The first will be professional, permanent management consultants either employed by firms or in a sole practice. The second category of consultant will be professionals in between jobs who are simply filling the time until the next full-time permanent role comes along. In the case of alliances, some of these people may even go on to become alliance staff people; we have already seen this happen.

ANALYZING THE CULTURE

Nonprofit organizations start with ideas. Whether the idea is as simple and universally accepted as the notion of educating children or as complex as preserving the artistic heritage of an entire community, the founding idea is the starting point. Eventually it gets developed into what is more commonly called a mission, and this idea gets communicated either formally or informally to its leaders, staff, and funding sources.

What carries a mission is values. These are largely implicit statements about what matters to the people associated with the leadership of a nonprofit. Values underlie behavior. If I regard something as important enough to be done, I will organize my behavior in order to get it done. I may not always be successful, but I will try. Similarly, over time the leadership of a nonprofit will organize it and direct it such that, generally speaking, it will be true to those underlying values. Note that values are embodied in action, not spoken words or even written policies. The true values of an organization, the ones that consistently drive it, are the ones that find expression in hundreds of specific actions (or inaction) by many different people every day.

Since many people in a nonprofit must take action reflecting its underlying values every day with little notice or advance preparation, they need some guidance as to the appropriate actions to be taken. The glue that links actions to values is what we call the organizational culture, and it is here that we see the greatest divergence among nonprofit organizations. It is entirely possible, and in fact it is likely, for groups of people all around the country to recognize the same general need for a specific nonprofit service at about the same time. It is equally probable that their true values will look a lot alike. Where they will diverge is in the ways they make those values work—that is, in the culture that they develop to link values to action.

The culture of a nonprofit invariably begins with the board of directors. They hire the chief executive officer and after that everything they do—even if it includes doing nothing while the CEO does everything—sets the tone for the organization. What this means is that nonprofit culture is normally the one thing on which there is greatest agreement throughout the organization, though it may not always be explicit.

We once worked with two different behavioral health centers that had every reason to merge their agencies. They were located in the same (relatively small) town within blocks of each other. They each had similar and in some cases identical funding sources. Discussions with board leaders on both sides revealed remarkably similar values; a college town, their service area was rooted in Vietnam War era political philosophy, and a good many of the board members themselves were just entering their personally and professionally productive middle age.

Where these two organizations differed was in their cultures. One was highly focused on what they saw as their public responsibility and related accountability, with former clinicians occupying the top managerial spots. They favored traditional means of organizing themselves and were noted for the slowness of their strategic reactions. The other was highly entrepreneurial and willing to take risks. Their fiscal performance tended to fluctuate dramatically over the years, and it seemed that management was always consumed with one or another grand plan such as rescuing a third

Tip: Where to See Organizational Culture at Work

There are many good places to look for evidence of a nonprofit's culture. The key is to look in as many as possible and to assemble what you find into a coherent portrait of the organization. Not every one of these places will yield insight, and some will contradict others, but overall the list represents a usable roadmap to the nature of the culture. In alphabetical order, here they are:

- Composition of board and management team
- Degree of centralization versus decentralization
- Demographics of clients
- Demographics of staff
- Financial investment policies
- Financial performance
- Geographic location
- Management compensation policies
- Number and type of management meetings
- Number of board meetings per year
- Philosophy regarding staff turnover
- Process for recruiting and selecting new board members
- Requirements of major funding sources
- Size of board
- Size of management team (especially versus comparable non-profits)
- Unwritten/unspoken hiring preferences

local agency from bankruptcy and bidding to take over the management of an inpatient psychiatric unit in the local hospital even though no one had asked them to do so.

The differences in management style were reflected in differences at the board level. There were explicit concerns about being able to "trust" the entrepreneurial executive director who, thanks to the other CEO's retirement, was slated to become the CEO of the merged entity. These frictions were compounded by the fact that the entrepreneurial agency clearly had the better management talent in place. The merger occurred, but blending the two cultures was not easy. Years later there were still tensions and dissatisfactions expressed by the more traditional agency's core board members.

Cultural differences between organizations considering collaboration need explicit and sustained attention. Jill Sherer, writing in *Hospitals and Health Networks,* cites studies suggesting that as many as 75 percent of hospital mergers fail if cultural issues are not taken into consideration.

Even in situations in which the success or failure of the collaboration is not at stake, potential partners need to be fully informed about each other's culture. One of the most reliable rules of thumb for post-merger implementation is that *the stronger culture always prevails.* This is not to say that the culture of the larger organization will automatically dominate, or that the loudest or flashiest culture will carry forward. Rather, it is the tightest culture with the most viable ways of transmitting it that will eventually color the newly merged organization and perhaps characterize the new organization totally.

The Role of Class

A major subcategory of cultural considerations are the differences rooted in socioeconomic class. In many ways, economic class issues are woven into the very mission of nonprofit organizations. Civic symphonies require large numbers of people schooled in Western classical music, and they therefore tend to attract the middle and upper class participants who are most likely to have been exposed to it. Conversely, grass-roots organizations inevitably take on the socioeconomic character of the geographic locale they seek to serve.

In view of the nonprofit organization's role as carriers of values, this dynamic should be no surprise. It becomes problematic mainly when it is not recognized and incorporated into planning the collaboration. Often unrecognized class differences are the real driver behind a lingering feeling of "us versus them."

Most observers of the evolution of nonprofit organizations during this century seem to agree that the character of boards has changed from small clusters of local elites united by common culture and values to larger and more diverse groups of people who have more ideas than relationships in common. This trend derives from the general tendency of the American elite class to be determined not so much from social position anymore as from cognitive accomplishment.

An enduring if subtle dynamic in mergers—less so in alliances—is that people in every position from board to staff who most readily identify with the class-related aspects of the service will have the hardest time accepting a potential partner who does not share the same characteristics. One nurse who worked in a medical-surgical unit of a hospital about to be merged with another put it bluntly. "We get a lot of our referrals from suburban doctors and clinics. They [the other hospital] get most of their referrals from the city. There's no way that any of our patients is going to be willing to wake up from surgery next to a crack cocaine addict."

Another dynamic in mergers that can complicate the process is that board members may very well have a different class perspective than employees. In large nonprofits they will probably have more in common socioeconomically with management than with the majority of people who work for the organization so they are liable to see major issues—including the need for a merger itself—very differently. Again, the antidote is recognize these differences from the beginning and to incorporate them into planning. One of the advantages of the Merger Committee/Subcommittee structure described later in this book is that it helps mitigate the effects of cultural differences.

Pitfall: Don't Confuse Culture with Governance

Culture is not the same thing as governance. Cultural issues are typically resolved long before governance matters arise. In fact, the tendency of a nonprofit to homogenize its value set is what frequently reduces matters of governance to a series of lopsided votes. In a merger of two strong and healthy agencies, questions of governance will be far less contentious if the organizational values are compatible.

A Quick Culture Check

Superficially, it is relatively easy to find out about a nonprofit partner's corporate culture: ask around. Rarely does informed public opinion completely misread an organization's culture. It may be a bit dated because there hasn't been time for it to catch up to the effects of a major change such as the departure of the CEO, but in general it will be reliable. Skilled analysts will also find evidence of culture in the large amounts of information on the public record about most nonprofits. Tax returns are available for the asking, and some states keep copies on file for public inspection. Bond prospectus documents, when available, make for tedious but enormously useful reading. Even marketing material, when read carefully, can provide strong clues as to what an organization's culture is all about.

Once a discussion is under way, valuable bits of information can be picked up from a review of the areas described in the tip box on page 96. For a fast gauge of the potential partner's culture try another approach. Engage the executive director and a few key board members in a discussion, explicit or not, of the agency's last three major decisions. How were the issues framed? By whom? At what point in the decision-making process? How was the decision finally made, or was it never made at all? Once made, how was the decision communicated?

All these questions will help get at the nature of the decision-making process in the organization and will reveal a great deal about its values. Just the issues that various respondents choose as the three most important ones and the degree of consistency among them will say something about the organization's culture. In the end, however, a judgment about organizational culture is just that: a judgment. All participants must make their own assessment of a potential partner's organizational culture and use it as the basis for future action.

BUILDING TRUST

Trust is easily the most underrated economic force in our society. Acts as simple as hiring a nonfamily member—someone who until recently was probably a complete stranger—and giving them control of assets and paying them money in return for future results are things we take for granted, but they are at the heart of industrial and post-industrial economy. Nonprofits, of course, hold it as a virtue to operate outside of the family business mode. To do otherwise would invite mistrust and perhaps risk violating the law.

Nonprofits are hothouses for trust. The Internal Revenue Service grants them nonprofit status and rarely attempts to second-guess the exemption unless prompted to do so. Funding sources give public charities money without the protection of a contract. Community leaders trust that nonprofits are doing something for the larger good. Boards of directors trust management to execute decisions in line with a larger vision. And so on. It is no exaggeration to say that the entire fabric of nonprofit organizations, more so than any other private entities, is based largely on an intricate web of trusting relationships.

The Tools of Trust: Disclosure, Consultation, and Collaboration

When two or more nonprofit organizations decide to collaborate, creating an atmosphere of trust is absolutely essential. Carefully selecting a potential partner can lay the groundwork for trust to grow as described earlier, but agencies interested in collaborating can also do certain things to accelerate the process.

Disclosure. The first step in building trust is disclosure. Nonprofit corporations operate in an environment of public account-

Tip: It Isn't Just a Matter of Being Nice

Saying that trust is all-important isn't just a knee-jerk vote for motherhood, apple pie, and vaccinations. It's also easier. When the parties share a high degree of trust their process will be free of much of the time-wasting digressions, requests for clarification and misunderstanding that thrive on mistrust. Think of it as a cheap productivity tool.

ability, a big part of which is the routine disclosure of information that in a privately held for-profit company would be unthinkable. Copies of corporate tax returns, for example, must be provided to anyone who asks, and information ranging from salaries to program costs are often routinely available through other public sources. Shrewd leaders make this high level of built-in scrutiny work for them, but some try to act as though they have no responsibility to the public. Needless to say, they are not good candidates for collaboration.

Disclosure is necessary throughout the process of collaborating, but it is pivotal at two distinct times. The first is early on in the process, when both parties are first contemplating a merger or alliance. The second point is when the parties conduct what is known as a due diligence investigation after they have decided to pursue a merger but before it has taken serious shape. We will elaborate on the due diligence process in the next chapter. For now we will focus on early disclosure.

Disclosure early in a merger—for reasons that will become clear later on, disclosure has greater legal weight in a merger than in an

Tip: Food Builds Trust

It's amazing how far a few dollars spent on bagels will go. Or crackers. Or grits, doughnuts, fruit, or pork rinds. It really doesn't matter. It is simply easier to get people talking and interacting over food. There's another reason why providing food works so well. Busy overscheduled people often like to schedule merger-related meetings for one end of the day or the other. Having breakfast food at an early morning meeting provides fast get-going energy, and eliminates a nagging worry for group members who got up too late to eat before leaving the house. At the end of the day everyone's energy is sagging and a plate of cookies—or a full meal, if it's appropriate—replenishes the batteries enough to get through an hour or two worth of business.

Sub-tip: Try not to let evening meetings run past 9:00 P.M. Concentration fades, fidgetiness sets in, and not a few group members start wondering if they'll miss their favorite TV show.

alliance—is largely an informal matter. Board members who meet to talk in broad terms about "getting together" should engage in it, as well as executive directors who play the same role. All parties need a reliable thumbnail sketch of the other to use in future discussions, and it should amount to a balanced portrait of the agency.

What should be disclosed? How detailed does one have to get? What things should be disclosed early in the process? Use what in other contexts is called a materiality standard: *if a reasonable person would make a different decision had he or she known a particular fact, it should be considered a material fact and should be disclosed accordingly.*

Consultation. Once two or more organizations have decided to form some sort of merger or alliance, they need to know that they will always have the most updated information about their partner or partners. The simplest way to know this is to agree ahead of time—verbally and ultimately in writing—that no major decisions will be made without the other party's knowledge.

This is a proposition best agreed upon early in the process. In many areas where nonprofits are involved, the pace of change is unusually fast and it may not take long for a major change to occur in one of the partners. Being so close to the issue, managers don't always recognize the implications of a decision or an external development. We were once working on an alliance between several elder care organizations. Unknown to most of us, one of the participants was also in discussions with a new and rapidly integrating health care network. When the participating organization made a long term commitment to the larger network and announced it in a meeting, the confusion was palpable and took a while to resolve.

Collaboration. Unlike the previous two principles, collaboration is a less functional necessity and more a symbolic one. In some ways it doesn't matter exactly how the parties collaborate as long as they do. Note that we are using the word collaboration here on a somewhat less grand scale. This is cooperation around the daily demands of management. Everybody likes a little help to get the job done, and a prospective merger partner is nicely positioned to offer uniquely valuable help.

Two of the easiest and quickest ways to get into the collaboration frame of mind involve human resources management. One is

Tip: When to Consult

It's not a bad idea to spell out exactly what the parties agree to consult each other about during the process of their alliance formation. Here are some possibilities (not an exhaustive list):

- Changes in accreditation status
- Changes in major leases
- Changes in office or program site space
- Collective bargaining status
- Insurance coverage lapses
- Major asset acquisition or disposal plans
- Major media attention planned or anticipated
- Major new positions being added
- Management and board of directors' role changes
- New programs or services, including *all* contracts
- Planned borrowing activity
- Plans to submit proposals/new revenues received
- Possible or actual litigation
- Public processes anticipated (e.g., license renewals, zoning variances, etc.)
- Significant budget variances
- Unmet tax liabilities

to share job postings. Simply being sure to send notices of open jobs to the other organization is a good way to build good will, signal that the prospective alliance is real, and possibly gain a good staff member or two in the process. Even "losing" a staff member this way can be a win if it places a friend in the ranks of the other group.

Another way to collaborate on a person-to-person level is to seek joint opportunities for staff development. This can be as simple as arranging interagency carpools to conferences or as complex as mounting a joint training program.

The Role of a Premerger Agreement

Consider putting all the preceding into a premerger agreement, sometimes called a memorandum of understanding. Not to be confused with the final merger agreement, a premerger agreement acts as a formal kick-off to the merger or alliance-building process (it tends to be more useful for mergers than for alliances, since most alliances don't change corporate structure). While it is not always essential, it will spell out a framework for mutual learning and collaboration. Generally, the larger and more complex the organization, or if the alliance being planned involves some type of nonprofit/for-profit combination, the more a premerger agreement will be necessary. The premerger agreement will acknowledge that the signatories plan some form of collaboration, and it will describe the responsibilities and roles each will have. If confidentiality is a concern, the premerger agreement will detail what is expected of the parties, especially if the process does not result in any formal collaboration.

CHAPTER EIGHT

Merger or Alliance? How to Decide

In structuring nonprofit mergers and alliances, as in all good architecture, form should follow function. Participants in the planning process to this point will know what they are trying to accomplish. It need not be expressed in complicated language or in legal terminology. It may not ever be explicitly summarized in a sentence or two, but it will probably exist as a collection of shared understandings and objectives that most participants would cite independently if asked to list their joint goals.

The title of this chapter imprecisely implies that there is always a discernible difference between mergers and alliances. Most of the time, there is. But in large systems knit together by contractual agreements or by a mix of ownership and management control arrangements, the distinction between a merger and an alliance may be functionally academic. In truth, most large entities in the modern business world that are regarded as monoliths are in fact more like a strategically allied network of smaller businesses. The underlying legal principle differentiating mergers from alliances is that merged entities usually share common control. Thus, there is a clear difference between mergers and alliances, and participants need to decide which path to follow. In principle, it is largely a matter of reasoning backward from shared goals, while incorporating various practical considerations.

The topics below are meant to suggest some of the common influences on choice of structure. The list is not intended to be comprehensive. Generic factors quickly give way to very specific influences that will not always fit neatly into one of the following categories. Nevertheless, these elements should cover a large number of the key factors agencies will consider when deciding how to organize their collaboration. When they fall short of describing a specific situation, they may perhaps be of some use by stimulating thinking about the factors that do matter.

CORPORATE CONTROL

Without a doubt, the pivotal factor shaping the choice of structure in a nonprofit collaboration is the nature of corporate control desired. The term management control here refers to actions taken at the corporate level in the C.O.R.E. model. In our framework, whoever has responsibility for corporate actions in an organization has corporate control. In freestanding nonprofits this means that control is shared by the board of directors and the executive director and by a management team, if one exists. In our model, *if the focal point of corporate control changes as the result of a collaboration, a merger can be said to have occurred.* If change occurs only at the economic, responsibility, or operations levels, it is an alliance or affiliation. Mergers are about transfer of the locus of control.

This question of what happens at the corporate level is behind most discussions about structure in a nonprofit collaboration. We are talking only about the legal and systemic levers of control here, the provisions in the bylaws and similar documents that set out who is responsible for what and how they exercise their control. A strong CEO or board of directors can exert more control than they are given on paper, but that is more of an interpersonal quirk not supported by the underlying legal structure.

For-profit mergers tend to focus a great deal on the structural aspects of management control: stock ownership, voting rights, and board composition, for instance. Management control comes from these things almost automatically. In nonprofits, by contrast, there are fewer structural sources of control, and they function more to facilitate the emergence of leadership than to define it.

What all of this means in plain English is that leadership positions in a nonprofit are not transferable. If I own a big block of stock in a for-profit company that's merged with a comparable size firm, I will still have a significant economic interest in the merged entity, though it will be diluted; if I were the single largest stockholder in the original firm I may even be the single largest stockholder in the merged one. Not so with nonprofits, because there is no universally recognized means for transferring interests. Depending on how things go, I may not even have a role in the new organization.

This is why corporate control is so critical to nonprofits considering a collaboration, and why they are reluctant to give it up. It's not so much that boards and management cling to specific corporate vehicles—if asked, for technical legal reasons, to close down a corporation that had run a respected museum for 50 years and immediately replace it with another new corporation with the same name, most wouldn't hesitate—but rather that they recognize intuitively that their interests are wrapped up in the existing set of relationships and legal structure.

This dynamic also explains why the idea of an alliance rather than a merger is so attractive to many nonprofit managers and their boards. The coming wave of mergers in the nonhospital health and social services field will undoubtedly include a significant number of strategic alliances for this reason. The impulse to retain control of the corporate vehicle is strong enough that there may also be some creative energies devoted to devising brand new ways of knitting organizations closer together without transferring corporate control. We will explore some current models of alliances in a later chapter, as well as some of the techniques for ensuring control.

A final note on management control in nonprofit organizations. We have pinpointed the essential difference between a merger and an alliance as whether the locus of corporate control shifts to another entity. But at some point the distinction grows murky. For example, do we call a collaboration whose members are integrated at the economic, responsibility, and operations level, and who share key board members a merger or an alliance? Technically, we may answer this by attempting to determine the amount of control that those common board members really possess. Sharing only a board member or two should make it an alliance, albeit a tight one. But if those board members also have an independent base of authority common to both entities, it begins to look more like a merger.

Sectarian health care facilities in many parts of the country are moving rapidly into this murky zone. Disparate nonprofits may share only a single board member and may feel and act independent of clerical authority. But when that single board member is the cardinal or the head of, say, the region's Catholic Charities agency, it could functionally be a merger. In fact, in some cases the social service side of religious hierarchies is moving to exert control over formerly freestanding agencies by way of the larger religious network. Collaborations like these are showing how subtle the nuances of corporate control really are.

SPEED

Without doubt, mergers are faster to design and implement. In purely legal terms, a merger can be done by filling out a few forms and filing them with the appropriate authorities. With the correct signatures from board members and other responsible parties, the merger can be done in a matter of days or weeks—on paper. Securing the practical advantages of a merger takes a lot longer. Of course, in the absence of a valid and compelling push from the outside—and it's hard to imagine what that would look like—speed should not be a major consideration in entering a collaboration anyway. Mergers and alliances are really nothing more than operations planning exercises, and haste rarely improves planning.

CORPORATE INDEPENDENCE

On the other hand, if corporate independence is valued by participants they must try to design an alliance. As noted previously, carefully designed and managed alliances can give participants many of the benefits below the corporate level in the C.O.R.E. model that mergers can offer. They can save money, do administrative chores more efficiently, and work closely on programs. What alliances won't do is break down the insularity of the corporate vehicles. Participants will still be individually governed, legal and fiduciary responsibility for operational results will remain with each entity, and alliance members will still have a separate identity.

Is this desirable? The simple answer is that it is desirable if participants feel it is. From a systems perspective, there are too many nonprofit agencies in fields such as health and human services.

There are valid historical and legal reasons for this situation; nonetheless, it is increasingly an accepted fact in many parts of the country. There are also many reasons to believe, paradoxically, that reducing the numbers of nonprofits will make the field as a whole stronger.

Still, people and organizations show a strong attachment to the modern fiction known as a corporation, especially when it is *theirs.* And mergers as a strategic choice are relatively little known or understood in the nonprofit field. Worse, the tactic has been thoroughly discredited by excesses and shortsighted blunders in the for-profit world. The result is that merging is not often considered a desirable or healthy option for most nonprofits.

In this conceptual vacuum, alliances can play a major role. Ultimately, some alliances will surely prove to be the warm-up phase to a multiparty merger. Others will help restructure everyday ways of delivering services while still others will serve to increase trust and a sense of bondedness among participants. Whatever their accomplishments, the form of collaboration we are calling an alliance will have provided an important and irreplaceable bridge to the new generation of service delivery systems.

MANAGEMENT FLEXIBILITY

The manager says: "Funding source regulations. State laws. Federal oversight. Labor laws. Employment taxes. Inspectors. With all the requirements I have to watch out for, I can barely move. Give me flexibility."

The various funding sources and inspectors say: "We're giving these nonprofits a lot of money and responsibility. We have to make sure they do a good job."

Flexibility is the deepest wish of most nonprofit managers, and when they look at a potential merger they see the possibility of bigger operations and less flexibility. They are right to be concerned. Although we know that there is such a thing as being too small to carry out a mission, we really don't know if there is such a thing as being too large. A manager looking at a potential merger may see the danger of creating an encrusted bureaucracy that is twice as large and three times as hard to move as either of the previous partners were separately.

This may be more an emotional statement than a supportable fear. The rugged individualism that characterizes so many managers of small nonprofits—often cloaked in more acceptable terms such as grassroots activism or lack of money—frequently comes with an abhorrence of (others') bureaucracy. With more than 90 percent of all nonprofits' budgets tallying less than $26 million, the truth is that very few nonprofits have even a vague chance of developing truly bloated bureaucracies. Most of the time what this fear expresses is both a worry that the organization will grow disconnected from its founding community's needs and the more subtle fear that current managers won't know how to manage the newly enlarged organization without resorting to the very things that drove them to small organizations in the first place.

The kind of flexibility that managers initially desire in a collaboration is not really to help them do things proactively and respond to new opportunities so much as it is to help them avoid entanglements. Some of those possible entanglements will be described below. It is usually only after a while that management (and then their boards) begin to see the proactive benefits of the collaboration if it is designed with maximum flexibility.

For example, the management services company model (discussed at length later) may at first seem to offer mainly a solution to tricky questions involving a merger between two organizations. Only if managers look beyond the terms of the immediate collaboration will they see that the model could also incorporate a third, fourth, or even tenth agency, and that there are no logical reasons for stopping at managing just two organizations.

ANTITRUST

Sophisticated managers and board members may have concerns about violating antitrust laws when considering either a merger or an alliance. In most cases, this concern will dissipate when the facts are analyzed. Antitrust regulation is intended to prevent suppliers from gaining unfair advantage over buyers. If otherwise independent businesses representing a significant portion of a market could agree on the amount of services to be delivered, their cost, and the means of marketing them to the public, those businesses would hold virtually all important means of control and thus an unfair advantage.

Most antitrust action in areas where nonprofits are active has occurred in the health care field, particularly hospitals. The Department of Justice has overall responsibility for initiating antitrust interventions, but large service providers or those who have reason to believe that their collaboration may involve possible antitrust violations will want to conduct their own preliminary analysis.

Note: Antitrust 101

Antitrust laws have roots in the late 19th century when Ohio Senator John Sherman helped pass the act bearing his name in 1890. The political goal was to outlaw massive economic cartels and certain competitive tactics. In 1914, the Clayton Anti-Trust Act was passed, dealing with mergers and proceeding from the same populist-inspired philosophy. Grocers, bankers, and breweries were some of the targets of antitrust enforcement until about thirty years ago, most of which revolved around the question of market share in the affected industry: too much market share concentrated in a single place equaled unfair competition and therefore was a prime target for antitrust enforcement.

After a time, observers began to question whether a dominant market share alone would demonstrably result in higher prices and less competition, and judges began considering the specifics of individual cases rather than trying to apply a single market-share measuring stick. One result of this shift is that the matter of antitrust law became a more subtle, negotiated affair. Another result is that the Supreme Court hasn't heard a merger case in twenty years.

As a consequence, trust lawyers operate in a kind of legal netherworld, shuttling between practical realities of mergers in the business world and the theoretical underpinnings of antitrust law. Nonprofit antitrust merger issues, especially as they involve nonprofits other than hospitals, seem virtually invisible.

Nonetheless, it may help to summarize what is known about this obscure area where philosophy, politics, the law, and economics regularly collide:

- Both the Department of Justice (DOJ) and the Federal Trade Commission (FTC) have national authority to challenge mergers. State attorneys general may also have this authority.
- Any merger with a value of $15 million and involving one company with annual net sales or total assets of $100 million, and another with annual net sales of $10 million must be reported to the federal authorities before it can go forward.
- Generally, the key to viewing mergers and alliances favorably is the existence of competition and alternatives.
- Anti-trust Policy Statements establish 'safety zones,' or clearly described arrangements which the two agencies will not challenge.
- For physician networks, the presence of shared risk, significant investments in managing and integrating care, or efficiencies benefiting the consumer are good protections against antitrust enforcement.
- Alliances of different types of providers—not just physicians—have no clear safety zones.

Significantly, federal authorities have challenged fewer than 10 percent of all hospital mergers. The rate at which they object to proposed mergers fluctuates with the political convictions of those holding the office, but it is hard to imagine a dramatic deviation from past practice. Readers interested in further information about antitrust issues should see "Tip: What Regulators Want" in this Chapter.

COLLECTIVE BARGAINING

The most volatile topic in any merger—other than who will lead the new entity—collective bargaining matters can threaten to derail the entire process. Even in situations where union issues are not unusually intense, the whole subject of labor unions is so emotionally laden and operationally complex that it can be a constant source of anxiety.

Tip: What Regulators Want

Antitrust regulators showed what they expect in nonprofit mergers in a case in Florida. Three hospitals in the Tampa–Clearwater area, two of which had already created a single health care system, engaged a consulting team to analyze potential savings from a merger. The results suggested possible savings of $80 million over five years, and the institutions decided to go ahead with a merger.

Antitrust officials saw it differently. Noting that the three hospitals were among the four or five largest in the 17 hospital market, they argued that the collaboration would unwisely diminish competition. An intense legal battle ensued, and its resolution created a strange three-headed creature.

Accepting the economies of scale argument, the legal solution was to allow the hospitals to collaborate fully on joint purchasing and other economic strategies. However, in order to preserve competition, the three institutions were forbidden to market jointly or share information about contracting and pricing strategies with managed care organizations. This Solomon-like compromise was by no means ideal, but it at least allowed the collaboration to proceed. It also created a living, operating monument to antitrust philosophy.

Let us wade directly into these dangerously swirling waters. The reason labor unions pose such a problem for many nonprofit administrators is rarely discussed directly, but it goes as follows. Labor unions have historically drawn most of their political support from the left. Many nonprofit administrators, especially those who began their careers in the 1960s and 1970s, have distinctly leftward political leanings.

So far, so good. Superficially, there would seem to be a fair amount of common ground here. However, on the whole, nonprofit administrators are a resolutely individualist lot. One of the reasons they may have gotten into the field was for the opportunity to make a large difference on the strength of their own ideas and hard work. Unions, on the other hand, must draw their power from collective action. So the 1960s advocate-turned-nonprofit-administrator who is thwarted by the 1990s labor union not only loses on a management question, but may easily feel like he or she is abandoning the values that brought him or her into the field in the first place.

The fact that labor negotiations take place on the dual levels of operations and ideology accounts for the ambivalence and unpredictability of some nonprofit managers in dealing with their unions. By contrast, for-profit managers are not likely to feel the same conflicts and so will tend to be more straightforward and "business-like."

Wading deeper, we turn to another delicate subject. Ask any nonprofit manager to assess the effects of a union on their organization, and at least two themes will probably emerge. The first is that the existence of the union limits organizational creativity and flexibility, and that this fact alone is frustrating even if relations with the union itself are acceptable.

The second theme may not be explicitly stated, but rather embedded in anecdotes and casual remarks. It is that the existence of the union, in some curious ways, actually makes the managers' jobs easier. That is, because it so precisely defines so many aspects of the employer–employee relationship, the union environment removes a great deal of the usual messy guesswork associated with managing people. Needless to say, this is another source of ambivalence for managers, since it offers the short term gain of reduced aggravation in return for the long-term loss of creativity and flexibility.

Nonprofit mergers will often turn on questions of collective bargaining. Predictably, when a unionized agency and a nonunionized agency are discussing merger, the latter will feel quite skittish. They perceive the union shop as almost tainted, they worry that the union will "take over" management in the new entity, and they privately wonder about the unionized agency's competence if they allowed a union to organize their employees.

For boards and management harboring these feelings about a unionized agency, we offer three words of advice: get over it. Unions are a fact of life in many areas of nonprofit management, especially since traditional areas of union organizing such as manufacturing are shrinking and being replaced by public and nonprofit targets. Unions can't be wished away, they're not entirely bad things, and most bargaining units are amenable to open, honest, and firm management negotiations.

The most important thing that nonunion personnel can do is to begin discussions with a clear-eyed set of expectations. Boards of directors and management personnel with no union experience tend to enter into merger negotiations with a unionized counterpart secretly hoping that the union will somehow go away. This is highly unlikely. Even under the most peaceful and stable of circumstances, labor unions do not typically decertify (dissolve) themselves. Once a merger discussion is announced, the resultant uncertainty and ambivalence is, if anything, likely to drive employees closer to their union.

Part of the reality that a nonunionized agency has to accept is that as soon as the merger talks are public knowledge there may be a union organizing drive among their own employees. Representatives of the organized agency's union will interpret the merger discussions as an open door to the other organization. Even if there is no formal drive, it would be wise to assume that informal organizing will begin as early as a few hours after the proposed merger becomes public knowledge.

Collective bargaining considerations can shape structure in subtle and not so subtle ways. The principal way this happens is through what might be called compartmentalization. In most cases, employers are organized by worksite. Simply because one program in one city is organized by a specific union doesn't mean that a different program run by the same agency in a different city will be organized too. This puts up a substantial barrier to easy organization, but it also means that there can be no smooth exchange of unionized and nonunionized employees such as may be desired between different campuses of the same residential treatment school.

The impulse to compartmentalize union employees in a certain site or sites may also lead managers to consider some form of alliance rather than a merger. While the informal channels of communication and therefore potential union organizing are still open in a strategic alliance, the lack of corporate unity will impede full-scale organizing. Since ultimate corporate control remains in different hands in an alliance, unionization of the nonunion shop is not a foregone conclusion.

On the other hand, if managers need to be free to move employees from site to site, they may be well advised—at least theoretically—to choose a full merger under a single board and CEO. This is due to the fact that one generally cannot mix union and nonunion employees in the same job classification at the same site. When all employees are unionized, they are subject to the control of the single employer. However, union contracts often include provisions prohibiting management from reassigning employees to different sites, so this advantage in practical terms may be neutralized.

Nonunionized management and boards would be well advised to seek out an experienced labor attorney if for no other reason than to simply act as a sounding board and resource. Not only is there a surplus of laws, regulations, and policies in this field, there are numerous practices and policies that only a specialist knows. For example, the National Labor Relations Board is frequently called upon to arbitrate disputes or advise on areas of employer–employee relations. Like any large organization, the NLRB in some types of disputes tends to behave predictably and in others it does not. Even the knowledge of whether one's case is on a well-worn path or if it could be precedent-setting is useful and can only come from a specialist. Their advice can be worth many times their fee.

LIABILITY

Nonprofits often enjoy an unusual degree of protection from liability laws, and preserving that advantage can shape the structure of a collaboration. Often the protection goes away if the tax-exempt entity engages in commercial activity within its own corporate structure or as part of a related entity's, so this is one of the reasons why for-profit activity is almost always carried on via a separate corporate entity.

GEOGRAPHY

Related to both liability and reimbursement, geographic considerations greatly shape collaborative structure. Many nonprofits doing business in another state—and sometimes even in another city—will find it advantageous to form a separate corporation. Two nonprofits from different states contemplating a merger may actually find it preferable to keep the two companies intact and use other ways of linking them

REIMBURSEMENT

It will come as no surprise to veteran nonprofit managers that reimbursement considerations play a major role in just about everything that some nonprofits do. Reimbursement regulations from government sources for health and human services are particularly detailed and can actually play a role in determining corporate structure. For example, Medicare pays for home care services on a fairly strict cost-of-service basis. The only way to financially justify expanding services into Medicare populations, therefore, is to charge a share of overhead costs currently being paid by other sources to Medicare services. The effect of this gambit is to free up monies that otherwise would have been spent elsewhere. The cleanest and most acceptable way of shifting overhead costs in this way may be to establish a separate Medicare-only corporation.

Foundation grant makers in the arts and education may be reluctant to support for-profit activity such as a museum gift shop. Government sources, especially state governments, can be especially swift about scooping dollars generated through other sources in order to reduce their own costs. Both practices are frustrating for nonprofits who compete for private revenue sources and may lead to the creation of separate corporations.

MANAGEMENT CLARITY

One of the secondary benefits of different corporate structures is that it often makes it easier to keep track of things. If the symphony orchestra is run out of the symphony orchestra corporation and the newly merged youth symphony is run from an entirely separate corporate structure, the job of keeping separate operations is much easier. Of course, it is possible to overdo this notion and to erect undesirable administrative barriers between the entities. Merger participants need to think through the implications of keeping separate corporate structures and decide whether the benefits outweigh the costs.

BOND COVENANTS

When large nonprofits need to raise capital for a construction project, they typically float a bond. Investors purchase the bonds in return for a steady stream of interest income over the next several years, and they also insist on certain conditions. Those conditions will vary according to each borrower, and they are written into the terms of the borrowing. Consequently, bond-based covenants can have a significant effect on everything from the merger's corporate structure to whether the organization can merge at all. Management staff involved in the bond issue tend to remember such covenants in detail, but if there has been executive level turnover since the bond was first issued it will be wise to check for possible restrictions.

Note: How Bond Underwriters Influence Corporate Structure

The nursing home had built an assisted living wing and a new independent living program on its existing campus when it turned its attention to a new assisted living project in the next town. To finance the project the growing agency turned to the bond market. Financing specialists were interested, but wary of the freestanding nonprofit's increasingly stretched financial position. To allay their concerns, the organization had to create a separate corporation solely for the purpose of holding title to the new development. For the next several years, until some of the debt was paid off and they could refinance, the agency had to hold two separate annual meetings, run two separate boards of directors, and keep a separate set of books for each company.

LOCAL REALITIES

Nonprofits are quasipublic entities and can sometimes be adopted by a town or city as their own. Museums, for example, have always represented the character of their surroundings in some way and often become community prizes. Years ago community hospitals were more or less forced to exist because transportation systems were nonexistent, outpatient physician care was almost unheard of, and civic pride was fierce. In these cases, the establishment of a local source of service was a natural and sensible response to the nature of the demand.

One of the things that occasionally accompanies such determinedly local service provision is equally localized control mechanisms. The land used for the museum may be publicly owned, for instance, or a long-ago capital gift may stipulate that the asset is to be returned if the organization ever stops providing services as described in the bequest. Provisions like these can powerfully shape the choice of corporate structure.

SALARY AND BENEFITS

Most nonprofits' single greatest expense is personnel compensation. A salary and fringe benefits package is like an organizational fingerprint, the unique result of the interaction of a huge number of factors. Even in the absence of collective bargaining, managers need to consider the impact of a merger on salaries and benefits. Nothing will use up extra cash as fast as making two different compensation plans identical. In view of the fact that most nonprofits operate frugally anyway, there unfortunately is usually little opportunity to change compensation practices dramatically. That being the case, managers must decide what to do about it.

The most common choice in our experience is to leave present practices in place, correcting the worst disparities as early as possible and attempting to adjust the remainder gradually. Another potential strategy, especially in rural areas, is to use the management company model to be described in a later chapter so as to reinforce the differences between the two organizations. Sometimes, there will be enough differences between the two merging agencies' labor forces and compensation practices that there will be no clear disparities.

REGULATORY POLICIES

Regulatory compliance is a fact of life for most nonprofit organizations, regardless of the service they provide. Regulation is particularly intense in health care, social services, and education, and it can cause planners to make different decisions about corporate structure than they otherwise would have made. Its effect can be magnified when combined with reimbursement policy.

Set-asides are a good example of how regulatory policy can make a difference in organizational structure. For many years governments tried to encourage the development of minority-owned or controlled businesses. Typically, they would "set aside" a certain percentage of government contracts to be awarded to minority vendors, including nonprofits, which they would certify after evaluating the minority status of the entity's ownership or board composition. To the degree that the certifications actually gave a competitive advantage, they were valuable designations.

If the government entity favoring minority enterprises was shrewd in designing its program—and most were—the key concept was minority *control.* As long as minorities either owned or were in control of a vendor it would be eligible for special status (in nonprofits, the equivalent test was the composition of the board). Consequently, a noncertified group merging with a certified group threatens this preferred vendor status if it dilutes minority control beyond whatever is deemed the acceptable minimum. It may help to leave government work eligible for minority set-asides in a separate corporation, so this is one way that regulatory incentives strongly influence corporate structure. However, keeping the work in a separate corporation may not help. Ultimately, minority vendor status may be one of the casualties of a merger that is otherwise highly desirable.

There are thousands of ways that regulatory matters can influence the structure of a collaboration, and most of those regulations are a function of state government. This means that the same set of circumstances in one state may lead to a different decision in another state. Exhibit 8.1, adapted from a report prepared for the

	Connecticut	*Massachusetts*	*New York*
Incorporation	None	File copy with Attorney General (AG)	None
Amendments to certificates of incorporation	None	File copy with AG 30 days after adoption	Notify AG
Mergers	None	Notify AG if material change in use	Notify AG
Sale of all assets	None	Notify AG if material change in use	Notify AG
Voluntary dissolutions	None	AG a necessary party in court	Notify AG
Removal of restrictions on assets	AG a necessary party in court	AG a necessary party in court	AG a necessary party in court

Source: Reprinted with permission of Harriet Bograd. Adapted from "State Attorney General Role in 'Life Cycle Events' of Nonprofits" Yale Working Paper #206, 1994. For more information, see www.bway.net/~hbograd/cyb-acc.html

Exhibit 8.1 Three States Attorney Generals' Actions: A Comparison

Mellon Foundation by the Nonprofit Coordinating Committee of New York, indicates just how differently three very similar Northeast states' attorney generals (AG) handle various "life cycle events" in their nonprofit organizations.

Other regulatory demands, such as licenses, inspection authority, and even operations or governance requirements, can be strong enough considerations to force certain corporate structural choices. Clear thinking about what the collaboration is intended to accomplish, a shared understanding of the nonprofits involved, and some good legal advice will be the best way to ensure that the architectural form of the collaboration follows its function.

CHAPTER NINE

Models of Collaboration: Merger

This chapter begins a series of chapters detailing distinct models for structuring nonprofit collaborations: mergers, management company models, strategic alliances, partnerships, and for-profit involvement. Each chapter will explore the basic structure, typical governance and management control devices, advantages and disadvantages, and special considerations for the model's use.

WHAT IT MEANS TO MERGE

In order to make sense of the options available for structuring nonprofit mergers, it would be helpful to step outside the field and look first at for-profit mergers. The headlines of the average newspaper are filled with a constant stream of stories about two companies merging with each other. They tend to talk at length about the personalities of the CEOs, the expected strategic benefits of the merger, the profits to be made by parties to the decisions, and many other things, but they rarely talk about how the merger is actually carried out.

Here's the nuts-and-bolts part that they don't cover. In the for-profit world, the choices for merger structure come down to two. One is for the acquiring company to acquire the target company's outstanding stock. This method gives the new owner control of the ownership of the organization, which in turn usually gives control of the board of directors. It is also possible to do what is called a "pooling of interests," which is an arrangement short of outright purchase but which still involves manipulation of the company's stock.

The problem with stock-oriented acquisitions is that, while they bring ownership and control, they also bring potential troubles. If stock ownership simply means that someone else gets to sit in the owner's chair, then any bullets and arrows aimed at the former occupant of the chair will be aimed at the new one too. Any liabilities (e.g., lawsuits or obligations to pay money to someone) incurred in the name of the corporation by the previous owner will be binding on the new one.

The way to solve this dilemma is to acquire only the assets of the corporation. If the company is a widget manufacturer, the acquirer purchases the widget factory, the widget distribution system, and the good widget name. As soon as the transaction is completed, the new asset owner can start operating out of his or her own corporation. The name of the company on the door doesn't even have to change since that is usually one of the assets purchased.

Of course, in practice, it is rarely that simple. Most owners will always want to sell stock, since that's what enables them to walk away most cleanly, while most buyers will want to purchase only the assets since it's less likely they'll drag in liabilities that way. Naturally, there are other considerations on both sides, but this represents the essence of the conflict and is why for-profit mergers and acquisitions are tricky things.

THE ESSENCE OF A NONPROFIT MERGER

Now fast-forward to nonprofit mergers. Stock questions become irrelevant because nonprofits don't have owners. So structuring a nonprofit merger really comes down to a question of how one gains control of another nonprofit entity. Note that we are talking about control in a legal sense. A nonprofit agency—or any other organization, for that matter—can be controlled for all practical purposes by people who derive their strength from sources such as personal charisma, longstanding relationships, or simply seniority.

If a nonprofit requires a substantial asset base to operate—museums and colleges demand buildings and significant other assets, for instance—then taking control of the assets gives functional control over the programs as well. However, many kinds of nonprofits need only office space and some routine business equipment. Taking control of the assets doesn't mean much. Therefore, control of the organization has to reside elsewhere. Ultimately, legal authority is given only to those officials who are regarded as official representatives of the community, better known as the board of directors. This is the reason that merging control of the boards of directors is the only reliable way of merging nonprofits.

The notion of change at the board level as the signal of a true merger ties neatly into our C.O.R.E. framework. Many activities such as marketing and fundraising get carried on at the corporate level, but the one common element of all nonprofits is that responsibility for the overall organization rests with the board. In a merger, the formerly separate boards become a single board of directors. Responsibility for governance remains at this level, but the size and scope of the entity change.

Structure

Merged organizations have the good fortune to be structured simply. There were two boards and two corporations before the merger, but afterward there will be only one. In most cases, one of the existing corporate vehicles will be the "surviving" corporation. The decision as to which will survive and which will dissolve should be almost purely technolegal in nature. On occasion, there may need to be an entirely different, third corporation created into which the previously separate corporations are merged. Ultimately, this is a legal nuance of little interest to managers and boards. The point is that a true merger's structure is simple and straightforward.

Control and Governance

Again, as with structure, there is little mystery about how the new entity's board and managers achieve control. The board has a fiduciary responsibility, just as each of the two predecessor boards had with the previously separate organizations, and they delegate management responsibility to staff members.

Governance is the area of real uncertainty, because there are no recipe cards to follow in merging two boards of directors. Often, in

Tip: Consider Keeping the Old Corporation

Digging in your closet you find that old raincoat hanging limply in the back, exactly where you left it when you bought the new one a few months ago. Seized by a sudden desire to streamline, you throw the thing in the trash. What happens a week later? Right. You lose the new one at the start of a record-setting five-day rainstorm.

In a merger, one of the two corporations is typically stripped of all its assets and eventually dissolved. But are you sure you won't need it? Sometimes, even in a full merger, there can be a need for a second nonprofit corporation to hold property, conduct training, offer services to certain types of payers, or do any one of several other legitimate management chores. The moral: until you can be sure you won't need it, consider keeping the old corporation around as a shell for a year or two. It won't cost much to maintain it and it may come in handy for currently unforeseeable reasons.

As for the metaphor, it isn't perfect. Donate the raincoat and get an umbrella as a backup.

fact, governance of the newly merged entity becomes one of the early sticking points between two agencies considering a merger. Part of the reason for this is because in the early stages the groups don't fully trust each other, and if the merger is handled properly, governance provisions eventually become less of an issue. But the other part of the reason is because governance and control really do matter to the future mission and effectiveness of the nonprofit—and so they really should be debated and resolved to everyone's satisfaction.

Questions about governance normally break down into three distinct areas: size of the board; composition, as in how many of them versus how many of us; and selection of officers. We will take each matter in turn and suggest tactics for resolving the inherent conflicts in each.

Tools for Determining Size. If boards of directors were cars, the best ones would look like midsized four-door sedans. Small, high-powered groups are too quick for their own good, and the lumbering 18-wheelers take a long time to get up to speed and even longer to turn. Research—and practical experience—suggests that the best size for a nonprofit board is in the 9- to 14-member range. This number gives the group enough members to compensate for temporary absences while remaining small enough to encourage widespread participation. The problem is that the natural tendency when faced with, say, two 15-person boards, is to head off possible conflicts by creating a 30-person board for the new entity.

The primary means of reducing such size pressure is for each board's leadership to take an active role in surveying their own premerger membership. At any one time, there are likely to be several members who are quietly seeking a graceful exit from the board, and the changes that a merger will bring can offer that exit. Having a heart-to-heart talk with each board member is a good way to gauge the collective interest in remaining with the postmerger board. There is a possibility that this tactic alone will solve the problem by reducing the boards' membership to a manageable level.

If not, and if the Planning Committee feels, as most do, that the best solution is to simply create a new board which is the sum of the old ones, then there are a few other techniques to consider.

Place a Cap on Total Size; Reduce Membership through Attrition. Capping total board membership at the sum of the two component boards will help prevent the problem from getting worse, and by preventing any new members from joining the board for a period of time it will set in motion a self-reducing mechanism. The risk is that the board will stagnate as a leadership vehicle, and that the original, or "charter" members will become a closed circle. In a subtle way, it also encourages continuation of any Us vs. Them feelings ("they're not making any more of Us so we'd better hold fast against Them"). Still, it may be preferable to gridlock if the board can't agree on total size.

Staggered Terms. It may help to assign staggered terms to different board members. Although this technique alone doesn't resolve the question of board size, it may help because board composition is associated with control. Stretching the transition period over a longer time may ease the stresses associated with a change

Pitfall: Missing Organizational Culture's Influence on Governance

A seven month long effort to merge two hospitals and their medical schools fell apart because participants could not agree on who would control the newly created medical school. Mount Sinai Medical Center and New York University entered talks aimed at merging their two systems and found that combining the two hospitals would be eased by the comfortable geographic distance between the two locations which permitted some duplication in the marketplace.

The medical school merger was different. The university felt that the merged school would operate just like any of its other schools, while the medical center envisioned a more independent, equal partnership. "The issue of governance was always fuzzy and nobody really focused on the differences," one insider told *The New York Times.* "There was always an ambivalent understanding of how the medical school piece would work . . . when we finally got down to . . . this piece we couldn't move anywhere with it."

Reading between the lines of this failed merger is not difficult. As a relatively young (29 years) medical school, Mt. Sinai had grown in prestige and amount of federal research funding, a useful barometer of respect in the medical world, while NYU had lost money. Compounding the problem, Mt. Sinai negotiators apparently felt they were not being treated as equals. A profound difference in cultures played itself out in the arena of governance.

in control. In addition, individual board members' actions or perceived interests may be an obstacle to effective collaboration but may have to be included in the final entity for separate reasons. Staggering terms gives members reason to hope that these problematic board members may eventually move on. It may also help by symbolizing the transitional nature of the newly constructed board, not to mention that the whole concept of term limitations is gaining credence in nonprofit boards as well as elective offices. Staggered terms as a strategy for limiting board size work best when linked with a cap on charter membership.

Ancillary Boards. Ancillary groups such as advisory committees or honorary trustees can relieve pressure on the Planning Committee to create a large board for the new entity. Anything that begins "Friends of . . ." will probably not be an effective substitute for full board membership, but for some members the idea of a less involved form of participation may be appealing. Often, high-visibility groups such as symphony orchestras and art museums will have an oversized Board of Trustees which is largely ceremonial and is separate and apart from the board of directors. For the board member seeking visibility with little commitment of time (but probably a significant commitment of money) this could be ideal. If a good ancillary board doesn't exist and the merged organization would be large enough to support one, it's a good time to think about creating one.

Board Composition

Next to board size, the stickiest governance matter to be resolved in a merger is likely to be the composition of the board's membership. This is one of the areas in a merger where it is very tempting to take a formulaic approach: "if we have 60% of the assets we should get 60% of the board seats," or "we own four buildings and you only own two, so we should get twice as many seats as you get."

Using simple formulas is clearcut, understandable, and very pragmatic. What is so attractive about formulas is that they *seem* to be fair. The problem is that they aren't effective. Done properly, mergers are about looking to the future. Formulas for board composition, however, look backward. Worse, there is no automatic connection between what any individual board member can offer and from which organization he or she came.

Our solution to these twin problems is simple, effective, and all but certain to be ignored. To counteract the regressive tendency of formulas, think of board members as strategic assets that need to be carefully matched with the newly merged organization's future needs. All things being equal, if a museum is moving more toward contemporary art exhibits and away from 16th-century Italian art, the professor/board member with a specialty in that area will be more strategic than the professor/board member who is an expert in Titian. Of course, the idea is to avoid having to lose any valuable resource, but sometimes choices must be made and it is always better to make them strategically than to wait for them to make themselves.

The second part of the solution is to sever the implied connection between individuals and their nonprofit of origin. There is a great temptation to choose between one president and the other, between one treasurer and the other, and so on. Often, participants feel pressure to start making these choices early in the process. We suggest waiting. In any task-oriented group such as the Merger Committee and its various subcommittees, people tend to take on roles with which they feel comfortable. People become leaders in response to a unique set of circumstances. Just because someone was a vice president of a predecessor organization does not mean that they could or should hold the same office in the new entity.

Over time, individual board members will tend to assume distinct roles in planning for the merger. If the Planning Committee can put aside for a few months its understandable desire to finalize officers while it concentrates on other tasks of the merger, there is a good chance that the appropriate people for those roles will emerge naturally.

Of course, this is not always going to happen automatically, nor will all parties allow it to proceed unhindered. No matter how well-intentioned the participants—and, make no mistake, when economics are at stake, good intentions can be overwhelmed—the integrity of the process must be protected. This is a good role for a facilitator. In fact, we would argue that the seeds of a failed merger are sown when one side or the other acts exclusively as the agent for its own interests and regards the merger planning process as a contest to be won. It is difficult for many board members, especially those with personal experience, to get out of the win–lose mentality that characterizes so many for-profit mergers. The thinking and action that follows this model can scuttle the whole process.

Advantages and Disadvantages of a Merger

There are numerous advantages to the straight merger choice, and a few disadvantages. The primary advantage is that it is simple to understand and implement. One need not worry about creating a new corporation or putting in place a structure that no one understands, as we will see is sometimes true of other choices. Because

Pitfall: "Winning" at Governance

For governance matters, one of the advantages that nonprofit mergers have over for-profit mergers is that no one organization can be said to have "won" since directly measurable financial gains to individuals are not at stake. Consequently, "winning" occurs largely on the ego battlefield, where the dynamics can be subtle.

For example, board members usually know that they have a fiduciary responsibility to the public at large, so very few will explicitly and visibly advocate for their own organization's selfish interests; to do so would be indiscreet. Nevertheless, sometimes board members are wedded to their own organization's way of doing things. To feel vindicated in this faith it is not enough merely to "win," one must be perceived by others as having "won."

To determine whether this is happening, look at the way symbols are handled. Organizations intent on being a dominant partner will tend to reduce or eliminate, at all costs, areas where the other nonprofit might have influence in the future. The new CEO will be "theirs," the new logo "theirs," the surviving information system "theirs," the board will be "theirs," and so on. In a true merger, even a dominant nonprofit will be able to signal its interest in partnership by carefully handling decisions with deep symbolic content.

of its simplicity, it takes less time to arrange. It is definitive—there is a single focal point of leadership, governance is straightforward, and the organizational boundaries are simply the sum of the formerly separate corporations. Mergers also have the advantage of being the tightest and most formal means of collaboration. They consolidate a lot of power in the service of a mission.

Mergers almost by definition tend to be horizontal by nature, meaning that they occur between similar organizations. They are excellent for creating more of the same. Consequently, they are the preferred tool for achieving economic size. The work of bringing two organizations together is so complex and taxing that if there are fundamental differences in operations it can become nearly prohibitive.

Predictably, the disadvantages of mergers are often the same as the advantages. Their simplicity, unity of leadership, and tightly knit nature are sometimes precisely the points of greatest worry for ambivalent board and staff. It is not uncommon for agencies approaching a merger to seriously pursue the idea of building in a "demerger" provision. Since in most cases demerging is like unscrambling an omelet, this offers reassurance that is more emotional than realistic.

Perhaps the greatest disadvantage of a merger is that it is somewhat limited in flexibility and sophistication. They are also time-consuming, as noted in a previous section. In truth, a merger can take years to gel. Should an organization's management feel it needs to be on a fast track, it may very well be disappointed at the amount of time that needs to be devoted to making a single merger work.

Special Considerations

Although it does not technically relate to structural considerations, the issue of the size of the merging parties can also be a factor. There are two ways this typically happens; either one of the nonprofits is much larger than the other, or they are arguably comparable in size. Different considerations apply in each case.

The Takeover Merger. When one partner is significantly larger than the other, the merger is rightfully seen as more of a takeover. In the takeover style of merger, the dominant agency by definition becomes the template for the new entity. The administrative infrastructure of the smaller agency either gets dismantled or its people and systems are absorbed into the larger organization's administrative system. The real suspense comes around questions of programming. The partners must choose how to organize the smaller nonprofit's services. Usually the decision is between operating the previously standalone nonprofit corporation as a new and self-contained program or parceling out its various services to different parts of the larger agency's existing service system.

This is a question of no small consequence. There are no automatically right or wrong approaches, but whichever route is taken will have a significant effect on the merger's success or failure. Operating the old corporation as a self-contained program is the quickest and clearest option, but doing so risks missing an opportunity to rethink the entire system of services and make it more integrated. Personnel in the old nonprofit-turned-program may also grow more ingrained and isolated, feeling that they have outlasted one management structure and so they'll be able to do it again.

On the other hand, reorganizing an existing operation is always a challenge. If program service people draw a distinction between what they do and the management of the old agency, there may be a kind of programmatic arrogance. Rightly or wrongly, they may view the merger as a sign that prior management failed, and this can increase their resolve to demonstrate their own competence. They may also fear for their jobs. These impulses of self-confidence and fear may seem contradictory but they can easily coexist and make for a potentially volatile mix for the entity taking over.

Merger of Equals. The other distinct merger model is between equals. Obviously there can be differences of opinion about what constitutes equality. Should it be based on total revenue? Asset base? Management team size? Public identity? For purposes of clarity, we'll simply say two nonprofits are equal if a reasonably educated outside observer would consider them equal.

There is another way for nonprofits to be viewed—and to view themselves—as equals, and that is if they share a common mission carried out in a franchise-like way. Many local chapters of nationally recognized charities are beginning to rethink their histories of operating as hundreds of small, autonomous units in favor of efforts to consolidate and strengthen their regional presence. Local affiliates or chapters of groups such as the United Way, Boy Scouts of America, the American Cancer Society, and ARCs have already merged, and of this writing there are indications that this trend could continue for many years as these groups position themselves for the 21st century.

The structural implications of mergers between equals can be more challenging than takeover mergers because they can catapult both organizations onto a different level of management from where either of them had been before. This change means systems of all kind must be overhauled. To take a concrete example, a nonprofit with 75 employees may be able to keep track of all the human resource management information such as vacation time and sick time tracking, personnel records and regulatory compliance with part time administrators, and a largely manual system. But if it were to merge with another 75 employee agency, the new entity would almost have to invest in automated human resources systems and more professional managers.

More important, a merger of equals may also force organizational and structural changes that will affect leadership. Structure here refers largely to programmatic and administrative activities. For any nonprofit to double in size over a period of two or three years is a daunting management task. Merging equal-sized agencies produces the same challenge overnight. Managers at all levels must grow with the new organization, including keeping pace with its changing structure.

For these reasons, it is critical to resolve service delivery questions at the front end of any merger between equals. For thoughtful Planning Committee members, there will be an inherent tension. On the one hand, they need to make sure that the operational needs of the new entity can handle the suddenly increased size (will the cash flow hold up? Do we need to get another payroll service right away? Can we still handle that huge Monet exhibit next year?) On the other hand, this is an excellent time to throw out the old ways of doing things and to bring in fresh perspectives and new ideas.

How to decide which direction to choose? For practical reasons, the answer is likely to be a blend of maintaining the old and creating the new. What matters is how they get there, because this issue is a miniature of the entire merger. It is especially critical in a merger of two equal nonprofits because there is no natural position of authority. Any one person's ideas seem no better or worse than any one else's. How they come to terms with a direction implicitly defines the new entity's values and sets a precedent for the process they will use for governance in the future. This type of merger is particularly well suited for an outside consultant to manage.

Focusing early and rigorously on the service delivery system in a merger of equals needs to happen. Rejuvenating and strengthening the system of service delivery is what mergers and alliances should do. It is necessary to get this planning done early, not just because it is central to so much else but because resource-related areas such as finances and space allocation are inherently limiting. If programming needs don't quickly dominate the way resources are distributed, they will quickly be dominated by it.

CHAPTER TEN

Models of Collaboration: Merger by Management Company

A second option for merging is what we call the management company model. This choice is also popularly known as a holding company, management services organization, transfer of sponsorship, or other names. The essence of it is that a formerly freestanding nonprofit corporation is managed by another party, and that both are under some form of common control. Often the considerations influencing organizational and legal structure described earlier do not line up neatly. Many times they are blatantly contradictory, and equally desirable objectives simply cannot be accomplished within a single organization.

The sometimes contradictory interests of advocacy and service provision are a good example. Associations for retarded citizens (ARCs) started out as advocacy groups and had considerable success. Some grew so successful as shapers of public policy that when it came time to organize a private system of care providers they were called upon to start providing services in addition to simply advocating for them.

Many who took on this additional role eventually realized that the demands of pure advocacy sometimes conflicted with providing services. Especially in a system so dominated by government funding, advocates whose organizations' main role was as a service provider did not always feel free to criticize or prod the very institution upon whom the rest of their organization depended for support. Some resolved this conflict by creating a separate corporation solely for the purposes of advocacy and a second one solely to deliver services. Both would be managed and governed by a single management company.

One might well argue that this is not a perfect solution, since it may be just a fictional legal overlay. Will I as an advocate truly feel independent and "pure" in my advocacy if I know that the person down the hall from me may lose her job as a result of my efforts? The virtue of a management company model in this situation is that it at least makes economic incentives clearer to everyone and is a reasonable midpoint between potentially compromised advocacy and none at all.

STRUCTURE

A management company model looks very much like the traditional organizational chart, except that the boxes on an organizational chart representing programs and services in a management company setting signify corporations. Exhibit 10.1 shows a hypothetical management company structure that may result after the kind of evolution that many ARCs have experienced in recent years. It represents four separate corporations, all of them nonprofit public charities.

The most significant thing about Exhibit 10.1 is the public's perception of it. Chances are that the ARC was the first entity of the four to come into existence. Its evolution into a four corporation management company structure could have evolved gradually, or it could have occurred almost literally overnight. How someone outside the organization perceives it now depends on the nature of

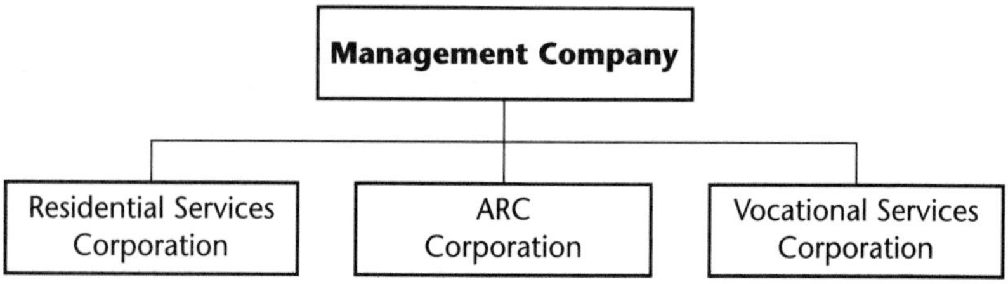

Exhibit 10.1 Sample Management Company Organization

their relationship to it. Parents with a newly diagnosed mentally retarded son or daughter may still see the ARC as an advocacy group and source of information. If their child is in a residential program, they may or may not see that program as an adjunct to the ARC. They probably wouldn't know and wouldn't care that it was a separate corporation.

On the other hand, the copy paper vendor would look at the management company as a large account, and the fact that it was providing management services for three human service companies would be immaterial. The owner of the building where one of the residential programs was housed would see the management company as little more than a post office box, and so on.

All of these perspectives are "right," but the size and complexity of the organization cause different observers to see the same picture in different ways. No one other than those involved with the management company is likely to have an overall vision of the organization. This is both good and bad, depending on one's starting point.

CONTROL AND GOVERNANCE

It is in matters of governance and control that some really interesting things distinguish this model from all others. Start with the board of directors. The theory is that, in a nonprofit organization, the board has a fiduciary responsibility for the organization. That is, they do not own the entity but must manage it as if they did. They also have control. Legal theory has it that a nonprofit corporation is composed of a membership that has some interest in the nonprofit's mission. From that membership, and possibly other sources, comes a board of directors which becomes the oversight body. Therefore, to control the corporation, one needs to control the membership.

How does one go about controlling the membership? If the entire membership happens to be composed of a single entity, and if that entity happens to be another corporation, then that other corporation effectively controls the board. Consequently, the easiest way to control a subsidiary corporation is to make the parent corporation the sole member of the subsidiary corporation.

This bit of legal legerdemain is at the base of the most common control mechanism in a management company structure. It offers the great benefit of single board control over multiple corporate structures. The parent company board needs only to become the sole member of another corporation to be able to exert control over it. This can happen either through a vote of a freestanding nonprofit or by the creation of a completely new nonprofit corporation to be the subsidiary. However it is done, the management company, or "parent" corporation, has complete control of the subsidiary.

There are other ways to insure control. A slight variation on the sole corporate member model is to simply appoint the same board to both corporations. Once this is done it is practically impossible to reverse, since the board would have to vote itself out of the subsidiary. In practice, this model may be little more than a theoretical variation on the sole corporate member model, since it doesn't offer any special advantages that the previous model cannot also offer.

It is also possible to link two corporations through the same management structure. Appointing the same executive director and/or management team to two different agencies gives de facto control. This structure might be used if a funding source insists on granting funds to a single-asset corporation. Federal programs such as some Housing and Urban Development (HUD) grants require that the money go to such single asset corporations, and there could be other compliance-related effects as well.

For example, one organization wanted to offer services in a different community. The political and regulatory climate in that community was such that it strongly favored "hometown" groups, so the solution agreed upon with local leaders was that a second "shadow" corporation would be formed with all the same leadership as the nonlocal parent corporation. This situation could also be flipped around: a local, formerly freestanding group could seek to merge with a larger parent by accepting that parent nonprofit's leadership team without changing the existing corporate structure.

Although helpful in dealing with things like regulatory dysfunction, this model has several pitfalls. One is that sharing management without changing board governance to match it is confusing and wasteful for professional staff. Another, and perhaps more significant, problem is that it shifts the true locus of control from the board to the staff level. Sharing management in this way unfortunately is also a golden invitation for double billing, in which the same executive director is effectively paid twice for doing one job. Finally, it makes function follow form. Management, in other words, has to act as thought it handles two different agencies when in fact it really is trying to operate a single agency under an appropriate legal umbrella. In short, this model may work as a temporary solution, or as an accommodation to quirky circumstances, but it could be messy in the long run.

A more common approach that doesn't change board control or corporate structure is for the parent company to sign management contracts with its subsidiaries. These management contracts could be as narrow or as expansive as desired. They may only supply a single executive or they could provide a turnkey package with everything from human resources and financial services to purchasing and marketing provided by the parent. Most nonprofits budget some amount of money for general and administrative costs, so some or all of these funds would go to the parent for goods and services that would otherwise have been acquired as an independent. The economic rationale is that a larger entity could provide the same services less expensively.

A final option for control involves special assets needed to do a job. If an asset such as a particular building is needed to deliver a service, controlling the building may amount to controlling the service. Although far less comprehensive than any of the previous models, this approach may be impractical in many circumstances. The exception would be if a nonprofit has an endowment so sizable that it dwarfs even the operating budget. In this case, managing and conserving the principal of the endowment becomes such a massive undertaking that the demands of the operating unit pale in comparison. Some major universities are in this situation.

ADVANTAGES OF A MANAGEMENT COMPANY

As an organizational design, the management company model is more robust than a simple merger. Among its greatest advantages is its flexibility. It offers single source management to corporations that could use it but that for a wide variety of reasons it may not be practical to meld into a single legal entity. Within the system one can use a variety of control mechanisms: single corporate membership for three subs, turnkey management contracts for two others, an individualized menu of administrative services with two others, a single paid executive for another, or an agreement just to manage the research laboratory of yet another.

Because these arrangements are usually invisible to program services, they can also feed off each other and lead to more (or less) collaboration in the future. The single paid executive may realize through management company meetings that two of the other subsidiaries need the services of hers, or the research laboratory management contract might lead to joint grant seeking. To some extent these are exactly the kinds of interdependencies that planners of the system may have envisioned initially, but it is the creation of a more integrated management environment that actually makes it possible.

The management company model can be expanded almost indefinitely. It will take some time to set up the management capacities needed to run a truly integrated management company/subsidiary relationship, longer in fact than it would take to do an

Note: Toward Truly Integrated Services

Those familiar with corporate America may recognize in these descriptions of the management company model some parallels with the business conglomerates of the 1950s and 1960s. These are the groups for whom "the business of business is business," and so it did not matter to these owners and managers what business their subsidiaries pursued as long as they were profitable.

The shortsightedness of this strategy is now becoming clear as many of these conglomerates fall apart or spin off some of their companies to be managed closer to home. Nonetheless, 21st century nonprofit entrepreneurs risk duplicating the same mentality on a smaller scale, with equally unsatisfactory results.

The solution is to keep in mind the objective of all this restructuring in the first place: integrated services and better value for society and the immediate consumer. There is no other good reason for creating all these corporate structures, devising suitable control mechanisms and persuading skeptical boards of directors and anxious staff to give it a try.

ordinary merger. Ironically, once the setup phase is completed, bringing in a new sub should take less time than a merger. The hardest part in that case is likely to be how—or whether—to incorporate the new entity's board of directors into the management company's governance.

A final advantage of a management company is the possibility for preserving local identity. While there is no reason for changing a successful local identity, even in a merger—why change something that's working?—it is easier and less emotionally charged for managers to keep local identities intact with a management company structure.

DISADVANTAGES OF A MANAGEMENT COMPANY

There are potentially significant disadvantages in using a management company. They start with the model's complexity. There really has to be enough at stake to justify the high level restructuring that must be done, with all its accompanying costs and time demands. Most of the time it doesn't make sense to create a management company–subsidiary relationship for just a few million dollars worth of programming. Legal and accounting costs alone to set it up and manage it may make it cost prohibitive.

The flexibility can also be elusive. Capital may not flow easily from the parent to subs, as planners may have hoped (lenders don't always agree that it should). Even though it may appear to be a good idea to put all these programs together in this way doesn't mean that the integration will actually happen, especially when the system is created by putting formerly independent entities together. Without good information technology to support the whole system, it will be hard to realize any gains, and at the moment good information technology is hard enough to put in place for a single entity, let alone an entire system.

Other, less concrete factors can influence the success of a management company model. Most notably, it could actually be an easy way to avoid the hard work of a merger. Of all the forms of collaboration, the management company structure is the easiest to create by top-down planning: record a few board votes, design a governance structure, and file the necessary forms. This tempting prospect can be a short term victory at the expense of true collaboration in the long term because it violates the principle that nonprofit mergers are planned top-down but implemented bottom-up. Already, some of the early systems put together in this way are beginning to fray. Usually the deterioration begins with the departure of veteran managers for whom the promise of the system gives way to the realities of no support and inadequate strategic management.

SPECIAL CONSIDERATIONS

Management company structures seem to work best as a means of vertically integrating organizations or to knit together entities that otherwise might be too different in some way to merge easily.

Vertical Integration

The management company model was made for vertically integrated systems. Its virtues are the reason why most large hospitals-turned-integrated-health-systems are now organized as management companies ("holding companies") with subsidiaries in diverse other lines of service such as nursing and rehabilitation, home care, and mental health. Their flexible and open-ended nature makes them ideal structures to take on the task of integrating an array of service providers under a single umbrella.

In the nonprofit field, "vertically integrated system" is virtually synonymous with health care. However, in the future there is every reason for it to include social services and other types of services as well. Once it is widely accepted in health care, it will also expand to fields such as education and public administration. This will expand the model itself. While health care is diversified by services (e.g., hospitals, nursing homes), education is diversified by population (municipalities for public education, adult populations for colleges and universities). Integrating services across different types of programs is a different matter than integrating services across populations, and so the management company model itself will expand its definition to accommodate the differences.

CHAPTER ELEVEN

Alliances

Nonprofits that want the benefits of merger without giving up the control should investigate alliances. Operating on the three levels of collaboration below corporate—operational, responsibility, and economic—alliances offer a compromise between a full-blown merger and no collaboration at all. For reasons that will shortly become clear, they are not as well developed in concept or operationally as are mergers, but there is no doubt that they are attracting strong interest.

STRUCTURE

In their early stages many alliances do not even rise to the level of a defined legal identity; we might more properly call them a state of mind, rather than a specific entity. If and when they do take on a recognizable legal shape, it is likely to be determined by legal and financial considerations as much as anything else. Alliances can take an almost unlimited number of shapes, and for that reason we must use it as a catchall term, applying to highly formalized structures as well as informal ones. A fully developed alliance may even look like a network of nonprofits, each with its own corporate structure but each participating collectively in one or more common tasks. To describe the options more fully, it might help to categorize alliances as either task-oriented or process-oriented. The difference is largely one of degree. To the extent that an alliance develops for the purpose of accomplishing a single defined job or series of jobs—for example, to mount a joint orchestra/

Note: How Much Should an Alliance Cost?

Financially, gun-shy nonprofits often want to know the exact cost of a new venture, and an alliance will be no exception. Unfortunately, there are no widely reliable cost estimates available, if only because different alliances will try to accomplish different things. However, we can suggest a framework for evaluating the possible costs.

Start with the two types of cash outlays an alliance typically requires: operational costs (e.g., consulting fees, studies, legal advice), and investments. Since an alliance by definition is an effort to gain economic advantage from bringing together large numbers of organizations, operational costs should generally be modest for all but the largest nonprofits, measured in the thousands and tens of thousands of dollars. This is getting-started money and should be viewed as an expense without any identifiable payback likely.

The sizable cash outlays are the true investments that membership in an alliance may require. The nature of these investments will vary but may include things ranging from equipment purchase to leasehold improvements to up-front money for staff. These ought to be treated just as one would treat any new venture, evaluating the cost versus the anticipated benefit. Keep in mind that, as a true investment some of these outlays will hold their value—rented space may be able to sublet if the venture doesn't work out, or the special software resold to another group.

Many groups will also want to hold down certain costs, especially staffing-related ones, by contributing sweat equity—the labor of one's own staff. This works best if there is really no other alternative, or if staff members are only asked to operate within their own comfort zone.

choral performance series—it could be considered a task-oriented alliance. Conversely, if it is put together to have an impact on an ongoing area of management we would consider it more of a process alliance.

The difference between task alliances and process alliances has to do with future expectations. In the former, there is little expectation that the alliance's life will extend beyond the task at hand. In the process alliance, there is every reason to expect that it will continue as long as it is useful to all parties. Since the orientation is to a process rather than a product or task, there is no telling exactly what path the effort will take.

This is one of the reasons why many alliances are so poorly defined and poorly understood. A merger has a distinct beginning, middle, and end. In a task-oriented alliance one can at least step back at some point and say that the task was accomplished or that it was not. But in a process-oriented alliance it is never truly possible to say that one is past the beginning stages—or that one is at the end. There will always be questions of whether to grow by adding new members, how to adapt to changing external conditions, and the general tasks of maintaining the internal operations of the collaboration. In short, the process will always continue.

Like mergers, alliances can be either horizontal or vertical. Horizontal alliances are likely to occur among organizations that already know about each other and have something in common such as a trade association. One can even argue that a trade association itself is a form of alliance, except that a good trade association is usually much more complex, involves more groups, and has broader goals. One of the key characteristics of these types of alliances that may distinguish them from vertical alliances is that they have a more inclusive, almost egalitarian flavor. Based on the premise that more is better, they will rely on economics and signals from the outside world to know when to stop. For example, health care providers desiring to contract with managed care organizations (MCOs) will know almost intuitively how geographically diverse the local MCO market is. There is no point in exceeding the geographic reach of the target health maintenance organizations (HMOs), so there will be natural boundaries built into this kind of alliance.

Vertical alliances tend to grow out of a specific market. They are put together for specific strategic reasons, so they will attempt to incorporate participating organizations that support that strategy. They may be large, but they will be far from open-ended. Rather, they will close to new entrants once they have achieved sufficient mass. Perhaps not surprisingly, vertical alliances in the health and social service field so far have found it difficult to grow programs,

Tip: Associations as Incubators of Alliances

Attention, associations of nonprofits: there is a role for you as originators of horizontal alliances. Associations have all the advantages needed to encourage the development of what we are calling horizontal alliances: knowledge of participants, access to them, mutual trust, keen awareness of members' operating environments, and public credibility. It may even be possible to make a buck or two through carefully crafted economic programs, in addition to the fact that it's just the right thing to do.

preferring instead to take existing ones over. Growth for these early players has been acquisitive rather than creative.

Which raises a fundamental question. What is the difference between a vertical alliance and a vertically integrated merger? To the outsider, probably very little. Whatever the origins and initial intent of collaboration, a vertically integrated merger—run by, say, a management company—will look very much like a large-scale vertical alliance. To say that participants in an alliance retain corporate control may be functionally irrelevant if more than 50 percent of the total referrals are coming from participation in the alliance. Separate governing boards in this instance grant independent authority, but reality suggests otherwise. It is for this reason that some of the larger integrated health care delivery systems can be seen as vertical alliances even though they may be portraying themselves to outsiders as the product of mergers.

CONTROL AND GOVERNANCE

Alliances are a good example of the way that management is evolving away from traditional command and control toward a more sophisticated tendency to shape and influence events through collaboration, communication, and consensus. In short, controlling an alliance is like herding cats. To the extent that one can control an alliance at all, the term will typically refer to things like the structure of the various committees and subcommittees, their composition and size, the agendas of the groups, the overall pacing, and the strategic goals.

Without a specific legal entity in place, controlling an alliance is a political and negotiation process. Virtually everything alliance members do will have to be voluntary because to pretend otherwise would be fruitless. The easiest things to agree on tend to be governance matters: each participant gets one vote, new members must get a certain number of votes to join, and so forth. This early stage formlessness is natural for a new organization, but eventually the alliance may need to choose a more definitive governance process, and it is at this stage that members must make hard choices.

ADVANTAGES AND DISADVANTAGES

Alliances offer many advantages to the nonprofit seeking the benefits of collaboration without giving up control. They offer enormous flexibility plus the power to bring to bear the combined weight of many similar organizations in the service of finding a solution to everyday problems like purchasing commodities more cheaply. They also offer a means of involving staff at all levels in productive, nonthreatening collaboration.

Alliances can be a good way to explore formal collaboration as a strategy for the next century. There is something reassuring about their strength-through-unity message, and they are quite compatible with the theme of social sharing that many nonprofit managers bring to their work. For managers and boards who are skittish about entering into mergers, alliances can be the next best thing. It may even be possible to participate seriously in more than one alliance. It is not hard to imagine a time when most of certain CEO's work would revolve around alliance partners in one way or another.

There are also disadvantages. Done properly, alliances take more time than a merger. Particularly without a formalized, operating legal structure, it is very hard to identify savings and other direct benefits of the collaboration. They can be highly unsatisfying for those who desire a clearcut beginning, middle and end to projects (who doesn't?). And the lessons of one alliance are not necessarily easily transferred to another.

CHAPTER TWELVE

Partnerships with Nonprofits

Unlike many terms in this section, the word partnership has a very specific legal meaning. In legal terminology, a partnership is simply an arrangement in which two or more people or entities agree to cooperate in order to achieve some common business goal, in the course of which they agree to share profits and losses. Tax laws treat partnerships as though they were a wall of light; profit, loss, deduction, credits, and the like simply go right through the partnership to the partners just as though the partnership didn't exist. From that simple formulation comes a wealth of possibilities—and complications. In this chapter we will concentrate on partnerships that nonprofits would be likely to form.

Two elements of the above definition of a partnership are worth noting. First, a partnership is not a corporation. This may seem a trivial distinction but for legal purposes it is huge. Corporations—nonprofit or for-profit—are treated very differently under the law than are partnerships. Everything from tax status to liability law to operations management is different in a true partnership as compared with a corporation.

Second, and this is implicit in the previous definition but is worth highlighting, partnerships are created for profit, not for charitable purposes. A nonprofit has just as much right to be a partner in a partnership as any other person or legal entity, but the act of forming a partnership for any purpose is so definitive that there is no point in making it simply an extension of one's preexisting tax exemption. Partnerships are intended to be vehicles for profit.

As legal entities, partnerships are rather curious affairs. To form a partnership, one need do little more than declare the existence of a partnership on paper, then go through the appropriate local requirements, if any, for starting up a business. Most of the subsequent paperwork produced in the course of a partnership is little more than the formal effort to solve mundane albeit critical operational questions like how the partners get paid, what services the partnership will offer, and who can belong to the partnership.

Part of the problem that nonprofits will have in even thinking about partnerships in the context of the structure of a collaboration is that the word itself already means certain things. There probably isn't a state in the nation where the government purchases services from nonprofit corporations and the two entities don't refer to each other as partners at least some of the time. And even the most casual collaboration between two nonprofits tends to be called a partnership. To complicate matters, partnerships may also be called joint ventures, split operations, alliances, and similar terms.

To acknowledge the obvious, we are using the word partnership in a very different way from its typical casual application. We do so deliberately. Partnerships in this context are definable legal forms that employ people, pay taxes, take on debt, and do a myriad of other things characteristic of other types of businesses. They are a bona fide choice for structuring certain collaborations, and a sophisticated way of fulfilling complex financial, economic, and legal needs of collaborating nonprofits.

Note: Partnerships versus Joint Ventures

The difference between a partnership and a joint venture is that a partnership is presumed to be an ongoing relationship, whereas a joint venture is a one-time affair. Tax laws treat joint ventures as partnerships. In practice, joint ventures usually involve blending things like services or resources, not property. Partnerships are more likely to entail property ownership and maintenance.

STRUCTURE

If the fundamental collaborative nature of partnerships is clear, the permutations on the way partnerships can be structured are almost endless. Many states have begun to recognize limited liability partnerships. In addition, provisions for governance, profit sharing, and management can be so different that they effectively create a whole other set of variables in structuring partnerships.

One of the virtues of partnerships is that they can be designed so flexibly. This flexibility can also be a liability if it's not handled properly. The best approach is the form-follows-function philosophy described earlier: decide what it is that the partnership needs to accomplish, then figure out how to design it to achieve that result. And be sure to get qualified legal advice along the way.

CONTROL AND GOVERNANCE

Partnerships are notoriously difficult to control, which is why they tend to be better as vehicles for holding property or distributing wealth than as active platforms for operations. If, by definition, everyone has a piece but no one is in control, there will be no clear line of authority. If there is no line of authority, then participants in

Note: Partnerships 101

Partners may be people, corporations, or other partnerships. Each partner owns at least one interest in the partnership, which is called a unit. There are two types of partners: general and limited, the terms having to do with the extent and nature of liability for what the partnership does. Every partnership has to have at least one general partner. There can be more than one general partner, and if so, one of them is usually designated as the managing general partner. Limited partners get their name from the fact that their liability is limited to the amount of their contribution to the partnership (typically the contribution is the same for all limited partners).

a partnership—even employees—are free agents, able to operate independently. The partnership as an entity has to rely on something economic to unite and shape collective action. That something will have to be gains such as increased referrals, shared possession of some otherwise unattainable asset, and so forth. The more sharply that goal is defined, the easier it will be to manage the partnership.

Ongoing governance of the partnership will be a challenge. The smartest thing that the nonprofit partners can do is to lay out ahead of time exactly how they will govern themselves. The specific provisions of routine governance can be just about anything as long as everyone agrees to them, they are in writing, and they are reasonably comprehensive.

An often overlooked note: someday the partnership will end. It may turn into a corporation or some other legal form, or it may just dissolve. It's a good idea to plan for that eventuality from the beginning. Organizational planners call this an exit strategy, and although it may seem unnecessarily pessimistic it makes a great deal of sense to spell out ahead of time under what conditions and in what way the partnership will end. It makes for smoother transitions, and it forces today's planners to think through the possible implications of today's decisions.

SPECIAL CONSIDERATIONS

The preceding material discussed partnerships as though they were always entities created to accommodate the intentions of two or more nonprofits to accomplish a specific collaborative purpose. The reverse is also possible if an existing entity puts together a partnership of nonprofits. Most often this kind of thing happens at the Economics level of the C.O.R.E. model, and it frequently involves a trade association or similar organization. Two examples will illustrate the application.

An association of nonprofits realized that the office supply business was highly fragmented, with the bulk of distribution carried out by a lot of very small corner "stationery stores" supplied by a much smaller number of wholesalers. By uniting its members, the association was able to put together enough business to deal directly with the wholesaler, thereby cutting out that small but expensive last stop. Best of all, the association could receive the same commission that the wholesaler already was accustomed to paying whomever won the accounts of those corner stores. In the eyes of the wholesaler, the association became just another salesperson; in the eyes of its members, it was the source of significant savings.

Does this arrangement sound very similar to Staples, Office Depot and other megastationery supplies distributors? It should, because it is virtually the same model. But this arrangement began in 1982, well before most of today's superstores even grew large enough to sell shares in the company. It isn't much of a stretch to see these superstores as today's "partnerships" with the consumer.

Another partnership was put together by a quasipublic authority that had previously concentrated on issuing state government-backed bonds on behalf of hospitals, clinics, and schools. Reading the trend toward deregulation in the electric power industry correctly, they set about to take advantage of the trend before it occurred. A year before electric power deregulation was to go into effect in their state, they assembled an impressive group of nonprofits, including but not limited to the organizations for whom they had issued bonds, and then issued a request for proposals on the group's behalf to purchase electric power supply contracts. While not complete as of this writing, the effort was conservatively estimated to yield a 10 percent savings in electric costs for the participants.

Again, we note that these models are not partnerships in the precise legal sense of the term. However, they are a good illustration of partnership-like structures that can be expected to grow more popular in the years ahead.

PARTNERSHIPS WITH FOR-PROFIT COMPANIES

Some collaborations will involve for-profit companies. Unburdened by owners and investors demanding wealth, nonprofit organizations have enjoyed a longstanding presumption of moral purity in the marketplace. While this may be eroding slightly due to well-publicized scandals, the fact is that nonprofits have a reputation in the average citizen's mind for taking action unskewed by narrow profit motives. To suggest that a nonprofit and a for-profit may enter into a true business relationship from which they can each profit in ways important to them is still well beyond most people and many nonprofit managers.

Yet, this is exactly what is going to happen in some nonprofits' new strategic collaborations. After all, the designation of nonprofit is a tax status, not a moral state. Even the most rabid ideologues would grant that it is possible for a nonprofit to engage in morally reprehensible behavior just as much as it is possible for a for-profit to hold to the highest ethical standards. And as business people of all kinds begin to understand the flexibility and partnering that will be necessary in the next century's economy they will start to appreciate the role that a well-managed community nonprofit can occasionally play in their business plans. The result will be an increase in the number of nonprofit–for-profit collaborations, and an increase in the numbers of nonprofits and nonprofit alliances that establish at least one for-profit subsidiary.

A side note here. We are not talking about head-to-head competition of the kind that sometimes leads for-profit companies to charge nonprofits with unfair competition. This happens when a nonprofit and a for-profit do the same thing and compete for the same customers, as when a YMCA operates a health club or a research institute develops commercial software. The kind of nonprofit–for-profit collaboration that will occur in the future is the kind that grows from the mutual awareness that each can easily do something the other cannot.

Mostly, the way nonprofits will get involved with for-profits is through partnerships. How those partnerships will be structured is likely to be determined by the income tax implications in the case of the for-profit, and unrelated business income tax (UBIT) for the nonprofit. Sometimes the nonprofit will want to be the general partner. Here, the acid test is whether a partnership advances its charitable purpose, since the Internal Revenue Service has stated that such partnerships require "close scrutiny" as the first step in its approval process. If the Internal Revenue Service (IRS) decides that the partnership does advance the charity's tax-exempt mission, it must then decide whether the partnership agreement allows the charity to operate in exclusive furtherance of the mission. While this may sound like a slight variation on the first test, it is different because certain provisions in a partnership agreement that otherwise does advance a charitable purpose may turn out to be in conflict.

Any time an entity becomes a general partner in a partnership it assumes certain liabilities, as well as the responsibility for helping the partnership make a profit. Either one of these demands can lead to conflicts with a nonprofit's tax exempt mission, so planners must be careful to structure the partnership carefully. As an alternative the nonprofit can be a limited partner, typically a passive investor. If a college, for example, contributed money to a partnership with a housing developer for off-campus dorms but had no responsibility for day-to-day management, it would get a share of profits but be considered a limited partner.

Partnerships with for-profit companies can take other forms. For instance, nonprofits might lend funds to a for-profit. They can also lease the rights to develop land they own. And, because the tax implications of nonprofit/for-profit partnerships can be so complex, they may find the need to create a whole new for-profit subsidiary that will in turn work with the for-profit partner. This strategy can protect the tax status of the nonprofit and make UBIT matters clearer.

PART FOUR

Seven Steps to a Successful Nonprofit Merger

CHAPTER THIRTEEN

Organizing a Planning Structure

To plan a merger it is helpful to envision the process as a collection of seven distinct clusters of activities that must be performed. We call them steps because that is a familiar metaphor for processes, but in reality they are more like seven different bases that must be touched before a merger can be declared a success. Some clusters of activities have to be performed constantly, while others are one-time only. This is not a linear process. Most of these steps will take place while others are occurring.

Successful nonprofit mergers and alliances are planned from the top down and implemented from the bottom up. A good Planning Committee and its subcommittees act as a kind of differential gear for these two potentially conflicting directions, assigning specific areas of focus and tasks to the appropriate parties and controlling the overall pace. In small nonprofits a single committee can handle most of the planning tasks itself, but in larger organizations a system of subcommittees is the only feasible way to incorporate all internal stakeholders in the process.

Many management activities are linear processes. Buying a piece of real estate is a step-by-step affair whose components are determined by a combination of laws, regulations, and lender requirements. Filing tax returns is a linear process. Hiring staff members necessitates following the same general steps each time.

Designing and implementing a nonprofit merger is not a linear process. Many tasks must be accomplished at the same time and there are typically false starts and dead ends, especially when par-

Tip: Make Ambiguity Your Friend

Two of the best things that any participant at any level can bring to the process of merging or creating an alliance is a high tolerance for ambiguity and a sense of humor—and the sense of humor is optional. The process is intrinsically confusing and often misleading, and its complex, nonlinear nature makes it hard for anyone to grasp it all. Is it actually going to happen? When? What's going on now? Who's in charge? These are all excellent, rational questions. The problem is that they rarely have clear-cut answers. Learning to recognize this fact and still operate is one of the most important things that participants can do.

ticipants have never been through the process before. What's even more confusing is that the same experience can look like a straight line or a hopelessly jumbled mess depending on the stage of the process and one's role in the organization. Still, a well-organized Planning Committee following the proven guidelines of this section can help smooth out and streamline the procedure.

AN INTEGRATED PARALLEL PROCESS

Think of a merger as an integrated parallel process. Steps are taken by different subgroups at all levels of the C.O.R.E. model at any given time. In March a team might be engaged in integrating information systems on the responsibility level at the same time that a marketing subcommittee might be planning a high visibility advertising campaign at the corporate level. Part of the support for the new marketing push may be a new database software package that cannot be installed until June, thus effectively delaying the marketing campaign until September. The two initiatives are inextricably linked by a joint timetable, even though every other aspect of their development will proceed on quite parallel and independent tracks.

Implicit in parallel processes is the expectation that each party will identify and pursue its own rational interests, which is why the first step is for each party to establish its expectations of the process. In all likelihood, an individual board and/or management team has spent a good deal of time discussing the possibility of some form of collaboration before it actually begins the process. Still, before things get too advanced it's a wise idea for the lead group—preferably the board, although possibly the management team, especially in larger and more complex organizations—to identify exactly what it is that they hope to gain from a merger or alliance.

A good way to do this is to take a sheet of flip chart paper and list the benefits the participants expect to come from the alliance. A word or phrase for each will do just fine. Chances are these will center on services and economics, such as "more stable funding," "opportunity to expand programs," and "staff growth." Then do the same thing with the concerns and fears. Often the reservations about an alliance will be expressed in intangibles such as "loss of identity," "loss of autonomy," and "overshadowed mission."

The positives speak for themselves, so it's time to do some careful thinking about that second list. Ask yourselves this question: "if we were to be able to achieve our hopes and desires, and if most or all our concerns were either allayed or neutralized, why would we *not* enter this alliance?"

Often, under close examination, some of the fears melt away. Loss of identity is a prime reservation typically expressed about a merger. Yet, on a very basic level it is often a nonissue. A program with a good reputation has built up some loyalty—yes, a brand name. Why would any new entity want to throw that away just because the corporate vehicle behind the program now has a different name? The program's services are the same, the staff are probably the same. So what if the color of everyone's paycheck has changed? Should all of those behind-the-scenes facts really matter to a program's identity?

Those two lists summarize the organization's interests in the merger discussions. The work of the agency's representatives on the Planning Committee then becomes to study those concerns and fears, figure out a practical way of expressing them, and engage the full Planning Committee in resolving them. The Planning Committee will almost surely succeed if it maintains a single-minded focus on achieving the desired outcomes of the merger while avoiding the negatives.

ASSEMBLING THE PLANNING COMMITTEE

It is time now for a discussion of how to assemble a Planning Committee. The goal of a Planning Committee is disarmingly simple: collect a workable number of leaders on both sides who are willing to devote the time and energy to the process for a defined period of time. Of course, as simple as the goal may be, the execution of it tends to be anything but simple.

The Planning Committee should be a workable size, meaning approximately four to eight people from each organization. Ideally, it should have a balanced representation of senior staff and board members, the precise mix being determined by such factors as the size of the organizations, board culture, and the time commitment required.

There is a temptation to select Planning Committee members from the board based on their positions, for example, president,

Tip: What to Do About the December Sag

Planning a merger starting in the fall? Expect a slowdown beginning around mid-November. Board members tend to be hard to schedule for meetings, and staff members take vacation time. By the second week in December, it's virtually impossible to have committee meetings of any kind. The pace will pick up again just after the New Year holiday, but since people weren't around to schedule anything in December, the meetings take a while to get organized. The result is that the two month period beginning in mid-November is a washout.

One way to make this period work for you is to plan a social event for the two agencies using the holiday season as the rationale. This works well if it is cast as a purely social holiday gathering—perhaps designed to replace a traditional holiday party or open house that one or both groups might have been having anyway—and there is no explicit pressure to accomplish anything. It's a good way to facilitate the kind of social interaction that is necessary to begin building trust during the mutual learning phase. Which, when you think about it, is actually accomplishing quite a lot.

treasurer, and secretary. Avoid it. Select one or a small number of board members based on their roles, not their titles. Do the same for management personnel. The Planning Committee needs to have the smallest number of influential people possible just in order to be a workable group.

The first few meetings are likely to have been haphazard and meandering. Once the groups decide to pursue a merger and assemble a formal team for studying it, they cross a boundary. A proposition which had formerly been abstract and highly speculative begins to take more concrete shape. People are identified and assigned roles. Meetings are set, tasks are identified. The participants make plans, consider possibilities, and subtly begin to think like a team.

This stage will not take long because participants are eager to get into the process and a Planning Committee is a safe and sensible way of doing it. Also, it needs fewer people than were involved in the initial considerations, and so it will be easier to mobilize. A full leadership structure in larger nonprofit mergers—meaning the complete array of subcommittees, task forces, and ad hoc groups that will be needed to see the merger through—will, of course, take longer to put together. Still, the initial planning group is the core of the effort.

SUBCOMMITTEES

In small nonprofit organizations, there may never be a need for more than the Planning Committee. If the parties are large or complex, subcommittees will be a necessity. The Advocates Health Care system in Chicago, the giant product of a merger between two large health systems, took almost two years to complete and involved 14 separate subcommittees. With subcommittees, the Planning Committee delegates most of its functional roles and becomes almost a kind of legislative body.

Planning Committee members should understand from the beginning which model they have chosen. Although the presence or absence of subcommittees is clear enough, members need to understand that the two models imply very different things for their day-to-day role.

The best way to structure subcommittees is to identify the work that needs to be done and then delegate logical groupings of tasks to subcommittees formed for the purpose. Subcommittee membership will usually be drawn largely from the staff ranks, if only because board members rarely have enough time to contribute to the effort. Also, since subcommittees focus on implementation issues, it is not necessarily appropriate to have a substantial board of directors' presence anyway.

Certain issues arise predictably during a merger (alliances also require subcommittees, but their Planning Committees tend to act more as coordinators than as rule-makers). Each of these matters can easily be important enough to be considered in depth during the implementation stage. Planning Committees need to decide early whether to concentrate on these issues and, if so, how to group them. Here, in alphabetical order, are some of the areas most likely to be identified by the Planning Committee as needing in-depth attention at the subcommittee level. Note that this is nothing more than a list of common areas of planning, not a list of committees. An individual Planning Committee may or may not find them worth assigning to a separate subcommittee.

Administrative Systems

One of the easiest challenges to identify in virtually all mergers is how the parties go about integrating their various administrative systems. These "back room" functions include such things as accounting, payroll, human resources, and purchasing, and integrating these services can take literally years. Taken as a whole, this is one of the more complex areas of a merger, and it should be approached with the expectation that true integration will take time and resources. At the same time, success here can mean a payoff for the new entity in savings and efficiencies.

Collective Bargaining

Collective bargaining agreements are important enough to demand their own carved-out focus within the larger area of human resources and staff development. Often there will be different unions involved, different contract cycles, different organizing styles, etc. The complexity here can easily get enormous and should be monitored closely by a subcommittee.

Communications

Communication is essential in any merger, and it will need to be done both internally and externally. The Planning Committee can be instrumental in establishing constant communication as a condition of the collaboration, but the best way to achieve it is through a subcommittee assembled for the purpose.

Compensation Planning

Not to be confused with collective bargaining matters, compensation planning will attract a lot of attention. The difference is that all mergers will involve compensation, but only a relatively small number will involve collective bargaining units. Compensation patterns are also likely to be very different between two prospective merger partners, and these differences can cause real conflicts. At the very least, compensation is a highly sensitive area for the new entity. At worst, it will take large amounts of money to even out differing compensation schedules. The role of the Planning Committee and any compensation subcommittee is to handle these differences as skillfully as possible.

Executive Director Selection

In some situations the Planning Committee will need to select a new chief executive officer. With two or more existing executive directors possibly competing for a single new position, this will not happen often. When it does, there may need to be a subcommittee dedicated to the task.

Financial Planning—Cash Flow, Budgets, Banking

In financial terms, a merger is equivalent to explosive growth. Ironically, explosive growth can be one of the most dangerous things to happen to any organization. The idea is to use the growth positively, of course, but the only way to do that is through careful financial planning. A financial subcommittee can oversee (though not carry out) such critical tasks as budgeting and cash flow planning. Part of financial management involves relationships with outsiders such as bankers and auditors, and carefully selected financial subcommittee members can be helpful here as well.

Fundraising

Fundraising professionals can easily get spooked at the prospect of a merger, worrying that it will be interpreted the wrong way. Interestingly, their donors do not always share that reaction. A good education campaign can help prevent defections, and in large organizations this may need to be a separate subcommittee.

Information Technology

Today, nonprofits of all kinds must have sophisticated information processing capabilities. Under the best of circumstances it can be a chore to get two different systems to exchange information freely. Yet, that is exactly what they have to do once a merger is official. Whether one is collapsed into the other or whether they continue to coexist in some way, information technology systems need careful planning. Given its highly technical nature, this subcommittee can rarely expect to see more than a token member or two from the boards of directors.

Organizational and Corporate Structure

Somehow, management must capture all of those promises of more effective operations. While organizational structure is largely a management responsibility, often with the help of outside advisors, designing the corporate structure is an appropriate focus for the boards' energies. In large and sophisticated merger partners or in alliances, this is where a lot of time may be spent.

Professional Development

As used here, "professional development" is a bit of a catch-all phrase for a large range of possible activities. In a merger of theaters, the actors' professional interests and desires must be considered—apart from any potential collective bargaining responsibilities. Hospitals and health systems are looking for ways to include their physicians in risk-sharing plans and are always seeking new ways of relating to physician practice groups. These questions are usually best handled as a delegated task of the Planning Committee.

Professional Credentialing

Closely related to professional development concerns is the possibility that the merger will raise a professional credentialing issue. It could happen when one agency is fully accredited and the other is not, or it could come about because seeking accreditation jointly was one of the prime reasons for the merger in the first place. Another comparable question arises often in the health and human services field when licenses required for reimbursement are tied to certain geographic areas and a merger may threaten the continuity.

Program Integration

One valid reason for a merger is the possibility of integrating previously disjointed programs. Programs can be linked in any number of ways, from using common management to shared market-

Tip: How to Find the Leaders

Having staff and board leaders on the Planning Committee is a desirable goal, but how does one go about identifying them? Use McLaughlin's First Law of Task Force Dynamics: the leadership of any committee or task force is never greater than the square root of its membership.

If a committee has 25 members, it will have no more than 5 leaders; if it has 15 members, there will be a maximum of 4 leaders. It may also have 3. Or 2. Or none at all. But the total number of leaders will never exceed the square root of the total membership. Why? Because there isn't room for any more.

Sounds glib, yes. But it works. Try it in any situation you can think of (let's see, if the United States Senate has 100 members. . . .)

ing to outright merger. A program integration subcommittee is a way to plan those linkages, usually in coordination with a group working on organizational structure. This is another subcommittee likely to have little or no board representation on it.

Space Usage

Almost inevitably, a merger raises issues of office space planning. The merger may create vacant space, force offices to be rearranged or cause leases to be renegotiated. Reducing costs through more efficient use of space can often help justify the merger in the first place. There is also the inescapable element of psychological attachment to certain places to consider, so this committee will be immersed in a complicated and sensitive area.

SOME SAMPLE PLANNING COMMITTEE STRUCTURES

The merging agencies' needs should determine the proper mix of subcommittees. No group of subcommittee structures is right for all situations, although we believe that there is a direct correlation between the amount of time invested in subcommittee work and the ultimate effectiveness of the collaboration. Exhibit 13.1 shows a sample of three actual Planning Committee and Subcommittee structures.

The first merger was between two medium size agencies ($3 to $5 million) that had had a long history of serving noncompeting markets in the same geographic area. They chose to use only the single Planning Committee and to do various administrative tasks in ad hoc groups of senior managers. Consequently, the planning committee was taxed to its limit; the positive side is that the new board began as an unusually cohesive group thanks to all the time they spent together.

The second merger also involved only a single Planning Committee, but in this case one party was considerably larger than the other, and the entire collaboration was tacitly designed as a takeover. The larger entity heavily staffed the Planning Committee, and the smaller organization, which had far fewer staff with whom to handle administrative tasks, had to play a minor role in the process.

Merger	Function	Composition	Description of Merging Parties	Assessment
1. Planning Committee	Overall monitoring	Board, staff	Two medium-size agencies	Committee was stretched thin
2. Planning Committee	Overall monitoring	Board, staff	One large, one small agency	Used consultants appropriately
3. Planning Committee	Overall monitoring, corporate restructuring	Senior management	Two medium-size agencies	Board presence on all committees was missing
Personnel	Compensation equity, benefits planning, policy rewriting	Senior management, middle managers		Highly technical issues
Management systems	Integration of existing systems	Senior management, middle managers		A long-term focus
Communication	Internal and external communication campaigns	Senior management		Especially important at front end—generated excellent publicity for the merger
Program Services	Integrating program; development of new initiatives	Senior management		A long-term effort
Real Estate Development	New initiative development	Executive Directors		Long-range plan

Exhibit 13.1 Sample of Three Actual Planning Committee Structures

The third merger was easily the most thoroughly planned and ultimately most effective of the three. Two agencies, each with program services totaling about $9 million plus contracts for processing $19 million of transfer payments (e.g., weatherization and job training) allowed all members of their senior management teams to spend at least two days per month on a relatively fast track merger. As a consequence, the merger proceeded quite smoothly and created a major new service entity for its area.

What is most important about subcommittees is not how many there are or what their area is, but rather the degree to which they can carry out the work of the Planning Committee. To do so, they need clear direction from the Planning Committee, resources as appropriate, and support from the members' respective agencies.

THE ROLE OF CONSULTANTS

One of the biggest differences between nonprofit mergers and traditional for-profit mergers is that the latter use consultants as agents of private interests whereas nonprofits use them as facilitators of the process. The difference is rooted in what's at stake. In Wall Street's mergers, great personal and institutional wealth is at risk, so it is only natural that participants want and need to have strong individualized representation. What is missing in these agent-driven transactions is a mediating influence. The stock market itself frequently plays this role, and sometimes the courts, but no other entity has a rightful claim to shaping the process itself as opposed to the interests of the participants. This is why the transactions frequently become adversarial affairs.

The situation is different for nonprofits, which are quasi-public institutions and in which great wealth is at stake only insofar as it is represented in paychecks. Even in the largest and most generous of nonprofits, a year's pay hardly constitutes true wealth. The other element at risk is institutional and personal ego, but that's not the kind of thing that consultants can reliably preserve anyway. Consequently, consulting in mergers and alliance development at its best tends to be a classic use of outside advisors as facilitators.

Consultants can bring two distinct advantages to a merger: an educated outsider's perspective and specialized knowledge and skills. Trusted consultants can offer unbiased feedback on any major aspect of a merger or alliance. It is also easier for them to adopt any number of roles—coach, planner, cheerleader, dictator, referee, beggar, or schemer, to name just a few—and during the course of the average merger there's a fair chance that several of these will be needed.

Using their position as outsiders, merger and alliance consultants can facilitate the process and signal participants when there's a problem. Without the same internal agendas as the participants—for one, the consultant already knows he or she is "losing" his or her job when the transaction is complete—a merger consultant can be a steadying influence. As more and more nonprofits choose to affiliate in one way or another there will come into being a steadily expanding pool of highly experienced consultants. Given nonprofit alliances' future as the new strategic planning for the 21st century, it is highly likely that strategic planning consultants of the 1970s and 1980s will gradually become merger and alliance developers instead. In time, there will be a more than adequate consultant supply.

This is not to say that nonprofits will never use consultants as agents of their interests. Mergers between very large and complex

Pitfall: Lack of Agreement about a Consultant's Role

Because the idea of a facilitator dedicated to a *process*—as opposed to a facilitator hired by and accountable to a single organization—can be new to many participants, it is important to be explicit about the expectations. A consultant hired to develop a nonprofit merger works for both organizations, not just one (otherwise, he or she is simply an agent). This means that there are joint obligations between the parties, such as candor, accountability for assignments—and paying the consultant. Without these explicit agreements there can easily be misunderstanding about who can expect what from whom. It helps for both parties to do everything regarding the consultant jointly, from introducing him or her to evaluating the work product.

organizations such as hospitals and (in the future) universities require specialized assistance to each party. Typically that kind of assistance is rendered by large law firms, but that is chiefly because nonprofit mergers tend to have been defined as legal affairs. What these large groups are really paying for is a temporary addition to their own professional staffs, and so in the future that same kind of support is likely to come from a number of potential suppliers such as investment bankers (large nonprofits usually have a sizable debt load), accountants and professional merger specialists as well as attorneys.

The absence of a chief executive officer (CEO) is also a good time for nonprofits to consider using a merger consultant as an agent. In this case the consultant will act in lieu of the CEO for merger-related items. Sometimes the consultant will act as a full time interim executive director too. We know of a hospital that, seeking to merge with one of many local systems, moved a board member into the vacant CEO chair in an attempt both to lead the organization and to firm up a merger. Often a consultant will be a valuable assistant to a sitting CEO who is simply not able to give the process all the time it requires.

Finally, a merger consultant can be an invaluable resource during the process itself. At the moment, relatively few nonprofits have gone through even a single merger, let alone several; a consultant who has been through the process knows where the problem areas lie and may be able to predict how certain issues will evolve. If nothing else, it can be a great comfort for participants to know that what they are facing is normal and to be expected. If desired, the consultant should also be able to go beyond simply providing knowledge and offer private strategic advice.

CHAPTER FOURTEEN

Mutual Learning

In any nonprofit merger there will always be surprises. Count on it. Perhaps that renowned curator at the other museum has been quietly planning an around-the-world sailing trip and announces it the day after the big merger press conference. Or the locked room in the basement of the dingy office building you just acquired turns out to be stuffed full of priceless artifacts from the Revolutionary War. Or your own 10-year controller is unmasked as a convicted felon wanted in two other states.

Surprises like these can and do happen at any time, but when they occur during a merger or alliance with another organization they can delay and possibly even scuttle the process. The momentum that two or more organizations build up when considering a structured collaboration is a very fragile thing, and a single surprise (negative or positive) can easily derail it. And it may not even be the unexpected thing itself that does the damage but rather the fallout such as broken trust and delayed decisions.

The antidote is to deflate the surprise factor. Most "surprises" are really just information that only a small number of people possess. Assuming good will on all sides, a major surprise discovered early enough can turn into just another obstacle to be overcome with good planning. By doing some homework, each party can expand the number of people possessing the information. The name of that homework is a due diligence investigation.

duedil.doc
matrixm.doc
sitinven.xls

Tip: Know What's Really Happening in the First Step

The most important thing that's happening during the mutual learning phase is rarely articulated. Most of the substantive knowledge necessary for the Planning Committee and the respective boards and management teams can be taken from the resource book and due diligence reports. Assuming that the participants actually read the material, the calendar time required for most people to absorb the information would be equivalent to a moderately diligent study weekend before college final exams. What is really going on—and what takes so much calendar time—is a gradual process of familiarization, trust building, and private testing of the merger proposal. This is why initial meetings tend to be scheduled somewhat leisurely. It's as though the participants are saying "let's pursue this idea, but let's do it so that we can back out easily if it really doesn't feel right to us."

WHY DUE DILIGENCE?

The term *due diligence* may be only dimly familiar to nonprofit managers, if at all, as one of those pieces of legal terminology that has made its way into broad public usage in recent years. It refers to the systematic investigation of an organization's operations. When Wall Streeters conduct a due diligence investigation it's usually to verify the presence and ownership of reported assets, to check for the possibility of unrecorded liabilities, and to assess in a deeper way the proposed fit between the two companies. Nonprofits conduct due diligence investigations for similar purposes but different motivations.

For-profit managers must be sure that the takeover target really does have the value that they initially thought it had. If the transaction eventually occurs there will be an exchange of money for value, and so they concentrate on the more quantifiable aspects of financial health. Matters of strategy and long-term value have already been factored into the decision earlier in the process, and at this stage can be most easily considered only if there is some way to build them into the fundamental financial evaluation.

Nonprofit managers and their board members need not worry about an exchange of money for value in most cases. They have a fiduciary role requiring them to exercise good judgment in the oversight of a quasipublic asset, so the true goal is more of a planning and management challenge than it is a matter of generating or protecting wealth. At best, they are free to ignore questions of private benefit and to act on behalf of the larger good, at least as they see it.

Another way of saying this is that the issues raised by a due diligence investigation will be almost purely political. That is, they will involve questions that will only be resolved through discussion and negotiation. Whenever legal ownership of assets is not at stake, values and philosophy tend to take on primary importance. Ideally, this frees directors and managers to contemplate benefits of a merger from the perspective of the true fiduciaries that their roles imply. On the other hand, it can also mean that issues raised may have no common basis for resolution, which can cause the merger to stall and eventually collapse. All participants should understand what's at stake in the due diligence portion of their collaboration.

WHAT IS A DUE DILIGENCE INVESTIGATION?

Incorporating a nonprofit or any other corporation requires one to follow certain steps in a fairly linear fashion as stipulated in various laws. Audits of financial statements are carried out in a manner prescribed by the auditing profession. Bonds offered for sale to the public by large nonprofits go through predetermined processes with specific standards for the terms of the offering and the means by which it is offered.

Due diligence investigations share none of these characteristics, and for good reason. What each of the above processes have in common is that they are initiated by the principal organization on behalf of some type of external interest group (such as the general public or the bond-buying market), and that they involve a mediating third party of some kind such as an investment or accounting firm. Over time, those interest groups have figured out exactly what they need to know in order to approve or evaluate or invest in the nonprofit initiating the transaction. Since hundreds of these projects take place each week, the formats have become highly standardized. Interest groups can usually find what they need with a minimum of effort.

By contrast, mergers between nonprofit organizations are inherently private affairs, despite the existence of their public tax subsidies. Third-party interest groups have no legal right to command disclosure beyond the generalized and relatively light responsibilities placed on all managers of quasi-public entities to operate with a certain degree of openness. Due diligence investigations, therefore, start with deciding what it is one needs to know and then figuring out how to learn it.

This is the heart of why due diligence explorations are not codified in the same way as other investigatory or auditing processes. Each potential merger partner will have its own special areas in which it wants more information about its peer. The design of the collaboration itself may suggest particular areas of investigation, and there are almost always unique characteristics about one or both organizations that bear detailed investigation.

The due diligence investigation is most relevant to mergers. When nonprofits collaborate without changing their existing corporate vehicles or the responsibility for overseeing them, such as in alliances, there is little justification for doing the kind of formal due diligence exploration we are talking about here.

Typically, due diligence investigations are carried out by outside advisors. Internal staff can be involved if the advisor permits, although one of the advantages of hiring outsiders is that they can be held accountable. Mixing internal staff with outsiders can blur the lines of responsibility.

Most advisors will probably have their own format for due diligence investigations, and it is difficult to make generalizations about one format versus another. However, there are certain predictable areas that need attention no matter what other issues may arise. For convenience, we will cluster these into a handful of distinct categories. In this section we will concentrate mainly on the areas of focus for the due diligence. Evaluating the results of the investigation and making plans for implementation will come in a later section.

mergInc.doc

General Legal and Corporate Matters

Start with the basics. Your potential partner should be legally incorporated, probably as a nonprofit, and it should have appropriate incorporation papers on file. The articles of incorporation detail the goals and purposes of the corporation and will have been filed as part of the original incorporation package. Bylaws should also be in place, although, unfortunately, they rarely are up to date. This is such a common condition it should not cause any particular problem, unless the organization has made some sort of key change in a major process or policy that will affect its ability to collaborate.

All nonprofits should have a functioning board of directors which meets regularly and keeps minutes. A good sign of the level of organization and professionalism of the agency is whether key administrators can easily lay their hands on the last year's board meeting minutes. A three ring binder full of board minutes is a reassuring sight for a due diligence team.

Here's an example of how a due diligence team should operate. Not only should there be a complete set of board minutes readily accessible, but they should support the major decisions actually taken by the organization during that period. For example, the board should have documented its decision to acquire a major asset such as a building. It should have noted when the agency received notice of a legal action against it, it should have documented the process and rationale for hiring the new executive director, and so forth.

Don't forget—if there are multiple organizations involved under the same corporate umbrella, there should be proper corporate documentation for each.

Tip: Check Authority and Approval Process Now

Since you're in the neighborhood anyway, this is a good time to check out each other's provisions and likely timetable for approving a merger. The bylaws should spell out who approves such measures and the notice for voting that management must give. This will save a bit of time and aggravation later in the process.

bylawcom.doc

FINANCIAL CONDITION

Not surprisingly, the greatest amount of work needs to be done in the financial area. The justifiable fear here is that the surviving corporation will take on hidden liabilities. The most worrisome liabilities are the ones a nonprofit partner doesn't know about itself. We once saw a promising merger fall apart because one of the partners' office managers had been quietly not paying payroll taxes in order to cover a cash flow deficit. It was a small agency and a relatively unsophisticated board of directors, and the shortfall was discovered by the other partner during its own investigations.

There is a fair degree of overlap between a due diligence investigation and other disclosure processes already required of a nonprofit organization, particularly its yearly audit. Consequently, the team should obtain at least three years' worth of audited financial statements; five years' worth would be helpful. They should study the trends exhibited in the financials, and benchmark them against other comparable organizations, if possible. At this point the details are not as important as the overall trends.

Many auditors issue management letters at the same time as their yearly audit statements. The team should obtain these letters,

fintools.xlw

Pitfall: No Unaudited Financial Statements

There is a secondary reason for requesting unaudited financial statements, in addition to the obvious search for knowledge: to see if management can produce them. Good nonprofit management requires constant financial self-awareness. If the agency can't produce unaudited financials for the purposes of a due diligence, they probably can't produce them for their own internal monitoring either. Computerized financial accounting packages will usually create financial statements at the touch of a button, but if the data has not been properly entered and maintained this capability is meaningless. If the statements are available but routinely late—for example, if the March unaudited financial statements are not available until, say, July—it means that management always operates as much in the dark as the due diligence team.

as well as any written management responses to them. Management letters can offer important clues about the nonprofit's financial management style and effectiveness. Sometimes nonprofits are audited by funding sources as well, so the team should obtain these audits plus a report on the current status of any audits not yet complete.

The team should request unaudited financial statements to supplement the audited financials. The latter are produced only once each year and so their specifics are quickly out of date. Ideally, unaudited financial information is produced monthly and routed to senior management and the board of directors. Along with that information should come reports on aged receivables, cash flow, and utilization of services.

If the nonprofit does fundraising of any kind, the team will want to look at that material. Pure financial information will reveal fundraising effectiveness, but the way that an agency presents its case to the public will be a window into the thinking of the agency that can't be captured in mere numbers.

Since nonprofits cannot sell shares of ownership to the general public, they have to generate capital through profitable operations or by borrowing it. Due diligence investigations must take into account the level and type of obligations the potential partner has incurred. Smaller nonprofits will have used the financial equivalents of convenience stores and medium size grocery stores for their borrowing—that is, commercial banks—but larger nonprofits such as hospitals and universities will use the financial warehouses of capital finance, the tax exempt bond markets. These arrangements require professional evaluation.

Yes, nonprofits pay taxes. In fact, unpaid payroll taxes are one of the reliable red flags in any close look at an organization; more on that later. In some instances, nonprofits engage in nonexempt business transactions which produce a taxable profit (unrelated business income tax, or UBIT). In all cases, the ground rules are the same: taxes must be paid, and if they are not, the new board of directors could be taking over a major headache. Due diligence teams need to check on the status of all taxes payable.

An integral part of the financial reporting system is the financial planning system, more familiarly known as budgeting. The first step is to verify that the agency does have a viable, operating budgeting system. The second step is to examine its outputs. Small and medium size nonprofits will probably have the most minimal of budgeting processes, but they ought to have one. We'll describe some things to look for later in this section.

A quiet but critical aspect of operations is insurance coverage. The average nonprofit of even nominal size will have a surprisingly large number of coverages, ranging from workers' compensation and malpractice insurance to business interruption insurance and directors' and officers' coverage. Figuratively speaking, the due diligence team should gather up copies of all the insurance policies in a big box and study them to make sure that there is adequate coverage in place and that no policy has unexpectedly lapsed. Practicality is another matter, and we'll try to reconcile the two later in this section.

Although it doesn't affect many nonprofits, a few service groups may need to maintain a sizable inventory in order to provide services. There may be reason to examine the extent of the inventory and its value in the transaction.

Assets

Part of the financial review, but an important enough area to be treated separately, is the assets of the corporation. In a for-profit merger the assets' value affects the ultimate profitability of the entire transaction. In nonprofit mergers the stakes are a bit different, but misreading the value of assets to be acquired could have a lasting effect on long term financial health. In the case of large assets such as buildings or art collections, there may even need to be a valuation. This is unequivocally true for for-profit purchases of nonprofit assets, but it may also be necessary in nonprofit to nonprofit transactions.

The team will want to verify ownership of major assets, including real property and any endowments that may exist. For a due diligence investigation, simple copies of lists that probably already exist would be sufficient, along with evidence of ownership, since the asset base doesn't change dramatically and confirming assets is usually part of a yearly audit anyway. Sometimes ownership of an asset will bring with it the necessity of making major routine expenditures such as 24-hour security, or it might be on the brink of needing a major capital improvement such as a new roof or the rebuilding of a wing.

Pitfall: Beware the Money Pit

Beware money pits, the assets that cause unexpected, unavoidable, and unpredictable investments. For instance, environmental laws in many localities are becoming so strict that simply owning polluted property can require an agency to make a major investment in fixing it. Waste disposal regulations are becoming more complex and restrictive. The Americans with Disabilities Act (ADA) may require substantial renovations to a program site. Historical preservation laws in some cities, particularly in the Northeast, can have the same effect: the first floor of one association's headquarters was decimated by a runaway car, but preservation laws forced huge delays in rebuilding while obscure craftsmen were located to recreate ironwork, and waivers were sought to permit less expensive replacements. Other less visible laws and regulations unique to a locality can effectively mandate a major capital investment. Due diligence investigators need to be sensitive to these possibilities.

Liabilities and Obligations

There is a whole range of relationships that potentially create obligations or liabilities for the nonprofit corporation. In addition to contracts to deliver services, there will usually be contracts to purchase services. There may be employment contracts, and agreements to purchase supplies. Larger and more complex nonprofits will have a variety of management contracts—agreements between universities and food service vendors, for example, or between nursing homes and pharmacy supply companies. Retirement plans, employee benefit options, and investment management agreements are still other examples of obligations that can be transferred to another organization. Restrictions on monies raised in the past can also affect current operations. These should be documented and reviewed by appropriate expertise on the due diligence team.

Contracts, Licenses, Accreditation

Many times government officials require nonprofits that provide education, social services, or health care to be licensed or accredited or both. Government funding agents also often set up long-term contracts under which they agree to purchase certain services at predetermined rates. For due diligence purposes, all three of these kinds of arrangements are critical to maintaining an organization's future viability.

Contracting for the purchase of services from nonprofits became extremely popular with state and local governments during the past thirty years, to the point that many agencies in the social services and some in the health care fields are largely dependent on such agreements for survival. Typically, a contract is put out for bid to a wide variety of possible providers and then signed by the winner and the government agency for a defined period of time. Renewals may be automatic or contested, but it is possible to amass enough contracts and get them routinely renewed to run a reasonably well-funded organization.

On the other hand, the funding source always has the ultimate power to withdraw a contract. Without contracts, an agency lacks a stable base of funding and could face bankruptcy. Further, it often takes only one or two lost contracts to create a public sense of failing confidence in an organization. The due diligence team should pay careful attention to the status of all present and recent contracts, with particular attention to any that have been terminated for any reason during the previous three years.

The status of licensing and accreditation can offer the same kind of insight into an organization, although loss of either is a much more serious situation than the loss of a single contract because it often leads to loss of the ability to generate certain types of revenue at all. This is an area that cries out for special expertise on the due diligence team to help interpret potential weak points.

Human Resources Information

No matter how large and complex the merger partners may be, human resources issues will play a major role. Quantitative information to be gathered here includes complete lists of all employees including positions, titles, compensation rates, benefit eligibility, collective bargaining status if any, date of employment, and employer-wide histories of workers' compensation and unemployment claims. Obtaining a copy of all personnel policies and related material should go without saying. Employment contracts, if any, are definitely in this category as well.

A fact of life is that some nonprofits will have a collective bargaining unit representing employees. A further fact of life is that, in practice, it can be very difficult to merge a nonunion agency with one that has collective bargaining agreements. We will go into the implications of this later in the section, but at the due diligence stage, team members need to be especially thorough about collecting information.

One of the most useful things the team can do is to talk to the managers and bargaining unit representatives. It can be very helpful to talk with former managers and long time or retired union members in order to get a history of union–management relations. Not only will the investigators collect valuable information, but they will also send a signal that they are striving for objectivity and fairness. It is essential that team members behave with utmost professionalism in this highly sensitive area. Collective bargaining matters can be volatile, and there will be plenty of opportunity for debating the substance of labor-related decisions later in the process.

hrcomp.doc
salcomp.xls

Pro Forma Financials, Including Cash Flow

Mergers are about the future. The due diligence team should pay attention to the projected financial effects of combining these two organizations. The way to do this is by putting together a set of pro forma financial statements, or a kind of financial dress rehearsal for what the new entity would look like. At this stage of the due diligence investigation, it is usually enough just to collect the information that would be necessary to do the pro formas. However, it may be easy to forget to compile the pro formas later on, so it is a good idea to consider doing a set now. That way, the merger committee can study the calculations and possibly suggest some variations. Obviously, this is one step that only needs to be done once together and not by each team separately.

Regulatory Filings

Finally, investigate the current state of required regulatory filings. Nonprofits in health care and human services are among the most regulated entities in our economy, so there is a reasonable chance that one or both of the merger partners will have a continuing regulatory obligation. Sometimes these arise from the tax exempt designation itself. There should be a copy of the IRS's confirmation of tax exempt status in the files, and there may need to be continuous updating for state authorities too. The top state official with nonprofit oversight responsibilities, typically the attorney general or the secretary of state, may have a filing requirement, and local property tax assessment officials may also require some sort of filing to keep current. The due diligence team needs to identify all of these requirements and verify that the potential partner has met them.

RED FLAGS

A due diligence investigation is very likely to turn up one or more items of concern. In fact, if a due diligence team does not discover at least a few unexpected twists, it may not have done its job properly. The important thing is not any one item alone, but rather how the parties react to it. The same situation in one merger may be a deal breaker, while in another it may be simply a moderate obstacle or perhaps no obstacle at all. Whatever the case, there are some "red flags" that warrant further investigation. Understand that these are only signs, and that they may not amount to anything at all. Here they are, in alphabetical order.

Balloon Loan Payments Coming Due

Look at the back of the audited financial statements, where there are a series of numbered footnotes. Find the section that describes future years' long-term debt levels. The dollar amounts should decline as the years increase. If one year shows a higher amount of payback than the years before, it means that at some point in the future the organization will have to suddenly start paying back more on its borrowings. Ask the agency's management two questions: (1) are you aware that you will owe an unusually large debt payment in the future? and (2) do you have a plan for paying it back? If the answer to the both questions is yes and the plan seems reasonable, move on to the next item on the agenda.

General Records Disarray

If no one can ever seem to find the files you requested, if the records are stacked everywhere in cardboard boxes, if nothing seems to work right in the partner nonprofit, it may indicate a more profound breakdown of systems. Ignorance isn't bliss in this case, just dangerous.

Indispensable Staff

The presence of indispensable staff should serve as another red flag during a due diligence investigation. One can infer the presence of indispensable staff when all questions seem to lead to the same individual. It could be the executive director, a business person, a program manager, or even a board member. Indispensable staff is an inevitable phenomenon in most small nonprofit organizations, and many such individuals are truly gifted. Still, if a partner organization seems to operate mostly through the brilliance and hard work of one or two individuals, it means a potential problem for the collaboration if the merged entity happens to lose them.

Lapsed Insurances

Life is full of risks, and there is an insurance policy available to cover most of them. One of the frequent symptoms of slipshod

Tip: Beware Hard Workers

Sometimes indispensability is a cover for something more sinister. If Margaret the silver-haired bookkeeper works 60 hours a week, never takes a vacation, and seems to have her finger on practically everything going on in the financial office, there is a faint, although distinct, possibility that she is—no other way to say it—a crook. Don't rule it out with your heart, rule it out with a few quiet tests. This is where professional help is necessary (and easier—you don't want Margaret angry at you when your longshot worry turns out to be wrong).

management is lapsed insurance coverages. Considering the complexity of many nonprofit operations, this is perhaps inevitable. The chances are that it was canceled to save money, or it was overlooked. Either way, the surviving corporation faces a gap in coverage. If a claim is filed during that period, the assets of the organization may be exposed to settle it. Worse, in some states, it may not even be legal for an employer to operate without certain types of insurance—workers' compensation insurance and unemployment insurance being two prime examples. Lapsed insurance coverages are important, not only for the substance of the threat they pose, but for the signal of mediocre management they send.

Loss of (Pick One): License, Accreditation, Large Donor, Large Payer

Here's another one that's important as much for what it says about the future as for the substance of the problem itself. Nonprofits simply do not lose major pieces of their operations without reason. If anything, authorities and funding sources may tend to stay with a nonprofit a bit longer than they should, so when they depart, it can be extremely significant. The details of the loss should be thoroughly aired and understood, and generally they should be disclosed to the full Planning Committee.

Maxed-Out Line of Credit

Lines of credit are intended to be temporary sources of capital. Any organization that is using all of its line of credit throughout most or all of the year is waving a big red flag. Check the cash flow, revenue, and expense estimates and management controls carefully here.

Nonfinancial Liabilities

The idea of nonfinancial liabilities is meant to encompass a wide range of things a potential partner should know about before committing to anything. In one merger between a small organization and a larger one, the small agency's office manager was one of the original founders who over the years had become disillusioned with the organization's direction. The office manager's quiet resentment, combined with poor financial skills, helped get the little

Tip: Beware the Little Secrets

Some will resist a merger for reasons that they will talk about only reluctantly. For example, the executive director of the small nonprofit may come in late and leave early every day. Or family members may quietly occupy numerous positions throughout the organization, fearing for their jobs if new management comes in. One executive director who has discussed possible mergers with smaller agencies refers to these as the "little secrets" of a potential partner that will be revealed only after trust has been established. More insidiously, they may not be revealed at all, but instead will remain unacknowledged sources of resistance. Keep this in mind when a potential partner resists or delays for apparently inexplicable reasons.

organization into some serious fiscal difficulties. In other cases, the nonfinancial liability may be something like a funder's unfavorable audit report that has yet to be released, or a donor list studded with questionable characters.

Payroll Taxes Unpaid

Most nonprofits have a payroll that amounts to as much as 80 percent of their total expenses. For every payroll dollar spent, the government demands a certain amount of tax payments, and it expects payment on a pretty inflexible schedule. When an agency runs low on cash, one of the classic responses is to not pay payroll taxes. This may work for the short-term (the *very* short term), but the government always catches up and the unpaid taxes become a liability. Worse, it's a liability that board members can bear personally. An unpaid payroll tax bill sitting in someone's drawer—or, more forthrightly, carried on the balance sheet—can be a sign of cash flow difficulties serious enough to scuttle a merger.

Qualified Audit Opinion

The quickest way to discern a red flag is by reading the first page in a nonprofit's audited financial report. The page takes the form of a letter to the agency from the auditors, and if the auditors have any major question about what they saw, it will be expressed somewhere around the third or fourth paragraph. If they say they cannot express an opinion, or if they qualify their opinion in some way, the smart reader will want to ask many additional probing questions.

Unacknowledged and Serious CEO–Staff Conflict

Bosses are rarely universally beloved, but occasionally there is such conflict between the executive director and the staff that it becomes a handicap. Merger talks can let this particular genie out of the bottle, as staff become fearful that their agency will be poorly represented (or the reverse). The due diligence team should be aware that they may encounter signs of this conflict. Ordinarily, it won't take much to get the full story.

Unexamined Accounts Receivable

For many nonprofits, the invoices they send to users of their services (called accounts receivable) represent a substantial corporate asset. Like any asset, they need constant attention. For accounts receivable, there is always the chance that they won't be paid. If the amount of receivables carried on the books isn't constantly adjusted to acknowledge the fact that a certain percentage will never be collected, it could present a misleadingly rosy picture of financial health.

Unreported Litigation

Nonprofit organizations may do good work, but, unfortunately, that doesn't protect them from getting sued. Like any business entity, nonprofits are subject to a wide range of potential lawsuits. Sometimes, state laws offer a degree of protection, and many juries are sympathetic to nonprofits, but a determined plaintiff who doesn't care about winning can still make life miserable for an organization. Suits involving wrongful discharge are one of the most common types, and malpractice and breach of confidentiality suits are common too. Lawsuits should be disclosed in the footnotes to audited financial statements, but it is a good idea to ask if there is any recent indication of court activity.

VALUATION

Rarely do transactions involving two different nonprofit organizations call for precise valuation of the assets. Since no one owns nonprofits or their assets, transactions between them do not change the fundamental fact that the assets are semi-public in nature. However, if those assets—or the entities that own them—are sold to a for-profit organization, it means that they are taken out of the hands of the public. In return, the nonprofit or its "owners," the general public, should be compensated. This question moved from theoretical to real, starting in the 1980s, when for-profit corporations began purchasing nonprofit hospitals.

It turns out that the question of putting a value on nonprofit entities being sold is just about the same one that buyers and sellers of other corporations have had to answer for years. The process is far closer to an art than to a science, but it is the best way the business community has found to make the benefit of ownership quantifiable. There are a handful of ways to derive an estimated value for a nonprofit that is being sold. One approach is to calculate the present value of the extra cash (profit) the entity is projected to produce over the next several years, and another is to simply look at comparable transactions.

Present Value of Cash Flow

Consumers instinctively understand that a dollar is worth more today than it will be worth tomorrow because its purchasing power is inevitably eroded by inflation. Plus, there is some hard-to-quantify value in having the ability to spend it sooner, rather than later. On the other hand, .90¢ may, or may not, be worth the same amount today as a dollar will be tomorrow. If one assumes the inflation rate for the next twelve months will be about 11 percent, .90¢ can in fact be said to be the equivalent of a dollar in one year. The .90¢ is called the present value of that dollar in one year.

The only obligation-free way of getting extra cash into an organization over time is by making a profit. Five-years worth of, say, a

5 percent profit on $1,000 will result in a total profit of $250, a tidy sum. But, the $50 profit in every one of those years is worth less than the $50 profit of the year before, because by the time it is produced, each $50 will have been worth less as measured in today's dollars. So the present value of 5-years worth of a $50 annual profit might be worth closer to $175 or $200, depending on the rate of inflation over that period.

This concept is at the heart of the discounted present value method of valuing a nonprofit. The approach calculates the amount of cash expected to be generated by the organization over each of the next five years, then figures out what each of those profits is worth in today's dollars and adds them all together for a cumulative net present value. This amount may be taken as a lump sum or modified in some way, such as by adding an estimated value for the entire period beginning with the sixth year forward (often this means simply doubling the net present value).

Comparable Values

A somewhat less promising, though equally valid, approach to putting a value on a nonprofit is to look for comparable transactions. Since the whole idea of for-profit firms purchasing nonprofits is very new (some states haven't even seen their first purchase, or conversion as it is known), seeking comparable transactions may be an inherently limited strategy. The process usually involves looking for transactions that have occurred in the last year or so in the same general market area. Valuation specialists look for organizations that were similar in size, profitability, market penetration, and related characteristics. After that, it is a relatively simple matter to put the details of each transaction side by side and make some inferences about the specific transaction under study.

Carrying out the Valuation

Obviously, valuing nonprofit to for-profit conversions must be done by skilled outsiders who have no economic stake in whether the deal occurs or not. The whole idea of nonprofit public charity status is loaded with such high-minded overtones that the issue can become extremely sensitive, especially in areas where there have been no previous conversions. Often public accounting and consulting firms are asked to value transactions like these.

The advantages of an independent valuation expert are multiple. Valuation consultants are accustomed to placing a value on assets poised for sale, including ambiguous situations where there seems to be little hard information available. They should have resources and a span of experience beyond that of any participants in the sale. Their independence will shield them from extraneous pressures, and it should be very difficult for aggrieved parties to question their motives. Finally, they can be more easily held accountable for the quality of their work.

CHAPTER FIFTEEN

Leadership Decisions

Somebody has to be the boss. In the Western world, we have yet to figure out how to make an organization work well over time without designating someone to be the boss. There is a strong collegial strain in much of the nonprofit world, and in some cases there is outright resistance to naming a single person as the leader, but we know of no other way. Someone has to be the executive director of the new organization, and the sooner the respective boards confront the question, the more likely it is that the merger will work.

Put another way; leadership of the new entity is such a critical question that, if it is not resolved early, the chances of a successful merger are cut by half. Moreover, the way the parties confront the question and answer it says a great deal about how they will work together in the future.

For obvious reasons, decisions about who will lead the new entity can take a long time. We define leadership here as including senior-most managers as well as the chief executive; regardless of the size of the nonprofits merging, this group should easily fit inside a small conference room. There are obvious tensions in the leadership decision phase, and we have already dealt with the chief executive officer (CEO) choice earlier. Specifically, leadership here refers to other managers, board members, and anyone in the organization who consistently provides some form of direction, whether or not they hold a formalized position.

The choice of other managers is usually easier and faster once the CEO choice is resolved. Still, there are often gaps left open and managers left hanging without clear communication about their status, and this can add extra calendar time. It is not out of the question that some senior positions will be undefined right up until and through the official merger date. Sometimes this is the result of ordinary bureaucratic or organizational snafus, but it may also be the deliberate decision of the new executive director to study a few incumbent managers in the merged entity before finalizing a role for them.

This is one of those areas where the boundary between merger planning and implementation is hard to define. Once the bulk of senior managers is chosen, the process can move quickly. In the best mergers, the group of staff who meet most regularly with the Planning Committee becomes the nucleus of the implementation management team. Sometimes the Planning Committee meetings end up transforming into the new management team meetings as soon as board members stop attending. A sign that the merger is going smoothly is that attendees at these meetings realize gradually that the sessions have turned from merger planning to operations management.

STRATEGIES FOR DECIDING WHO WILL BE THE BOSS

The very best way to handle a conflict over the chief executive officer position is to prevent it from occurring. This means that there has to be a clear-cut choice for the top position. There are many ways to get to this state. The preferred one is to time the merger talks so that one of the agencies has a vacant executive director position. The CEO of a nonprofit organization is the closest thing to an owner that this field can offer. Even if the incumbent has no strong will to lead, the very fact that someone is in the position is a potential stumbling block. This is why many merger discussions are triggered by the departure of the CEO.

If one of the positions is not open, the next best alternative is for one of the incumbents to have a clear and desirable pathway out of the organization. Retirement often provides that option for an executive, especially since many of the current leaders of community-based nonprofit organizations founded in the 1960s and 1970s initially assumed the executive director role when they were in their forties and may now be ready to retire. Hospital chief executives by contrast tend to be less rooted in a particular community, so their options may lead them to a different geographic area altogether.

Often the leadership question is resolved before the respective boards or management teams get involved when the two executives, sensing the desirability of a merger, work out their own arrangement. Not uncommonly, the leadership arrangement is part of the initial merger package proposal presented to the boards. For this to happen, the executives usually need a history of trust, mutual respect, and compatible skills and interests. When these arrangements occur, they are often the strongest possible outcomes, since the principals designed them and are more likely to be committed to making them work.

One trio of executives representing three merging agencies agreed ahead of time that one of their number would become the new executive director, the second would concentrate on program services, and the third would retire. Another pair decided to split duties on the basis of their long-term interest areas. One would concentrate on daily management and strategic direction, while the other would focus on developing his growing political contacts and network that had historically been responsible for much of the success of his agency.

Key to all these kinds of arrangements is a frank discussion and shared understanding of the respective individuals' strengths and interests. In fact, sometimes the best course of action to follow in resolving leadership conflicts is to give the parties a bit of time and space to work out their own plans.

If both executives are viable candidates who want to stay on, the Planning Committee will get its first personnel challenge. Again, this is a relatively unusual situation. Few active, in-place executive directors will pursue a merger if it appears that doing so will lead them into a competitive situation that they have little chance of surviving. Of course, outside forces such as a farsighted board of directors or an aggressive funding source may force consideration

Pitfall: Co-Executive Directors

Two steering wheels only work on big fire trucks.

of a merger in spite of the executives' self-interests. It is reasonable to anticipate that more executive directors will face this scenario in the future as mergers and alliances become more commonplace.

Resolving a leadership impasse is an ideal job for an outside party. Merger consultants will often fill this role nicely and spend a fair amount of time working through the intricacies of the leadership choice. Under special circumstances, this function might be performed by a board member or someone connected to one or both of the organizations, but explicit neutrality is very important and is easiest for outsiders to offer.

SOME TOOLS TO ACCOMPLISH A LEADERSHIP TRANSITION

Whoever actually facilitates a resolution of a leadership conflict needs to have some tools at their disposal. Here are some of the classics.

Mediation and Negotiation

No matter who does it or what it's called when it happens, merging two CEO positions requires effective mediation and negotiation skills. The job of chief executive is so complex even in a small organization that rarely do the heads of two collaborating nonprofits have identical skills and interests. Typically there will be an internal/external split. One director will have strength in external affairs such as fundraising, political networking, or public relations, while another will be strong in programming, financial management, or operations. Personalities and management styles will also differ markedly, as will personal needs. All of this provides fertile ground for negotiation and mediation.

Often there is a clear choice for the new executive director position and the effort goes into convincing the candidate not chosen (and his or her supporters) of the wisdom of the decision. A useful approach with the latter candidate is to ask him or her to describe in some detail how they like to spend their working time. Do they enjoy running meetings, speaking to groups, working on a computer, marketing programs, or networking? Chances are that their preference will be a valid way to perform a management position.

If so, the Planning Committee should give some thought to structuring a position that will enable that individual to contribute in exactly the way that best suits their talents and needs. If a face-saving way can be found to describe the importance of such a position, it will go a long way toward easing the transition.

Alternatively, each candidate might be strong in complementary areas and the effort must go toward deciding collectively which strength set will be needed for the corporation for the next few years. This is where the Planning Committee must show some leadership, because there is no right or wrong decision. Assuming intangibles such as personal style and character are not issues, the primary job is identifying the best match between the tasks needed to be accomplished and the candidate best suited to accomplish them.

Employment Contracts

Only a minority of small- to medium-sized nonprofit executive directors have them, but employment contracts may be a way to ease the transition to a single chief executive. They express the serious intent of the new board, as well as a means of demonstrating sincerity when a former executive director is asked to stay on in a different role. Candidly, they also remove a major reason for a nonselected executive director to sabotage the process.

Tip: Dealing with Disappointed Supporters

There are bound to be some hurt feelings when a group of supporters' candidate is passed over for another. Sometimes support for a particular executive director candidate is really support for something else that that person was expected to be able to deliver, such as a strong voice in governance or a symbolic message to program staff. If that is the underlying theme of the vote, it may be able to be handled in other ways. For example, if the issue is representation of a particular program or geographic part of the service area, it may be possible to structure the governance structure so as to accommodate the concern.

Consulting Contracts

Consulting contracts are similar to employment contracts except that they are intended to be time-limited. They function essentially as a long term subsidized job-hunting period but have the added advantage of keeping some institutional knowledge in-house temporarily without a long term commitment. They also invite abuse, and so should be used sparingly.

A New Corporation

Some forward-thinking organizations have dealt with the transition challenge by giving one of the executive directors an entirely new corporation to develop. Obviously this tactic will only work if the executive is an entrepreneurial type, but if so, it offers several advantages for all parties. It brings proven talent to bear on developing a new service arena, which, if successful, will ultimately benefit both the manager and the parent nonprofit. It allows the individual to continue calling himself or herself an executive director (never underestimate the power of saving face, even for those who claim not to be bothered by what seems like a demotion). And it creates a focal point for energies apart from the day-to-day operations that the executive is now expected to leave.

Farewell Parties

A good technique for recognizing an executive's contribution while bringing closure to it is a plain, old-fashioned party. Espe-

Pitfall: Artificial Competition

Sometimes a board of directors will make a point of conducting a search for the new executive director. They will invite the incumbents to apply but make it clear that they want to interview other applicants too. Unless there is a demonstrable concern about both candidates' abilities—in which case the matter should be dealt with directly and not as part of the merger process—this is not a wise idea. Why fix something that isn't broken?

cially when a manager has chosen to retire, a grand party planned carefully and publicly in advance is an excellent way of turning the new page in a way that it can't be easily turned back.

ONCE THE SELECTION IS MADE . . .

Once the selection is made the agreed-upon executive must begin to take command immediately. Given that the two organizations are still not officially or even functionally merged yet, this requirement is admittedly a difficult one to fulfill. At a minimum, the selection should be announced internally, with all board members and others who played a significant role expressing their support. Next, he or she should meet individually with all key managers to assess their abilities and interests in playing a role in the new entity.

At this point in a merger, there will probably be no formalized basis for the executive of one corporation to actively manage the other. In fact, there can be no guarantee that the merger will even go through. Consequently, if a designated individual is to fill a

Tip: To Pay or Not to Pay?

The new executive director is chosen and informally begins a leadership role with both organizations prior to the actual decision to merge. Should that person be paid?

Symbolism is terribly important here. Generally, it is less complicated if the designated individual simply incorporates the new duties into his or her existing ones. For the other corporation to reimburse the chosen executive director's corporation makes it look as though there should have been an exchange of value (money for services), rather than a mutual investment in a shared future. In any case, if there is some compelling reason for one corporation to pay the other for an executive's time, it should be regarded as a shared expense. The shared executive director should never personally profit from the transaction, or the whole rationale for the merger could be questioned.

CEO-type role for another organization at the same time, it must be done largely through symbolic actions.

He or she should take the predominant executive role in the Planning Committee. Gradually, the executive director appointee should replace the merger facilitator. The new CEO should take every opportunity to be seen both internally and externally in some connection with the other entity, though taking care to stress that the merger is still in the planning stages. Physical presence means a great deal at this stage. Even if the new executive's presence is peripheral to a meeting, it helps reinforce the notion of an impending change.

CHAPTER SIXTEEN

Structure of the Merged Entity

The new entity's structure, both corporate and organizational, is the aspect of collaboration most likely to catch an outsider's eye. It is also the subject of much premature internal speculation, perhaps for the same reason that it appeals to outsiders—it's the easiest way to grasp the impact of the change. To skilled outside eyes, the choice of corporate structure is often obvious. To insiders, the choice of organizational structure—that which is represented on the organizational chart—is often almost as obvious. Half the time spent here is frequently the result of each side getting the other to understand its needs.

Choosing an appropriate structure for the merged entity is largely a technical matter shaped by financial, legal, and other considerations. This stage can take several months because it has everything to do with process and nothing to do with technical issues. Participants need to educate themselves enough about the options to make an informed decision, and then the decision itself needs to be okayed by many different parties. These may range from regulators to funding sources and from lenders to outside attorneys. Some of these parties may have to be consulted by law, while others need only be consulted because of internal politics.

We have already covered the question of structure thoroughly in a previous section, so it is not necessary to repeat it here. What has not been covered is the process by which the structure is determined. We will touch on this subject lightly before moving on to communication strategies.

Computer experts know that the proper way to computerize a business application is to decide what needs to be done, select the software which will do it, and finally, purchase the hardware that will best run the software. It is much the same with corporate and organizational structures during a merger. Wise managers will concentrate first on what they are trying to accomplish through the merger. Gain market share? Amass clout for use in negotiations with funders? Cut costs? Secure new programming? Only when they have identified goals and objectives to be achieved through the merger will they begin contemplating how the new entity or entities should be organized.

This is usually not nearly as easy as it sounds. Often board or staff members feel strongly about one type of structure over another. Frequently, board members will have had some personal or professional experience with a proposed model, and their eagerness to advocate for or against it is hard to contain. Compounding this problem is the fact that matters of corporate structure are like driving a car: it looks easy, and everybody has his own opinion about how it should be done.

The best approach is preventive. Try to secure the Planning Committee's agreement to postpone a decision about corporate structure until later in the process. At the very least, it should not happen until the CEO job and most senior management positions have been filled, and the due diligence phase completed. Shore up that agreement by providing education about the various options available. Dedicate a half-hour of one Planning Committee meeting to an invited guest (an outside neutral expert) who can explain the major possibilities and their advantages and disadvantages. Constantly remind over-eager Planning Committee members of the commitment to weigh all the facts before choosing a corporate structure.

In some ways, the most powerful thing that merger planners can do is to make the choice of corporate structure a largely uninteresting, technical matter. In order to do this, the planning dialog has to be kept at a high enough level that participants can think through the implications of various scenarios, being able to explore each one with confidence. For example, the discussion should be framed as "will our newly merged entity be strong enough for us to expand into the neighboring state?" rather than "well, the neighboring state refuses to work with foreign corporations, so we better incorporate something right now." Legal and financial advisors need to play a support role in these discussions, which means that they should be primarily technicians. It is easy for boards and management teams to be intimidated by technical knowledge of this sort. To avoid it, one needs an unswerving focus on what is trying to be accomplished, not how it is to be accomplished.

Naturally, staff and senior managers will be far more interested in the new organizational chart than in the nuances of corporate structure. One of the reasons for resolving the leadership of the new entity as soon as possible is that it permits the new CEO to begin establishing the internal organizational structure. Since mergers tend to occur most readily between similar organizations, the suspense is not likely to center around the boxes on the organizational chart. Chances are they will look like the old boxes, although perhaps more plentiful. The real suspense will be who fills them.

Usually the continuing CEO will create an organization that looks like an enlarged version of his or her old one. Almost as predictably, he or she will be inclined to bring the former complement of managers into the new positions. This is completely understandable, but the shrewd executive director will sense the enormous political implications of his or her actions and will actively seek to place the other agency's senior managers in demonstrably important positions.

Tip: Consider Title Upgrades

One way to take some of the sting out of people not getting the precise roles they had envisioned in the new entity is to upgrade titles all around. This is why many nonprofits outside of the health care field are now beginning to use a title, such as vice president, to a greater extent than before. Title upgrades can buffer some of the upset that may go along with a merger. It is an added bonus that some changes in title can actually reflect the employee's role a bit more precisely.

And you thought it was only those silly people in Fortune 500 companies that used important-sounding titles . . .

Often an immediate problem arises because the new executive director wishes to place a former number two position in a comparable role. The other agency, having given up its "claim" on the executive director's job, feels that one of its people should hold the second position in the new entity. One way to balance off these potentially divisive sentiments is to use the organizational structure to create opportunities for a senior management team that is large enough to accommodate members from both agencies, yet small enough and efficient enough to get the job done.

No matter how small the organization nor how idealistic the staff, prepare for gamesmanship at this stage. People's jobs, reputations, and self-esteem are on the line. Inescapably, talking about positions and roles in a new structure means talking about real people. Worse, it's hard to hide or be subtle. Some proposals for structure will be blatantly self-serving, and resistance to any proposal is never far away. If it is true, the newly appointed executive director can gain much leeway with the promise that no one will lose a job through other than attrition.

FORMAL AGREEMENT

The timetable required for formalizing the merger agreement shows the starkest difference between calendar time and process time. This step is easily delayed for mundane reasons. Missed phone calls, inopportune sicknesses, misplaced faxes, unclear minutes—these are just a tiny sample of the things that stretch the calendar time needed to write up an actual agreement.

There is no universal format for a merger agreement. Nor should there be. Since every merger is unique, the intentions and details will vary. The state oversight agency, such as the attorney general or secretary of state, may have forms for this purpose, or it may require certain material to be covered. This is the point at which participants will be very happy if they have kept careful notes throughout the process. Usually the merger agreement itself will be the first time all the various points have been collected in one place. The simple act of collecting them, documenting them, and discussing the final draft is frequently a wonderfully focusing exercise.

Tip: The Value of Paying an Outside Attorney

At the risk of sounding like a shill for attorneys, we will say that the agreement formalization stage clearly shows the value of using paid outside legal advisors, rather than a board member who happens to be, say, a first rate insurance company attorney. We saw one merger in which just such an arrangement was made, and the attorney—or, to be precise, his partner who was covering for him—forgot to file the merger papers at the appropriate time. The oversight was not discovered for several weeks and led to much avoidable confusion.

As difficult and time-consuming as the merger agreement may be on a technical level, the biggest time-consuming step can be the two boards' discussion of it. Be sure to leave ample time for prolonged discussion by one or both boards. There should be no surprises at this point, but many times there will be a need to fine-tune the exact written expression of a point that was agreed upon much earlier.

CHAPTER SEVENTEEN

Communication Strategies

When stockholder-owned companies decide to explore a merger, it's generally a hush-hush affair. Premature disclosure of the proposal can have a major impact on stock prices—good and bad—and on a myriad of other direct and indirect aspects of their businesses. In addition, top executives who hold significant blocks of stock must observe strict regulations governing nondisclosure, including under what circumstances they are allowed to sell the stock or buy more. In short, the economic stakes are unequivocally high, and there is every reason to keep a lid on the process until the appropriate time.

Not so for nonprofit organizations. For these groups, there is a noticeable lack of incentives to keep quiet about their plans. Which is not to say that groups considering a merger should broadcast their initial discussions, just that there is no compelling reason to go into high-secrecy mode.

There are a few reasons for proceeding cautiously when widening the circle of those knowledgeable about a potential nonprofit merger. The first is that it is simply more workable that way. If smaller groups need not be concerned about external reaction too soon, they can usually get more done. Another reason is that stakeholders, such as funding sources, may react negatively to the news unless they are approached privately first. Finally, there may be unique reasons in any given merger for initial secrecy.

Since nonprofit mergers are best planned from the top down and implemented from the bottom up, the communication strategies that best serve them involve a constantly widening array of people. Communication throughout the course of a merger or an alliance development process not only eases fears and makes things go smoother, it also increases the chance of lasting success. For analytical purposes, it is best to separate communication strategies into internal and external communication campaigns.

INTERNAL COMMUNICATION

In most cases, initial discussions about a potential merger will take place between only a handful of people such as the executive director and two- or three-key board members. Ordinarily, there should be an explicit understanding among these people that the idea is confidential at this point; again, the intent is to keep the early planning manageable, not to exclude. Early on in this process, the full board should consider the idea; if confidentiality is a concern, it may be wise to adjourn a board meeting and convene in an informal session.

The next step is usually to talk with the other board of directors. Generally, this will involve a small delegation from each agency meeting in a comfortable site for preliminary discussions once the respective executive directors have laid the groundwork (i.e., establishing a complementary view of the environment and the role of a possible merger in strengthening the shared mission). Then, it's time to report back to the respective boards. This process may actually occur two or three times before the parties reach agreement to go on to a more formal attempt at collaborating.

Communication with senior staff tends to be personal and in groups. Note that, with nonprofit mergers being so frequently initiated by staff, this type of communication may well occur before communication with the full board of directors. The idea is to get senior staff focused on feasibility and implementation. Note that the term *senior staff* is a loose one. In small nonprofit organizations, it may mean simply anyone in a position of responsibility besides the executive director. In larger organizations, it can mean a whole layer of managers.

Internal communication with the full staff about the merger should be formal and should come from the executive director or chief executive officer. The first official announcement of the col-

Pitfall: Home Turf Is Over-Rated

Perhaps it's because of the lack of serious economic incentives, but in our experience, nonprofit boards and their staffs rarely worry about neutral meeting sites for the Planning Committee and just pick the most comfortable and convenient meeting room. This is probably because there is usually a basic trust between the two parties, or they wouldn't have started merger talks anyway. The fact that neutral sites usually cost money may have something to do with it too.

laboration in medium- to large-sized agencies will almost certainly be written, and it needs to do a number of different things. First, it needs to lay out the case for the merger, explaining how changes in the larger environment have created the conditions leading to the collaboration effort. It should explain how the project will position the organization to cope with those changes, including examples of what might be accomplished with the merger that could not

Note: The Power of Vision in Communication

When the executive director announced the merger at the mental health center's program staff meeting, one of the staff members turned to her friend and in a stage whisper said, "Maybe it's time to get a job at that inn in Maine."

Later that afternoon, the same staff member was overheard in a hallway conversation discussing the information presented at the morning session. "They say after the merger, we'd cover three quarters of the county's population and service 85 percent of the Medicaid population. Imagine how we could put some of these programs together . . ."

The moral: there's no substitute for a positive vision in internal communications, especially in the first face-to-face meetings about the merger. Which is not to say that there's anything wrong with inns in Maine . . .

Tip: Characteristics of In-House Written Communication

Make it substantial. No one wants to read self-congratulatory pieces or see blurry photographs of the executive directors smiling together. Give readers the substance, do it quickly, and move on.

Corollary: boring is better. The truth is, many merger details are pretty boring stuff. The principle is, people want to know it, not dwell on it.

Keep it short. One page is always good, two at most. Anything longer begs to be ignored.

Write simply. Write for the average seventh grader. It's what daily newspapers do, and it works. Some word processing software packages can estimate the reading level on which a piece was written.

Tackle controversial issues. Everyone knows where the controversies are, so you might as well score points for confronting them directly, especially if you can't resolve them quickly or fully.

happen without it. Finally, it should show what can be expected to happen to staff in general. The message here is reassurance, if appropriate, or a straightforward explanation of any bad news that's already known.

Well-designed meetings are another valuable internal communication tool. Once the board has given preliminary approval to the idea of a merger and senior staff have been incorporated in early discussions, it is time to announce the initiative to staff. Given the proper atmosphere, a successful meeting can explain far more than any written document, and it will do much to reassure hesitant staff. Ideally, a series of departmental or small meetings should be held on the same day in the two collaborating agencies to announce the merger talks.

Who should speak at the meetings will depend on the style and politics of the organization, but whoever it is (there should be more than one speaker in most organizations), they should lay out the rationale for considering a merger. They need to be scrupulously honest about where the process stands and about any specific plans for the future, which means they will be saying, "I don't know," a lot. Above all, they need to avoid making any commitments, unless they are absolutely sure that they can be kept. At the same time, they need to be as reassuring and positive as possible, especially about possible lost jobs. The best way to do this without making unrealistic commitments is to talk in terms of intentions and desires. For example, instead of saying, "no one will lose their job," the preferable way to say it would be "we do not intend to lay off any direct program service employees unless it is absolutely necessary."

For most agencies, a regular written document will be the cornerstone of ongoing internal communication. It need not be fancy—in fact, sending out a slick publication would probably give the wrong message anyway ("now that we're growing into a larger organization, we can afford expensive cosmetics") unless both organizations had that type of publication. A simple letter from one or both executive directors should do it. Interestingly, some nonprofits going through a merger find that the merger newsletter eventually a regular in-house publication.

EXTERNAL COMMUNICATION

For a nonprofit organization, there are two audiences for external communications; funding sources and the public at large. Each audience is composed of smaller interest groups that may need an individualized communication strategy. Funding source types will typically include donors, service users, and purchasers of service. The public at large is generally represented only by the media and one or more regulatory bodies.

Donors

Development directors often respond to internal news that a merger is being considered with strong fears about what it will do to the donor base. Usually they're wrong. It's a logical and understandable fear, but it reflects the kind of management-centrism that occurs when professionals consider external developments solely from their own viewpoint.

Donors give money to a nonprofit because they like its mission. They may have been cultivated by individuals, they may feel a kinship with certain executives, but in the end if they are operating with sincerity, it is the mission that they care about. Another way of framing the question is this: ask yourself if the average donor cares more about the nonprofit's: (a) corporate structure; (b) management team; or (c) mission.

To ask the question is to answer it. In a properly structured merger, (a) and (b) may or may not change, but (c) should stay intact. Professionals' fears about donor losses are a way of saying that donors' major connection is with a particular corporate structure or a certain manager. This is a misreading of most donors' intentions when they develop a relationship with a nonprofit.

At the same time, individual donors may need special attention, particularly at the time the merger is announced. Development staff should be included in announcement planning. For instance, it may be helpful to make personal contact with a handful of major or influential donors on the day the merger is announced—or even the day before, if it can be done discreetly. Unequivocally, within a day or two, all regular donors should receive a written communication about the merger, its rationale, and the explicit wish that they continue as donors after the merger. This is especially necessary if the agency will be perceived as being "taken over" in the merger.

Service Users

Service users are likely to greet the news of a nonprofit merger with indifference, as long as it does not involve major changes such as building or program closings. Their greatest interest is usually continuity of the services. A subset of this concern is composed of pragmatic procedural questions—do I need to renew my membership with the new organization? Can I keep my doctor? Will I need to go to a different site? Communication with them should stress the seamless nature of the transition, if that's true, and provide ample guidance for any changes they may need to make.

Purchasers of Services

We distinguish between service users, who are direct one-at-a-time consumers of the nonprofit's services, and purchasers of services, who are outside institutions such as governments and businesses.

In the health, education, and human services fields, governments are usually the largest purchasers of services, from nonprofit organizations. Naturally, they have a stake in how those services are delivered. The way that they define that stake and their level of sophistication about purchasing services from private nonprofits determines the best communication tactics to use with them.

Although different purchasers will react to the prospect of a merger in different ways, one nearly universal statement about them all is that they should get a courtesy call. Why? Call it business common sense. When a single purchaser is responsible for a significant piece of an agency's revenue, it is wise to engage that entity regularly if for no other reason than to signal respect for their interests. Deciding how and when that call is made in each case is the important part.

Beyond the question of business common sense is the current likelihood that the merger of two of their nonprofit service providers will be a rare event for many governmental purchasers. While this will change in the coming years, in some areas of the country, it will be novel and potentially threatening for the purchasers. After all, they had probably just made the decision to use private nonprofits as service providers sometime in the past two or three decades. At first, the purchasers were the ones with all the financial and management know-how. Their service providers were almost certainly loosely structured, informally managed, generally untutored, and maybe even naive. In short, they were dependent on their government funders for more than just funds. Now, those same nonprofits are taking the initiative to restructure their own operations and may even be talking about a new way of doing business that could appear to diminish the governmental unit's control over them.

Don't underestimate the importance of this interpretation or the likelihood of its occurrence. Most governmental units and their managers, especially mid-level bureaucrats, are still firmly rooted in the industrial model of command and control over their service providers, as though the latter were simply extensions of themselves rather than a fundamentally different and vibrant service delivery system. Those operating with the command-and-control mindset may object to such profound private initiatives as mergers and alliances because they fear that it will somehow reduce their relative position or importance. Officials objecting to these moves

Note: Nonprofit to For-Profit Is Different

All this information is keyed to nonprofits merging with other nonprofits. In some cases, there will be a for-profit entity involved, and that opens up a whole other complicated area for consideration. Nonprofit to for-profit conversions are an entirely separate type of transaction and will be treated separately in a later section. From a communications perspective, the major difference is that they usually require legal approval from the governmental official in charge of the state's nonprofits (such as the Attorney General or Secretary of State). Predictably, that process is highly public and ultimately political in nature. Depending on how many a particular state's nonprofit community has undergone, the process may be more or less predetermined.

need a great deal of hand-holding and constant reassurance about the motives and competence of the principals involved in the merger. Nonprofit managers seeking to arrange a merger in these circumstances need to go well beyond a courtesy call.

On the other end of the continuum are the purchasers who treat the restructuring as little more than a signal to change a few addresses and phone numbers on their database. Their interests tend to be maintaining orderly housekeeping, and they will be easy to work with as the merger or alliance develops. One can presume that such an approach will be characteristic of most governmental purchasers eventually, as they learn how to leverage their role as purchasers without getting deeply involved in the operations of their contracted service providers.

The General Public, as Represented by the Media

Happily, or unhappily, depending on one's perspective, the media is not usually very interested in nonprofit mergers and even less in alliances. As a result, managers get a lot of room in which to maneuver before a story becomes interesting to the media. The downside of this fact is that it may be hard to get coverage if it is desired. Without a hook—the media term for a reason to read a story—there is little incentive to pursue the angle.

There are exceptions to this general situation. Big nonprofits in any field will frequently attract media interest simply on the basis of their size. Being the first in the area to announce a merger will sometimes be enough, although this is getting harder to do. Also, an instantly recognizable nonprofit name will generate media interest.

The media business can best be viewed as a gigantic commodity production system. Individual news stories enter that system, get measured against its expectations and the economics available to cover it, and then get processed through to a conclusion. Most nonprofit mergers don't even show up on the large systems' radar screens, so if there is to be any coverage, it will occur in small market print or radio outlets. In a few cases, the merger will be a large story for its area, so that's when media-conscious managers can count on some intense exposure.

The real challenge of an external media campaign related to a merger is not getting a particular amount of coverage, but rather, how well and how consistently one can control it. Reporters will do a certain amount of their own research, but they do not expect to become experts in the field. Rather, they want an easily understandable framework and a clear story line. If the agencies contemplating the merger can provide that, the resulting coverage will tend to conform to it. Failing to provide it, the merging partners risk losing control of the public dialog.

An example will illustrate the point. A major teaching hospital and a major municipal acute care hospital decided to merge. In the hospital industry, mergers are frequently the precursor to attempts to build integrated health care delivery systems. The principals of both hospitals knew this and had the germ of a long term integrated system in mind, but the political and operational chore of merging two such dominant institutions was overwhelming, and they did not present in any way the longer term goal.

The result was that opposition to the merger, largely from the two different and competing collective bargaining units involved, focused on the collapsing of the two hospitals, rather than on the larger and much more important effort to build a uniquely integrated care delivery system. Had the leaders of the effort used the media to lay out their larger plan and attempt to convince the public of its soundness, two things would have been different. First, the opposition would have had to target the plan and spend en-

Tip: What to Do When the Press Picks Up the Scent

Occasionally, the local media will be keenly interested in a nonprofit merger and will approach management before management is ready to make a public statement. When this happens, deflate the conflict angle. The media outlet—it will almost always be a newspaper or perhaps a radio station because nonprofit mergers are not visual events—may be interested in the story because they believe it will lead to massive job loss or some other bad thing. If the merger is really just an extended planning effort, which it probably is, the media hook disappears. No reader of a general newspaper wants to read a story about endless subcommittees where the worst conflict is over bagels versus donuts for the 7:30 A.M. Planning Committee meeting.

If the reporter is still interested anyway, play for time. By gauging how far along the outlet is in developing the story, you can estimate how much time you have in which to take charge of the coverage with all the local media. Alternatively, if you're willing to play a cute media game, you can offer to work closely with the reporter to develop the story as an exclusive—but only according to your timetable. A word of caution on the latter strategy—it will only work in media markets where there is a clear dominant outlet. Even then, you risk incurring the wrath of all those other media folks that were left out. Professional public relations assistance is invaluable here.

ergy showing how it would not work rather than snaring management in the no-win minutiae of layoffs and union negotiations. Second, with management staking the higher strategic ground, critics would have seemed diminished in comparison. Although the merger eventually went through, it would have been much smoother with a more effective communication strategy.

Communicating with Regulators

Communicating with regulators involves different considerations than the type of communication described up to this point. The regulator, who is likely to be the state attorney general, secretary of state, or some such government official, is accustomed to communicating through policies and how-to materials. It should be fairly easy to find out if there is a formalized procedure governing the type of merger you envision and, if so, how to make it work. Unless your situation falls outside the pre-established guidelines, regulatory communication should be largely a matter of following instructions.

The one exception to this idea is when the merger involves a unique twist on the usual nonprofit-merging-with-nonprofit route. One of the more common twists is when a for-profit company purchases a nonprofit corporation. Initially common among nonprofit hospitals in the South and West, "conversions" are spreading to health maintenance organizations and hospitals in all parts of the country. The first ones in each state are the most difficult because regulators have yet to work out the legal, financial, and operational procedures needed to monitor them properly. Once established as an accepted practice, conversions are likely to be more straightforward in subsequent transactions even though they may still be individually scrutinized.

CHAPTER EIGHTEEN

Implementation and Evaluation

While the legalities of the merger process are black and white—entities are either legally merged or they are not—the management aspect is not as clear cut. In fact, except for the official acceptance of the merger plan and whatever filings are required by the overseeing state official, there is no universal measure of when a merger can be said to have taken place. Entities can go on indefinitely with two of virtually everything they began the merger process with, and as long as there is no agreed-upon plan or set of benchmarks for declaring the effort a success, no one can argue.

At the same time, there is a point beyond which two previously separate organizations can be regarded as a single one. Like the point in focusing a set of binoculars when the two images blend suddenly into a single view, there will come a time when participants realize that the merger has taken hold. This is likely to happen when the new entity is called upon to make a major decision such as hiring a new executive director, entering into a new banking or other professional relationship, or any one of numerous other situations that require people to focus single-mindedly on the future without regard for the past. It will happen with both personnel and the board of directors, although where it occurs first is impossible to predict.

The legal requirements for merging nonprofits can usually be fulfilled with a minimal amount of time and effort and, although it is important not to overlook them, the major energies should be devoted to achieving the merger's promise. Just as computer software and hardware need to be constantly upgraded, merger implementation can never truly be said to be "done." It is the integration and empowerment of nonprofit programs that is the goal, and ultimately the time line of any single merger along that path becomes somewhat of an arbitrary designation.

In truth, post-merger implementation will probably occupy the nonprofit field for at least another generation beyond the impending wave of mergers and alliance development. The fact is that we are not even close to being able to fully live up to the promise of mergers and integrated services. We don't have the administrative systems, the management know-how, or the information systems that will allow us to fulfill that promise. In most cases, these things don't exist. In the case of information systems, they may exist, but nonprofits in their old forms didn't appreciate the need for them, couldn't use them, and couldn't afford them anyway. From an historic perspective, mergers and alliances are little more than a massive restructuring effort that will get the nonprofit system to a point where it can make real use of new ways of organizing service entities.

This chapter will identify crucial areas for implementation attention. Readers should be aware that what follow are not recipe cards, nor foolproof formulas for implementing a merger. Instead, these points should be taken as guidance for how to proceed in key areas. Unique circumstances will change both the problem areas and what to do about them, so readers should be prepared to make appropriate adjustments.

REDEFINED OR REAFFIRMED MISSION

Since the merger process itself is a kind of oversized strategic planning exercise, a common vision should have been developed throughout the whole time. Still, the process is not always conducive to producing a clear, carefully thought out statement of vision and mission for the new entity. If such a statement does not already exist, the Planning Committee should make devising one a high priority.

Tip: Get Them Involved in Picking a New Name

One pleasant way of getting both about-to-be-merged staff groups in the spirit of the merger is to solicit their ideas for naming any new entity that may arise. This can be done in the form of a contest, an agency-wide brainstorming, or just an extended shared project.

NAME

As with strategic direction, the choice of a name or names for the new entity may have been implicit in the merger planning process. The two points to remember here are simple ones: (1) you do not have to change any name as the result of a merger; and (2) you can change the name if you want to. Often merger planners will assume that a name change is automatic. But why? No matter what the name of the new corporate entity may be, the names of the two previous corporations can still continue as program names without the "Inc." after them. This is especially helpful when loss of autonomy and identity are crucial issues in the merger planning process.

SALARY AND BENEFIT DISCREPANCIES

It will come as no surprise that, in a field where 60 to 80 percent of the average nonprofit's expenses are personnel-related, resolving personnel issues is critical to the success of a merger. We will also state, right at the beginning, that there are rarely fully satisfactory answers to the personnel issues that arise. The best course of action is to recognize the inherently unsatisfying nature of this aspect of the merger and strive to set up a process that will secure as reasonable an outcome as possible.

Salary inequities are the hardest of merger issues to resolve. It is not usually financially practical to bring the lower-paid employees up to the level of higher-paid ones, and it is impossible and typically undesirable to cut higher compensation levels in order to cre-

Tip: Personnel Inequities Soak Up Economies

Often, funding sources such as governmental entities will expect to see dollars freed up (for them) as the result of a merger. Typically this expectation will be expressed with varying degrees of conviction. Funders watching a merger with hopes of savings need only look at the differences between salary levels of the partners. Compensation and benefits discrepancies alone will often soak up all of the economies a merger may achieve.

ate savings. The result is that salary inequities must be dealt with around the margins, often with largely symbolic means.

For instance, managers may choose to soften the worst of the discrepancies. Requiring two people, formerly from different organizations, to work side by side with very different compensation plans destroys morale. In these limited cases, management might correct the worst of the differences. It may also be possible to compartmentalize the lower-paying jobs—often from the same organization—in a definable way and treat that program or site as a kind of feeder system to the better-paying positions. This requires a fairly explicit statement from management that this is what is being done and that movement from one program to the other is acceptable.

A powerful and more affirmative method for dealing with salary gaps is to use the merger to create new opportunities for staff. Often there is a reason that a group of staff members are paid less than their peers. It may be that their collective skills and experience have less market value. Creating new programming and guiding those employees in that direction, with proper screening and training, can be a way of softening salary gaps.

Perhaps the most common way of dealing with salary discrepancies in larger organizations is to leave them in place through the kind of vertical mergers that are almost indistinguishable from tight alliances. There is ample reason why managers would want to do this, and most of it comes from very practical motivations. For instance, a university which takes over a series of day care centers will almost certainly keep a separate corporate structure for day care rather than pay university wage scales for day care work.

Ideological or emotional motivations aside, financial and legal ground rules are just too strong to do otherwise.

STAFFING LEVELS

Setting proper post-merger staffing levels is critical for eventual success. Saving money through staff cuts alone is never a sufficient reason for a merger. It doesn't need to be. The challenges facing most nonprofit organizations in the future, and the benefits to be achieved through greater integration, are so enormous as to dwarf the benefits of saving a few dollars through cutting staff. To put a different twist on it, if the only value that two nonprofits can get through merging is to shed a few positions, then it would be a short-term strategy that may not be worth it.

That said, there will almost certainly be an opportunity to create savings by eliminating unnecessary jobs. If one accepts as a given that nonprofits exist to provide a needed service to the public of some kind, and if that service has demonstrable value, then the core staff group delivering those services will see relatively few reductions after a merger. Most redundant jobs tend to be found in middle management and what we would call generic positions.

Generic positions are those posts found in many or all nonprofits and business entities. Nonprofits compete for generic employees in the same labor pool as other employers because those employees' skills are applicable to virtually any setting. A well-trained bookkeeper, for example, should be able to function as well in a foundation as in a bank. Middle managers, on the other hand, tend to have more restricted options and, therefore, tend to be more difficult to handle. Those just outside the executive director's previous inner circle can be the toughest because they will feel most vulnerable. They are also the ones most likely to oppose a merger (in action if not in word) since they have the most to lose.

The tools of choice for working with these middle managers are attrition and long lead times coupled with plenty of signals. If the job market is at all favorable, some managers unwilling to go through a merger will have found other positions by the time reassignments must be considered. One of the benefits of the subcommittee planning structure described earlier is that participants get to spend some time with each other. During the course of planning sessions, they find out whether they can work with their peer or a potential supervisor from the other side. Everyone develops a shared impression of others' talents and abilities, so by the time the new CEO and management team begin selecting personnel, there may be a collective understanding about who will be selected to do what. For those unlikely to get a future position, the planning framework is a way for them to begin getting that signal.

Why not just lay off staff? Why try to accomplish reductions through attrition? This is one of the areas where nonprofits differ almost completely from their proprietary counterparts. In organizational terms, nonprofit organizations are almost pure political entities. To move a nonprofit forward requires substantial agreement on vision and values, all the nonfinancial things that have to substitute for the profit motive. Nothing detracts from organizational commitment faster than a round of layoffs. Needless to say, this is not the most economically endearing characteristic of nonprofits, but it is a reality. Layoffs and firings are always an option to cope with fiscal crises, but it's better to find subtler ways of reducing staff—even if it means having to work harder at it.

INFORMATION SYSTEMS

Another major area of potential implementation conflicts is information systems. This one is especially vexing because it masquerades as a technical choice when in fact it is more stylistic and cultural. Rarely are there black-and-white or right-and-wrong answers in information systems. Instead, there are newer technologies and older technologies, and there are system choices which make one type of management activity harder and another type easier.

For example, there are now quite powerful low-end commercial accounting software packages available that many nonprofits use. They are typically easy to use, flexible, inexpensive, and efficient. These kinds of packages are called horizontal applications because they are widely available and can be used across a variety of industries. They tend to be developed by commercial software companies that also offer other types of software. The other kind of software is designed expressly for a particular industry, such as nonprofits. They are called vertical applications and are usually developed with a particular industry in mind.

Either choice can be effective. Ultimately, it comes down to a question of management preference; since no package is universally satisfying, what strengths in the software does the agency seek and what disadvantages is it willing to put up with? Merger implementers should be aware of this central question and not just assume that the choice of one package over another is a matter for the technicians.

The other major aspect of information system choices to keep in mind is the economics of merging the systems. In this regard, merger planners must keep an absolutely relentless focus on the future. Often one agency will protest that it just invested thousands of dollars in a new computer system, or that it recently upgraded the wiring in a building now slated to be sold as a result of the merger. This is a frustrating by-product of mergers, but it is not a reason for choosing one alternative over another. Financial analysts have a useful concept they call *sunk costs.* It means that an outlay of money made in the past cannot be retrieved, nor the decision altered. The money is gone no matter what one may do today—it has been sunk and nothing that anyone can do is going to change that. Certain information system investments are going to be sunk costs during a merger, and acknowledging as much will help everyone move on from there.

NOTES ON TIMETABLES

Board members and managers about to begin a merger process usually want to know how long it will take. It's a reasonable question, but a difficult one to answer. This is because mergers can be measured along two kinds of time. The first is calendar time, and this is self-explanatory. The second kind of time we call process time, which we define as the time spent in merger-related meetings, preparation for meetings, individualized discussions, outside research, and so forth. Process time is relatively short compared with calendar time, but since it must occur in preplanned segments and since the completion of one segment often depends on another, process time tends to stretch out on a calendar.

Tip: Set Effective Dates at the Beginning of a Quarter

Routinely, partners in a merger or alliance need to establish effective dates for various milestones up to and including the effective date of the formal restructuring itself. When setting such dates, keep in mind that the underlying rhythms of all businesses tend to be divisible by quarters. Nonprofit fiscal years are likely to begin on July 1, October 1, or January 1. Certain tax reports are due each quarter. Insurance policies are often renewed as of January 1 or July 1. Special provisions in a loan or other banking agreement are often written to take effect at each quarter, and so on. Collaboration planners should therefore set any dates, over which they have control, to be either January 1, April 1, July 1, or October 1.

Another reason why it is hard to give a reliable estimate of calendar time is because it is frequently difficult to say when a merger or alliance process "starts." Is it when two or more agencies begin talking with each other? Does it begin when they agree in principle to pursue a merger or alliance? Or when they sign something? Can the process be said to have begun with the preliminary discussions, or when the management team or the boards first got together? Each one of these milestones can be seen as the beginning of the process.

In some ways, it is even harder to decide when a merger is completed. When the final legal papers are signed and filed? After a year or some other arbitrary amount of time? On an operations level, mergers can be said to never end. US Airways, one of the major airlines in the country today, is actually the product of six different mergers beginning in 1968. Some of their administrative systems *are still not merged.*

That having been said, we will also argue that it is easier to predict the amount of calendar time likely to be involved in a merger than is commonly assumed (by their nature, alliances are harder to predict). The reason is because at some point, process time tends to have diminishing returns. Consequently, a merger process lasting for more than about 6 to 9 months is in danger of not working at all.

Tip: Rule of Thumb for Estimating Calendar Time

Here's a rough rule of thumb for predicting how long a merger will take:

The total estimated calendar time for a merger between two nonprofit agencies is equal to three months plus a month for each merger subcommittee.

To make this work, the Planning Committee must first identify the major areas needing focused attention as part of the merger planning process. Each area then gets assigned to a separate subcommittee created for the purpose, as described earlier. Since there's a certain amount of work that needs to be done, regardless of the size of the participants, adding three months to the number of subcommittees gives a workable estimate of the overall timeframe.

Naturally, larger and more complex organizations can be expected to take longer to bring together. Mergers involving public or political entities can be virtually guaranteed to take more time. Still, for most groups interested in moving expeditiously and yet

Pitfall: Don't Confuse Process Time with Calendar Time

Those who fancy themselves as "goal-oriented" (such as business people on the board) will tend to reject the need for much process time. They often believe that the only process involved in a nonprofit merger is the one mandated by the state official in charge of nonprofits and nonprofit mergers. Since this process is usually very narrow and primarily for reporting purposes, it can often be handled quickly and can be mistaken for a goal. However, mergers entered into for strategic reasons and to bolster the ability to serve a mission take time to reach their potential. The real goal should be realizing potential, not achieving compliance.

Steps	Who?	1996: O N D — 1997: J F M A M J	Start	Finish
Mutual Learning		10/2 2/3	10/2/96	2/3/97
Planning Structure		10/29 11/26	10/29/96	11/26/96
Leadership Decisions		1/2 4/2	1/2/97	4/2/97
Entity Structure		12/4 2/28	12/4/96	2/28/97
Communication		10/2 6/24	10/2/96	6/24/97
Formalizing Agreement		4/18 5/18	4/18/97	5/18/97
Implementation & Evaluation		12/30 6/24	12/30/96	6/24/97

Exhibit 18.1 Planning Committee Schedule (Sample)

taking the time to examine critical issues, the process itself should take place relatively briskly.

Each one of the seven "steps"—or activity clusters—described above starts and ends in a different way at certain points throughout the merger process. Since they are not linear steps, more than one activity can and should be happening at the same time. Each of the seven steps typically has a number of smaller substeps or ongoing processes, many of which will vary tremendously according to circumstances. Exhibit 18.1 shows a hypothetical timetable as it might look for two nonprofit entities contemplating a merger as of a specific point in time.

CHAPTER NINETEEN

Common Sources of Resistance

Every merger encounters resistance. A merger is a big idea, and big ideas are never accepted unanimously by any group of thinking people. It can take many different forms, be active or passive, and it will come from a virtually unlimited number of people and institutions. The important thing is not whether the merger encounters resistance, but how it is handled. And the key to handling resistance is understanding it. Most resistance to the merger proposal will come from one of the two big E's: ego or economics. These two big E's are large indeed and require a clear-eyed response. This chapter will explore some of the more common sources of resistance, why the resistance is probably occurring, and what to do about it.

The idea of economics in this context is probably self-evident—fears of job loss and salary or benefit reductions are natural companions of the merger process. Ego as a term is normally associated with individuals, and that form of ego is absolutely a factor in resistance to a merger. The biggest and most effective source of ego-based resistance is likely to be the executive director who doesn't want to have to send out Christmas cards announcing that he has just been demoted to assistant executive director. Close behind is the board president who "doesn't want to be known as the last president of this agency."

But there is another type of ego at work here as well, and it is a more group-oriented phenomenon. Most commonly, it gets expressed as pride in a group such as a department or even the whole organization. It can also be expressed as a strong preference for a certain management style or an ideology, concern for "the community," the vague assertion that "their services aren't as good as ours," or even an impatience to "get this process going." Whatever the exact expression of this kind of ego, it can be a powerful source of resistance (note that, in the example of impatience cited earlier, it may paradoxically lead to resistance by creating it on the part of the other organization).

Ego-based resistance can only be dealt with symbolically. The smaller organization in a merger may feel less like it is being taken over if a majority of meetings are held in its office, or if the new entity adopts its name. The time and place of the Planning Committee meetings may be symbolically important ("our board always meets on the third Tuesday of every month"). The use of names in the new entity is of utmost importance, and so on. The enduring point here is that, like it or not, much of the richness of the merger dialog occurs on a symbolic level. Participants who are not aware of this or who operate as though it doesn't exist run the very real risk of slowing the merger and possibly scuttling it altogether.

BOARD MEMBERS

Chronologically, the first source of resistance is likely to come from board members themselves. Given the fact that board members of nonprofits should have no routine financial interest in their organization, their resistance will come from questions of ego. Since board membership is inherently an act of giving, it may seem strange to say that board members operate egotistically. But, as any veteran nonprofit manager can attest, they do. In this case, ego often means the institutional identification that board members feel, although it can also refer to the raw personal ego stake that some develop. Here are some paraphrases of the way board members operate out of ego:

> *"This organization has been around for 112 years, and it's going to be around for another 112 years."*
>
> *"If we merge with them, the quality of our services will go down."*
>
> *"I refuse to be known as the last president of this organization."*

Ego expressions can be negative too:

"We'll get swallowed up if we merge with them."

"Why would they possibly want to merge with us?"

Several things make board member resistance easier to work with than almost any other kind. In general, one will not find a more sincere group of well-meaning people than board members of nonprofit organizations. Whatever their personal styles or ideologies, they usually want to do the right thing for the people and the community they serve. Most are keenly aware of their fiduciary responsibility. In many types of nonprofits, the board members are conceptual and analytical, tending to make decisions on the basis of rational arguments rather than impulse or emotion.

Pitfall: Board Members' Conflicts of Interest

He was a former mayor, a local businessman, and a tirelessly public-spirited citizen who knew as president of the local battered women's shelter that his program was much too small to survive on its own and needed to merge with a larger agency. Unfortunately he was also the program's landlord, and he had lost a sizable amount of money modifying and maintaining the building. Seeing the larger merger partner's enviable cash balances up close for the first time, he sensed an opportunity and went after it. Enlisting the help of a local politician and friend, he mounted a campaign to get the new entity to reimburse him for his uncovered building expenses. Through sheer persistence and careful maneuvering, he ultimately won some money from them.

Mergers create the potential for conflicts of interest where none existed before. The above case was a clear conflict of interest even before the merger and probably could not have been avoided with any amount of planning. The mayor–landlord's role was a form of hidden cost, and the main thing the larger agency could have done differently is understand from the beginning that they were being set up, and that this was a price of the merger.

At the same time, boards can be difficult. Most often this takes the form of a kind of genteel totalitarianism in which a single cogent opposing voice can stop the majority from taking a particular course of action. These boards desperately want not only consensus, but unanimous agreement. Unable to incorporate differing opinions into a strategic direction, they choose no direction at all.

The upshot of all this is that boards need to be sold on the idea of a merger. And why not? They are the ones with the legally constituted authority, and they have every right to consider such a major decision carefully. Someone needs to present the facts to them. They may need and want guidance in interpreting those facts, and they will certainly want to debate the idea. If the initiators of the merger—usually management or perhaps funding sources—have made their own decision on the merits of the case, the board can reasonably be expected to come to the same conclu-

Tip: The Reluctant Board Member

Occasionally, one or two board members will be unalterably opposed to the idea of a merger. To deal with their resistance, determine whether the individual is opposed to the proposed merger or to the idea of merging in general. Be forewarned that the individual will almost always say that it is this particular merger they oppose, not the idea itself. If that is true, and if their opposition is rooted in principle rather than a conflict of interest or some other hidden agenda, it is worth spending some additional time with that person. If it is ultimately impossible to gain their support, ask that they at least not actively oppose the process. Identify their concerns and make an attempt to incorporate them, but make it clear that dissenting opinions are valued and that the process will go on.

If the opposition is more general but cloaked in concern about the proposal of the moment, the director may be able to be politically isolated from the rest of the board. Sometimes their personality will accomplish that anyway; hardheaded stubbornness rarely builds strong coalitions. If not, wavering supporters might be turned away or neutralized by carefully accommodating their individual agendas. It's not pretty, but it works.

sion. If they don't do so after a careful, nonpressured review, then the proposal may deserve at least a rethinking if not tabling.

UNIONS

It is an unfortunate and ironic trend that organized labor, which began the 20th century as a force for social change, is passing into the next century as an increasingly defensive and reactionary political movement. Often this posture grows starkly clear during a merger. Unions are potentially rich sources of resistance because they have both ego and economic reasons for opposing collaboration.

Many nonprofit managers are fundamentally sympathetic to labor unions even if they are angered or disillusioned by some of the day-to-day realities of a collective bargaining environment. This leads to a quiet ambivalence on the manager's part, which can play itself out in erratic behavior in union relation matters. It can also lead to a downright hostile environment if both senior management and union personnel let personal feelings get in the way of businesslike dealings.

Unions have economic reasons for opposition because most are struggling to survive, and anything which threatens to reduce income from dues threatens the union itself. It would not be unrealistic to expect that, in medium- to large-sized nonprofits with sizable unions, losing a few hundred members might translate into losing one or more positions at union headquarters. Of course, a merger alone rarely results in the decertification of a union. Rather, the threat comes when two nonprofits proposing a merger have comparable staffs represented by different unions.

Again, the preferred strategy is straightforward, merits-of-the-case negotiation. Realistic managers and board members won't go into a merger hoping that it will get rid of a nettlesome union. In fact, it may end up expanding the number of unionized staff. A more practical expectation is that a sensitively handled merger process may improve the overall level of union–management relations.

MIDDLE MANAGERS

In mergers, as in life, there is no group more conservative than the newly arrived. Those who have just recently made it according to the old rules don't want them changed. This is the ego aspect of manager resistance. The economic motivations come from the fact that people who have been smart enough to earn a management job are smart enough to figure out that it is their ranks that are the most redundant and, therefore, the most susceptible to job cuts.

The ticklish part about manager resistance is that it is rarely explicit. Many times there is little or no verbal resistance at all, perhaps because reluctant managers realize that it would be foolish to directly oppose the merger process once it gets started. Instead, the ostensible verbal agreement is subverted by inaction, delay, and diversion. After a while, resistant managers usually stamp themselves as such by the fact that they never actually accomplish the things they are assigned throughout the merger process.

About the only positive thing that can be said about resistant managers is that they help make certain choices clearer. Managers who passively resist the merger process practically guarantee that they will have no meaningful role in it or in the implementation phase. Moreover, they risk marking themselves as expendable in the future, thereby accomplishing exactly what they tried to avoid by derailing the merger—job loss. This is not to say that reluctant managers should simply keep their mouths shut and go along. Sincere, principled resistance can actually be constructive, but ultimately the smart manager will try to lead the parade, not keep it from starting.

FUNDING SOURCES

Government funding sources act as a proxy for the open market in many nonprofit arenas and so are instrumental in forcing the conditions in which mergers are advisable. For this reason, higher levels of government funding agencies usually do not resist a merger. In addition, it is legally and politically wise for them to maintain official neutrality anyway. They are rarely in a position to demand or block a merger, and a statement of neutrality from them is as close to approval as one is likely to get.

The story is different deeper in the bureaucracy, however. Field office managers, in-house attorneys, and even financial analysts sometimes feel threatened by the prospect of a merger, as they should be if they see their job as one of maintaining command-and-control authority over the groups they fund. Strategic mergers consolidate power in the private nonprofit sector, and in return for giving up a measure of short term control, the government official gains the ability to profoundly shape and influence the future. This should be an appropriate trade-off for governmental work in the new information age, but not all officials see it that way. Happily, these guerrilla control efforts usually extinguish themselves although it may require a little careful exposing of them to hasten the process.

BANKS

Banks can have a great deal to say about a proposed merger, although it's a bit unfair to call them a source of resistance. Any proposal which can potentially change the ability of their customer to repay a loan—for better or worse—will attract their attention. Usually they will have written into the terms of the borrowing the requirement that the bank be notified of any impending merger or change in the borrower's corporate status, so complying with this clause triggers a discussion (it's a good idea to do it earlier if possible). Fortunately, banks' interests are straightforward. Prove to them that the merger will have either no effect or a positive one on the banking relationship, and wise bankers will accept the merger with little objection.

If banks can be said to resist a merger, it is most often not voluntary. What tends to trip up a smooth transition is the bank's own bureaucracy. At the heart of this problem is that the human beings working for the bank may not know how to adapt their own policies when two nonprofits merge. Fortunately, with good will and persistence on both sides, this problem can largely be made to disappear.

REGULATORS

So far, regulators seem to intervene in nonprofit mergers only when there is a proposal to sell nonprofit assets to a for-profit firm.

These conversions, as they are known, are a growing trend for reasons discussed earlier. We will explore the regulatory aspects of changing from nonprofit to for-profit status later in the book. When regulators raise questions about a nonprofit to profit merger, it may be because it causes confusion or noncompliance in some area of regulation, such as licensure.

PART FIVE

Strategies for Developing Alliances

CHAPTER TWENTY

The Seven Stages of Alliance Development

Unlike mergers, alliance activity occurs only on the operations, responsibility, and economic levels—in other words, below the corporate line in Exhibit 5.1. Whereas mergers of nonprofit organizations usually have some type of strategic purpose (including survival, the most strategic purpose of all), successful alliances will produce tactical advantages such as economic savings and streamlined services.

By their nature, alliances are far more open-ended and inherently ambiguous than outright mergers. In the latter, a defined number of parties work toward a clear-cut goal, and they either achieve it or they don't. The product is the end result, and at least one can say that the most intense period of the merger process has a beginning, middle, and end.

For practical reasons, alliances are difficult to organize, motivate, and shape. But the thing that makes them even more difficult is that leadership in an alliance derives, not from an assigned position or role, but rather, from a delicate mix of personality, organizational identity, and resources. This same mixture is true of internal leadership in any nonprofit, but at least there the leaders have a predefined positions and roles to reinforce their credibility. Alliances have no such positions or roles and so must depend on the political skills of their members.

Alliances are not new ways of conducting business. It just seems that way because they tend to operate out of sight of the average consumer. In the for-profit sector, there are examples of alliances created for very mundane purposes which have grown to be highly successful. Decades ago, a group of cranberry growers on Cape Cod, Massachusetts, got together to find ways of getting their crops to the market. The eventual result was the Ocean Spray company, a very successful cooperative which over the years has evolved from being a harvest management tool to a well-known consumer products company.

In a different industry several decades ago, a handful of industrial paper distributors (largely family-owned businesses) realized that they needed to do something to help counter the huge economic advantages that other larger publicly held distributors (and the paper manufacturers) enjoyed in the marketplace. They formed an alliance to mimic some of the advantages of larger size while still maintaining their independence as private businesses. Today, Network Services is a 70-plus membership organization whose members are its owners, and which has a history of giving regional firms a way of competing for what might otherwise be unreachable national accounts.

CATEGORIES OF ALLIANCES

Alliances can be categorized based on their purpose. Either they are task-oriented alliances or process-oriented. Task-oriented al-

Tip: Alliances Can be "Premerger" Experiences

Even if alliances create no other value, they can serve as preparation for full corporate mergers. The kind of close cooperation and mutual learning that occur during the building of an alliance lays crucial groundwork for a full merger. No matter what the stated purpose, a successful alliance will help build trust between participants and open communication that wouldn't have existed before.

The other side of this dynamic is that it can be manipulated. One or two major nonprofits in an alliance may use it to position themselves as logical senior merger partners for some of the other participants. Usually, however, participants will see through such manipulation, and it may actually backfire on the empire builder.

liances come together for a specific purpose such as the development of a proprietary software package or the submission of a collaborative proposal. Process-oriented alliances, on the other hand, have no end product. Value is derived from the process itself and whatever victories it achieves along the way. There may not even be a set of clearly defined parties involved in the project, and there is not likely to be any strong legal bond between them until they achieve a sophisticated level of operations.

SEVEN TASKS OF ALLIANCE DEVELOPMENT

Since alliances typically involve a number of nonprofit organizations, they are considerably more complex than mergers, especially when it comes to starting them and focusing their collective energies. On the other hand, because they do not have to involve loss of corporate prerogatives or chief executive officer positions, they tend to be popular as an alternative to mergers. It can be expected that many nonprofits in the future will participate in at least one major alliance. Already many such collaborations are forming for a variety of purposes, and more are forming every day.

Unlike many other institutions in nonprofit management, alliances are market-driven. When alliances are formed but never quite get anything done, the market is speaking. What it is saying is that there is not a demand for what the alliance can provide. This is ultimately why alliances fail to get organized, although it is usually blamed on disinterest or a general inability to "get our act together." In these instances, the alliance's focus was usually not sharp enough or its focus lacked a compelling argument.

Alliances are not a way to be "just a little bit pregnant." Smaller nonprofits tend to like the idea of an alliance because it seems to offer an alternative to what they perceive as the distasteful option of a merger. Alliances' strengths lie below the corporate line in the C.O.R.E. model, meaning that they can most readily affect economics, administration, and program operations. Rarely can improvements—even dramatic ones—in these areas substitute, over the long term, for the power of a change in strategy at the corporate level. Alliances are at their best in helping members find new and better ways of doing what they are already doing.

As in mergers, we see seven tasks of alliance development. The following model is offered not as a prescription for how to develop an alliance of nonprofits (although it could be useful in that regard), but as guidance about the nature of the collaborative challenge facing alliances of nonprofits. These are the seven tasks:

1. Mutual exploration and analysis
2. Synthesis and tentative planning
3. Working committee structure development
4. Quick victories
5. Institutional buy-in
6. Work-plan by areas
7. Formalized operational structure

The following sections will examine the seven different aspects of alliance formation that we have identified. Again, there is no linear sequence of events intended, nor is it necessarily desired. Different objectives can and should be accomplished simultaneously. For example, an alliance may very well achieve a quick victory, even before it has completed its planning and analysis. This is likely to happen incidentally, as when the process of planning together coincidentally identifies an objective that can be achieved outside of the alliance process itself. Operations personnel may identify a joint venture that can be put together quickly, such as a response to a request for proposal (RFP). Or perhaps a foundation grant could be submitted jointly. Properly conceived and managed, the process of alliance development itself can produce synergies and pleasant surprises at any time.

Stage 1: Mutual Exploration and Analysis

Someone has to speak first. An alliance will only get started when one or more individuals takes the initiative. In many ways, this may be the hardest part of alliance development. Suggesting collaboration may seem like a risky act: what if the colleague is offended? Uninterested? Steals the idea? As the pace of formal collaboration among nonprofits quickens, managers are more likely, at least, to be familiar with the idea, and this should help facilitate the initial discussions. Still, someone needs to take the lead. Who should it be?

A few characteristics will often be typical of a nonprofit manager who initiates an alliance development project. The first and most important is personality. It takes a certain kind of person to make the first move. In addition to being comfortable with what others see as a risky situation (a perception they do not always share), alliance initiators, in our experience, are often innovative thinkers with a great deal of initiative. They tend to be young or, if older, relatively new in their field. Either characteristic helps them avoid seeing things in predictable ways.

Closely related to personality type is that alliance initiators almost always have to be respected by their peers. Respect gives initiators credibility so they can share the idea. Respected initiators are more likely to be trusted by otherwise skeptical or disinterested administrators.

As a practical matter, alliance initiators tend to be associated with larger agencies. Managers of smaller nonprofits tend to be unable to spare the time to devote to such a highly speculative long-term project. Representatives from larger agencies are also well-positioned to do the little things that make a difference such as hosting meetings, dedicating secretarial time, or copying documents. While there is no reliable definition of large or small measured in dollars in this context, it might be said that agencies in which the executive director has at least two organizational layers between himself or herself and program workers are about the smallest ones capable of subsidizing alliance development.

Finally, the alliance initiator needs to have internal "permission" to start alliance discussions. Even though alliances don't change corporate structure or lead to job restructuring—not right away, anyway—the executive's staff needs to be supportive if only to permit him or her to spend the time necessary to get the effort underway. Similarly, the board of directors needs to be attuned enough to the environment and willing to allow the time investment necessary.

So far, we have spoken of the alliance initiator as a practicing nonprofit manager. People in other positions can play the same role. One of the most interesting of these alternatives is the trade association. For many years, nonprofits have been joining together in membership organizations with the explicit intention of accom-

Tip: Decide Who's In, Who's Out

An early fundamental problem of alliances with more than a handful of members is that it may be very difficult to tell which organizations count themselves as members and which do not. Inevitably, some early planners will want to be highly inclusive and free-flowing, while others will want structure. In any event, different participants will go through their internal decision-making processes at different times and in different ways. The question of who's in and who's out may be answered quite differently at different times, depending on where participants are in their decision-making processes.

The best way of resolving this problem is to devise a symbolic way of indicating membership. Have participating organizations sign an agreement. Issue a public document with everyone's logo on it (graphic designers will cringe at that suggestion). Issue certificates of membership. Or—the most symbolic and the most real—spend the same amount of money on something for the alliance. This could be a membership–capitalization fee, a consultant's report, or any number of things. Nothing makes an abstract idea more real than spending money on it.

plishing broad goals as a group that no single entity could accomplish on its own. These trade associations, although nonprofits themselves, have as their explicit goal the betterment of their members.

The roles of the traditional trade association are fairly standard. They include lobbying relevant governmental units, public education, member education, and joint purchasing of goods or services. In some fields today, as a result of members' restructuring, trade associations are beginning to consider including the creation and maintenance of alliances and networks of members in their services to members. There are two reasons why this is happening. First, associations' classic role as packagers of information (including lobbying) is being undermined by the explosion of telecommunications. Now, it may be possible for nonmembers to be informed of changes in the environment just as quickly as association members, which diminishes one of the strong arguments for membership. Second, associations' methods and successes in areas such as joint purchasing and newsletter production are being copied and improved upon by for-profit competitors, and so associations must seek new revenue sources. What organization is better positioned to facilitate collaboration among a group of nonprofits than an association of them?

Funders may also encourage the formation of alliances. Although their interests are not typically as nitty-gritty as those of their recipients, visionary funders can be a good source of support, advice, and money for formal efforts at collaboration. Sometimes they can go even further. The Wilder Foundation in Minnesota, for example, responded to a change in state law encouraging the formation of health care provider collaboratives by helping to create Care Choices, an alliance of several long-term care providers. It followed up the project by placing an executive on loan to the alliance to act as its coordinator.

Other groups can also serve as alliance initiators. In Ann Arbor, Michigan, an unsightly abandoned railroad bed-turned-junkyard was the impetus for a community-wide collaboration between various groups to build a nonprofit shared services building. Today, Nonprofit Enterprise at Work (or N.E.W. Center) is a major catalyst in the community, bringing together disparate groups for training and advocacy, as well as, the more mundane functions of sharing copiers and support staff.

Deciding on a Purpose. The next logical question after the matter of who initiates the collaboration is who should belong to it. This question is best answered after clarifying the alliance's purpose. The inevitable tension is between an open membership policy in which anyone who wants to join can do so and an invitation-only group. The discussion is likely to have ideological overtones. Nonprofit managers as individuals tend to have highly egalitarian instincts and a strong dedication to the public good. Typically, this philosophy leads to an open membership policy. The other approach is to limit membership in order to keep control of one or more aspects of the alliance.

The C.O.R.E. model offers a guideline. Planners should consider how high up on the continuum they ultimately want the alliance to reach. If the alliance has strictly economic goals, an open membership policy is best. At the other extreme, if participants can envision doing joint marketing at some point or even considering mergers with each other, they will be well-advised to be selective about who participates. Holding the alliance out to the market as one entity for marketing purposes means that quality has to be reliably defined as the lowest common denominator. To ensure that quality standards are easier to enforce in the future, the alliance will want to be selective in the present.

Models of Alliances. The characteristics and intent of the organization initiating the alliance will have a great deal to do with the shape that it takes. This is not to say that alliance planners should consciously try to replicate a particular model, but rather that a given set of circumstances will tend to play out in the same ways each time. When a strong and stable nonprofit acts as the alliance convenor, using its own staff to coordinate and support the work of the group, the alliance will tend to look like a hub-and-spoke model. Here, the initiating nonprofit will be at the center of the effort, and the major relationships will be the ones between it and the other participants instead of those between participants themselves.

In the hub-and-spoke model, the convening agency becomes something like the anchor store in a shopping mall. It should be noted that just being stable and fiscally strong does not automatically make an agency an alliance leader. Instead, it is the combination of these characteristics with a more intangible commitment to leadership that makes an organization the pivotal entity in the development of an alliance. Ultimately, the drive to assume this role comes from an unpredictable combination of personal and organizational characteristics.

This model obviously encourages paternalism, a trait which rankles managers of smaller organizations. There is little sense pretending otherwise. The best hope is that ultimately a "swallowing up" of the others can be forgiven if the lead agency sincerely uses its resources to advance the common good—and the executive director can successfully communicate trustworthiness, credibility, and restraint. It also doesn't hurt to incorporate people, as well as, ideas from the smaller organizations if the lead agency merges with its former colleague groups.

A second model of alliance structure is the loose confederation of agencies. This is more likely to happen when at least some of the participants are similar in size and strength, or when the alliance is initiated and nurtured by an outside force such as an association or consultant. It can also take shape when some of the organizations' managers have known and trusted each other for a period of time and decide to turn that relationship into a more formal one. The confederation model can also come into being when the members share a common trait such as nonprofit status, religious or other affiliation, or simply geographic proximity.

Mutual Learning. Once the initial members of the alliance have been identified, they need to begin sharing critical information with each other. This is roughly equivalent to the due diligence stage of a merger, with a few exceptions. First, the proper goal of this part of the process is to learn as much as possible about each other. The same is true in a merger, except that in an alliance, the learning should be focused more below the corporate line in the C.O.R.E. model and less on corporate matters. Program compatibility and the possibilities for integration, for example, will be more important at this stage of alliance building than will the state of each agency's bylaws.

Another difference between a due diligence investigation and the mutual learning phase of an alliance is that the learning has to focus on broader and more qualitative issues, as well as quantitative. What is the stated vision and mission of the agency? What are the values of the respective participants? What are their strengths and weaknesses? How will the alliance fit with the established management style? Is it a valued initiative or just another set of meetings?

At the same time, there are many quantitative areas appropriate for exploration. One of the most important of these is the nature of the members' market areas. All concerned should have a good understanding of the programs and services offered throughout the alliance. A good way to display this information is in a matrix format so that it can be read at a glance. A representative sample of program marketing material can help show how the organization has positioned its services. Information about how services and programs are organized such as organizational charts, are necessary, as is descriptive information about board members and senior managers. If the service requires a significant physical site such as a private school campus, some

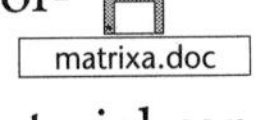

overview information about it would be helpful. If there are any quality benchmarks or indicators in the organization's field, they are extremely useful. Financial information, especially in the form of an analysis, is a must so that all members can see and understand their individual and collective financial plusses and minuses.

All of the above should be in writing, preferably collected in a single document or set of documents in three-ring notebooks for easy replacement and additions. At least one copy of the document goes to each participating agency. Ideally, it becomes the background for group discussion.

Note that task-oriented alliances will go through the same kind of process as listed above, except that they will focus intensively on one particular area to the exclusion of almost everything else. For example, an alliance whose major task is to create or modify software for use by the group will need to explore the capabilities and limits of each member's information management systems, including hardware, application software, and personnel competence, as well as the ability to invest in major capital assets.

A persistent question in a process alliance is whether representatives of each organization should visit the others. If the group is too large, or if a consultant has been engaged to develop the alliance, this may not be necessary. But if there are a small number of participants, it may be practical to introduce each individual to the other participants' programs. One way to do this is to hold meetings at each agency on a rotating basis, planning time for a tour the first time each site hosts a meeting.

Board Involvement. It is wise for each organization to involve its board of directors during this stage of alliance development, if only on a "for your information" basis. Since the work of alliances will involve noncorporate changes, managers may be tempted to avoid early discussions with boards about them, on the grounds that exploratory discussions do not need board approval. Not only is this missing the point of CEO–board relations (boards exist to do more than just "approve" projects), but it also misses an opportunity to build support that will be useful in the future.

An inescapable reality of nonprofit management today is that virtually all boards of directors—not to mention managers—will need education about collaborative relations, including mergers and alliances. This is a logical way to involve boards at an early point. Ideally this education will occur either before a specific alliance is proposed or as part of the early stages of considering whether to join it.

Stage 2: Synthesis and Tentative Planning

Alliances need to take the results of the first stage and fashion out of them the broad outlines of a direction. At this point, the direction need not be concrete or even highly specific, and usually it is not. If the first stage has confirmed that their purpose seems feasible, task-oriented alliances may be able to eliminate this step altogether and begin committee structure planning.

Alliance participants may feel the first stabs of frustration at this stage. For one thing, membership may still be fluid. Alliance leaders may not have emerged yet, or those who are emerging may not be acceptable to the group as a whole. Another source of frustration is that objectives probably have not been identified. Yet another frustrating aspect of the synthesizing step is the persistent and often unspoken skepticism that this whole effort will even work. In response to all of these legitimate concerns, one must counsel patience.

Agreeing on Objectives. Just as a single nonprofit functions best when it has a vision and clear-cut tactics for achieving that vision, an alliance needs agreement on broad themes and objectives. Articulating a common vision could be relatively easy because it is what brought the entities together in the first place. In many areas in which nonprofits are active today, the shared idea is to find ways of coping with reduced funding. Many arts organizations need to find solutions to rising economic size requirements and reduced governmental and corporate support. In health care, the hope is to use an alliance to deal with managed care.

Social service agencies anticipate the same kind of impact from managed care in their area as is occurring in health care, and in addition, they often have to counter the effects of government cutbacks and restructuring such as welfare reform. Such challenges tend to forge agreement over what needs to be done well before an alliance is attempted.

With general agreement over strategy in place, the alliance can begin designing ways of getting there. Again, the C.O.R.E. model

Note: Why Strategic Planning Sometimes Isn't So Strategic

Strategic planning was the darling of the for-profit world in the 1970s and 1980s and still exerts significant influence there. It has had a spillover effect for nonprofits as these historically nonstrategic organizations realize the benefits to be gained from thinking strategically.

Strategic thinking is essential for success as a nonprofit, so this embrace of planning is encouraging. But in truth, most strategic plans are not strategic at all but tactical—what will be accomplished, how, when, by whom, and what they need in order to do it. These are all matters of objectives and logistics—the stuff of management, in short, not the stuff of visionary leadership.

Alliances have the advantage of not needing to dwell on the strategic level terribly much. That part—equivalent to the corporate level—gets done largely by the convening of the alliance. They can therefore put together the kind of plans which are really just means toward accomplishing strategic objectives. Ironically, this may have been what they were calling strategic planning in their individual organizations anyway.

can help. In a brainstorming session, based on the mutual learning already done, alliance members will almost certainly be able to identify dozens of potential ways to collaborate. Although the brainstorming should be done without regard to the C.O.R.E. model so as to make it as innovative and unconstrained as possible, the next step is to categorize the objectives on the four levels. The actual objectives identified could be endless, but we will present some of the more common ones in terms of the model in Exhibit 20.1.

Two things are important about alliance objectives. First, they will almost certainly change several more times in the coming years as conditions change and objectives are accomplished. Second, and more important, in a sense, it doesn't matter what the objectives are at this formative stage. What is of lasting value is not so much the specific objective, but rather the process through

Corporate
- Market jointly
- Agree on a name
- Devise a common logo
- Seek contracts for providing services together

Operations
- Seek funding for joint programs
- Run programs jointly
- Devise shared quality standards and benchmarks
- Train staff jointly
- Seek accreditation together
- Agree to provide assistance in the event of program emergencies
- Share equipment or temporary staff needed to run operations

Responsibility
- Agree on common information exchange standards
- Share key administrative staff
- Agree to share job postings
- Use common job descriptions
- Implement a wide area computer network
- Devise e-mail communication systems
- Implement disaster recovery plans

Economics
- Purchase goods and services jointly
- Share office space
- Borrow money together
- Run transportation systems together (buses and vans, etc.)

Exhibit 20.1 Alliance Objectives

which it was created. The more subtle but ultimately long-lasting work here is to build a foundation of mutual trust and understanding beginning with the boards and managers of participating nonprofits.

Discuss a Timetable. Although process alliances are inherently open-ended, they still need the discipline of a general timetable to shape and monitor their progress. Experienced managers know that timetables established at the beginning of a project are worth about as much as yesterday's newspaper, yet the exercise of discussing the expected time frame will help mold future efforts and prevent misunderstandings.

More often, there is no external reference point for determining time frame. This is why process alliances need to impose a time frame on themselves, either through mutual agreement or as part of an outside consultant's work. Even if the deadline is privately regarded with skepticism, at least it is a way of holding everyone minimally accountable.

Sometimes there is a natural deadline set by parties outside the control of an alliance. In the early 1980s, when the Reagan administration drastically revised the way that the federal government channeled funds to nonprofits and their state funders, reducing the total amount in the process, the ultimate deadline was no more than a year or two away depending on the local vagaries of government funding. When the same thing happens today, alliances know that their deadline for effectiveness is measured in months or perhaps a year or two at the most. The same kind of certainty, though less precisely calculable, occurs in a health care market when the percentage of people in managed care plans of some kinds is growing at a consistent yearly rate. An alliance between environmental agencies at the operations level to respond to local disasters, such as oil spills, has an obvious deadline measured in hours and days.

Board Involvement. Once the alliance members familiarize themselves with each other and begin discussing future direction, participating organizations who have not already done so should engage the board of directors in the process. This would be a late start for a board, but it can still fulfill its responsibilities and make a contribution to the effort. Managers should make sure to do some catch-up education and show how the alliance would fit with overall strategy. For their parts, board members must be careful to keep an open mind about the alliance taking shape. Their overriding responsibility is to make sure that management is entering into an arrangement consistent with previous discussions about the agency's future.

Pick a Name. Perhaps the single most important thing that alliance planners can do at this point to establish momentum for the future is to pick a name for the blossoming project. Having a name for something gives so many obvious benefits that it is easily overlooked. Because it gives outsiders a way to refer to the project—no

Tip: Avoid the Name Drain

Certain words are already becoming overused as nonprofits form alliances. Words such as choices, partners, network, care, and even alliance itself are creeping into names just as the culture of the 1960s influenced new nonprofits' names during that decade. When choosing a name, be smart and forward-thinking. Early alliances can afford to try using some of these obvious choices because there is little competition. Later alliances in a given market area need to be a bit more creative.

small benefit considering that an alliance is an abstract process rather than a building or even a corporation—it marks the beginning of an external identity.

Picking a good name is not easy. There is a reason why large national firms pay millions of dollars for research into potential brand names. Nonprofits historically do not have those advantages and so must operate by collective intuition. In all likelihood, the choice of a name will be ad hoc and a matter of divided opinion. It doesn't matter. It can always be changed, and the real point

Note: Less Charisma in Alliances

Single nonprofits—and, by extension, two nonprofits seriously considering merger—can sometimes get by on the strength of a single charismatic leader. In fact, some nonprofits are implicitly organized to take advantage of strong individual leadership—a rubber stamp board, small or at least simplified operations, an intensely private orientation—and they operate best this way.

Alliances, on the other hand, rarely succeed solely on the strength of a single leader. By nature, they disperse decision making, take a longer time to achieve their goals, and resist concentration of authority in any one place. Charismatic leaders tend to avoid such situations, and if they get involved at all, it is usually as a noteworthy, but definitely part-time, participant.

of selecting a name is that it gives everyone something to hold onto.

Stage 3: Working Committee Structure Development

In the first two stages of alliance development, it is natural for a single group to handle most of the planning tasks. This group is analogous to the Planning Committee described in the section on mergers, and for convenience we will refer to it this way. Generally the membership will be the chief executive officers or other high-ranking administrators of the member organizations, and there should be some continuity among them.

This committee operates, by nature, at the corporate level of the alliance. That is, it consists of executives with overall responsibility in their own nonprofit's planning strategy for the alliance and matching objectives with people and resources available to them.

Except in the largest of alliances, there will probably be no reason for any other group to work on corporate level collaboration. This means that the committee must play a dual role. For operations, responsibility, and economics collaboration, it must assign, delegate, and coordinate. For corporate matters, it handles everything. The difference may seem slight, but it is not. The committee has to be extremely clear about when it is acting in a coordinating role and when it expects direct results from itself.

Governance. In the beginning, there is not likely to be much of a concern with governance, mainly because the members of the Planning Committee will be too preoccupied with getting to know each other and exploring what the alliance might accomplish. If there is any single decision to be made at this stage requiring a more or less formal statement of position, it will probably be the hiring of a consultant or part-time staff person. Still, regular decisions have to be made by the group, and the way they make them says a great deal about the nature of the Planning Committee as a governing body. A few principles can be deduced from those alliances already in operation.

Resistance to Creating "Bureaucracy." Many managers will be acutely aware of the inherent tension in their attempt to get the benefits of being a larger organization without actually becoming part of one. No matter how large the member nonprofits may be, there will usually be a tacit expectation that formal operating policies and procedures will be kept to a minimum. To do the job, after all, members need to be able to control their alliance directly, without a lot of intervening layers of management or procedure.

Sophistication and Formality Reflect the Membership. Organizations usually prefer doing intercorporation business with other organizations that think, act, and look like they do. This is not a reflection of a mindless club mentality, but of simple economics. The independent auto mechanic will do business with individuals and small local businesses because that's the nature of who he is equipped to serve. The multinational agricultural combine needs to do business with large companies because it is not designed to serve individual farmers. As a result of this tendency, alliances will look like their members. Universities will use skilled specialists from a variety of disciplines to create a formal, legal entity with staff of its own and possibly even capital assets too. A dozen small day care centers will use no paid staff and will try to put the alliance together without incorporating until it is absolutely necessary.

One Organization, One Vote. For practical reasons, alliances tend to be determinedly egalitarian in their decision-making process: one agency, one vote. Why not? What other basis exists for making decisions? Even if endowments or sheer revenue size counted for much in the nonprofit world, few nonprofits would get involved with an alliance partner who insisted on judging their balance sheet, rather than the organization.

It is a wise idea for the Planning Committee, in its role as the corporate collaboration planners, to have its relationship with the alliance subcommittees clearly defined. It can be expected that the Planning Committee will operate like a board of directors. This would mean that it has at least technical veto power over the subcommittees, and that their work is framed as a recommendation to the Planning Committee. At the same time, the alliance needs to find ways of either making decisions quickly (not a strength of any group) or of delegating sufficient authority to the subcommittees that they can make a certain level of commitment without getting

Tip: Forget Roberts' Rules of Order

Many nonprofit board members and some managers feel that meetings should be conducted according to Roberts' Rules of Order. These durable rules of procedure were initially created for large parliamentary bodies, not small groups of managers or board members. Alliance boards are problem-solving bodies, not public entities. If Roberts' Rules are needed to keep order, the atmosphere may be too divisive to get anything done anyway.

explicit clearance from the planning group. Otherwise, the process will get bogged down in a mass of approval requests and authorizations.

Characteristics of Subcommittees. While subcommittees will vary according to each situation, there are some characteristics of certain types of subcommittees that are reliable enough to guide alliance planners. These are not goals for a system of subcommittees, nor even necessarily desirable characteristics. What they do represent are traits that alliance leaders are likely to see emerge as the process unfolds.

Operations. One of the quiet realities of nonprofit management is the sense of isolation that many professionals feel. The size and nature of many nonprofits often mean that there is only one or two of most professional jobs in each organization—one social worker, one physician, etc. Designed and communicated properly, a subcommittee that focuses on some area of program operations can be a welcome experience for many of these people. The key is to establish that participation in the alliance is not expected to cost people their jobs—they won't, in short, be down-sizing themselves out of existence.

Unless there is a ready-made opportunity for collaboration, operations subcommittees are likely to be slow to act. There are several reasons for this. Program people—whether they are curators, librarians, therapists, performing artists, or teachers—usually have chosen to concentrate on what they do because it is what they enjoy doing. Asking them to even participate in a manage-

Tip: Continuing Education for Operations Professionals

Many types of professions commonly found in nonprofit organizations require their members to get continuing education in their field, and most licensing programs have explicit requirements for continuing education. One way to motivate and reward program personnel for participation in such planning would be if their professional societies would accept such work toward their continuing education requirements. Although month-to-month committee meetings are unlikely to be eligible for credit, the education sessions that should be part of the early stages of the process may very well qualify.

ment task may seem so unnatural that it takes time to adapt. Also, many program-oriented people are deeply ingrained in the intricacies of their normal funding stream without even knowing it. Arts people have NEA grants, community development program managers have the Community Development Block Grant, social services types have a variety of federal and state funding streams, and health care personnel are used to the dictates of Medicaid, Medicare, and private insurance.

Depending on the size and complexity of the alliance, there could be several program subcommittees. Health care facilities and some social services organizations bring together so many diverse professional and paraprofessional program service staffs that their opportunities for collaboration are often easier to handle in logical groupings of professionals. Then, the problem is to establish an overall coordinating mechanism such as an oversight committee.

Responsibility. By contrast, administrative personnel are likely to spawn only one or a handful of subcommittees. Largely this is because financial and administrative staffs in nonprofits tend to be much smaller compared with program staffs. Also, administrative matters are usually easier to centralize or to control through a small group of people. One budding alliance of mental retardation/developmental disability service providers pondered with some surprise, the following insight. Owing to the fact that three to five agencies out of the forty in the area provided services to well over 70 percent of the consumers, a subcommittee composed of just one individual from each of the 3 to 5 agencies could effectively set and enforce standards for the exchange of computer information.

The most difficult issues for these types of subcommittees will often be the ones involving things over which participants have little control. In particular, individual nonprofits often must work within a reimbursement system, and, more often than not, that system is controlled by government authorities far removed from participants' day-to-day operations. Any attempt at standardization must somehow take these realities into account. In the end, some activities may need to take place on a different level—such as state-wide—or not at all.

The subcommittee on administrative matters could easily turn out to be permanent. There is always more that can be done, and individual members will speak each other's language, thereby making communication easier and more pleasant (administrative staff can suffer from the same professional isolation that program people frequently feel).

Economics. Because economic collaboration is so unique to specific goods or services, collaboration on this level may tend to occur through a series of ad hoc task forces. Administrative staff may know a great deal about how to buy copier paper, but they will almost certainly be at a loss when it comes to purchasing industrial paper supplies such as paper towels and toilet paper. Fortunately, the process of economic collaboration is straightforward and can be applied to almost any product or service.

Once the alliance planners have identified a product or service for economic collaboration, they can follow these simple steps:

1. Identify which members currently purchase what products or services from what vendors.
2. Exclude any existing vendors from the above list if they are currently not performing satisfactorily; add vendors who may be appropriate, but who do not happen to service any member organization at present.

3. Identify the list of the most common items the alliance wishes to purchase. Consolidate items as much as possible, and be sure to compare similar specifications. Be sure to identify non-quantifiable specifications such as service requirements.
4. Send the above information to the selected vendors, asking them for a written quote.
5. Compile the responses and analyze.
6. Select a manageable number of finalists for an interview.
7. Choose a vendor on the basis of the written quote and the interview.
8. Notify all alliance members of the choice, detailing a target date for the changeover.

The economic subcommittees have the power to be highly successful and influential. One alliance of seven nonprofits identified opportunities to save as much as $50,000 collectively just on the basis of issuing joint RFPs for dairy products, bread, industrial paper, and plastics. Moreover, because economic subcommittees can

Pitfall: Beware the Cherry Picker

Sooner or later—and for a successful alliance, it'll be sooner, rather than later—a losing vendor will attempt to cherry pick the group. They will do this by belatedly undercutting their competitors, by offering special deals to certain members, or by doing things like appealing to the board of directors of a former client that just decided to go with the winning vendor. The best way of dealing with this attempt is to warn members ahead of time that this may happen and to constantly remind them that they will find true clout only in tight unity. Failing in that, the second-best way is simply to shine a spotlight on the vendor's actions (quoting the salesperson, sending around copies of proposals for sweetheart deals, etc.). Often the group's members will react negatively enough that the vendor's attempt at cherry picking will be self-defeating.

involve a full range of personnel from all levels of participating members, they are an excellent way to build support for the overall project. Once formerly passive or possibly disillusioned staff have the chance to participate in a meaningful and straightforward joint purchasing exercise, they can readily become champions of the process among their peers. In this way, the economic subcommittees have value well beyond measurable dollar savings.

Stage 4: Quick Victories

bidsuma.xls
vendors.xlw

At this point, the notion of integrated services and strategic collaboration will seem awkward and untested to many, including some of the participants themselves. Consequently, the concept must be sold. Board members need to be reassured that collaborating in some way is worth exploring even though there can be no guaranteed return on the effort. Even among the participants, not every executive director will be comfortable with the prospect, nor will all their management staffs.

The solution is to shoot for some quick victories. What do we mean by this term? Anything positive and traceable to the alliance that occurs within about 90 to 120 days of the official beginning of the project. These could be savings from a very focused joint purchasing project, or the importing of a highly regarded speaker made affordable by all members' helping to defray the costs. An early victory may happen when members collaborate on a joint proposal submission or share the cost of acquiring a valuable piece of software.

Quick victories prove the concept. They show that something of value is feasible in the short term so that members can see that longer term benefits are even more promising. They also create a sense of momentum. Staff actually involved in the early success can feel justifiable pride, while those who were not involved may begin to see the possibilities in their own areas. But—most important of all—quick victories get people's attention. This is no small feat in most organizations. Those early victories act like little billboards attesting to the success of this previously abstract and vague process of an alliance.

Often the quickest victories are economic ones. Different participants discover they share the same supplier and that combining their business gets them a lower price. Or they realize that the

Tip: Getting Vendors' Interest Is a Victory Itself

Most vendors figure out very quickly that an alliance can mean new business, so it doesn't take much to capture their interest. Whether they knew it or not, their previous success with participants may have depended on keeping them fragmented. They understand the prospect of greatly expanding their share of business by bringing in the other participants, even if they're at the risk of losing what they have now to another vendor who captures the full group.

same vendor has given each participant a vastly different deal which can be standardized to everyone's benefit. It is difficult to analyze purchasing patterns and carry out a rebidding process within a short time span; planners would be well advised to stick to one or two clearly definable areas (e.g., "dairy products," or "copier paper"). Still, just identifying the possibilities can be considered a victory.

Economic victories tend to be attractive to boards of directors as they consider whether to join an alliance, or to foundations potentially interested in funding the transaction costs of collaborating. Sometimes a less direct and quantifiable benefit will appeal to management. Ironically, program managers, who will often be most resistant to any collaboration that appears to affect their professional autonomy, may embrace an alliance readily enough to offer some quick victories in an area such as training. Administrative staff, who can be expected to be tentative or actively resistant later on if the collaboration ever threatens to reduce administrative positions, will tend to accept early collaboration if it involves new projects. Seeking new software or pursuing a type of professional accreditation that no member currently holds are examples of this less threatening type of alliance activity.

Stage 5: Institutional Buy-In

No matter how well-intended or stable some participating organizations and their managers appear to be, an alliance must move

Tip: An Idea for a Foundation Proposal

The reality of alliance development is that, to be successful, participants almost always have to spend money in the beginning. This can be particularly painful for organizations hoping to see savings up front. One solution is to approach a willing foundation with a proposal to fund the start-up costs of the alliance, especially an economically focused one. The central idea is that the foundation money could be leveraged—if $10,000 spent now to get the alliance up and running leads to a process that offers collective savings throughout the alliance of $50,000, the funder can be pleased to have created five dollars in savings for every dollar donated. This can be a very powerful argument, and it is perhaps more compelling for alliances than for mergers, where the savings are likely to be less visible.

aggressively beyond its formative stages to insure what we call institutional buy-in. Of necessity, the early days can only involve one or two individuals from each organization, but once the outlines of collaboration have been set, the budding alliance needs to create widespread support within each member organization.

To understand what needs to be done to gain widespread institutional acceptance of the alliance as a way of getting things done, it is helpful to examine the barriers to institutional acceptance and what can be done to lower them. We can identify several predictable barriers: lack of understanding of the concept of alliances; lack of communication about the specific alliance being proposed; interruptions in leadership; and lack of demonstrable benefits. We will discuss each in turn, along with suggestions for how to deal with them.

Lack of Understanding of the Concept of Alliances. The participation of some potential members in an alliance could conceivably be prevented by board action. Half-hearted support for participation can often be traced to lack of knowledge on the board's part, which in turn comes from inadequate understanding. The solution is for individual boards of directors to have a basic understanding of alliances, how they differ from mergers, and what they can reasonably be expected to accomplish. This is knowledge of the head; the next section will deal with knowledge felt with the heart.

Ideally, several months before the management of each participating agency proposes membership in an alliance, it will begin a process of education with the board of directors. This might take the form of special minicourses embedded in board meetings or outside speakers at the meetings. It could be done through disseminating written material, sending board members to conferences and seminars, etc. The exact format of the presentation is not as important as the fact that the material gets presented and the board members have a chance to consider it as an option for the future. No binding votes need be taken at this time. Nonmanagement staff can be informed through existing communication vehicles such as newsletters, staff meetings, and the like.

Lack of Communication about the Specific Alliance Being Proposed. Board members and others connected with the agency may have intellectual knowledge of alliances, but what will really make a difference to them is to know how it will affect their own organization. This is knowledge of the heart, and it is equal parts calculation and inspiration. Without a shared vision of the alliance's benefits, it will be seen as just another quirky idea of the executive director's.

Although at this stage the alliance will probably not have a plan in place, it is quite reasonable to communicate a broad overview of the alliance's direction. If the previous type of preparation was successful, the various constituencies of the nonprofit will be able to fill in the blanks between concept and execution. The problem here is that there is likely not to be a large amount of material available about the alliance except the initial analyses which may be impractical for broad audiences. Fortunately, the same education vehicles mentioned above will help get the message across.

Interruptions in Leadership. Few developments can destroy a growing alliance's momentum faster than leadership turnover. Not surprisingly, the most critical leadership disruptions occur among the planning group. Departures from some of the subcommittees can often be overcome once the groups are accustomed to working together. The alliance is most vulnerable at the point when the original leaders have begun to coalesce, but they have not achieved widespread acceptance of the alliance at all levels in all the participating agencies.

There are a few solutions to leadership interruptions. The strongest grows out of accomplishing institutional buy-in. When managers and staff are accustomed to participating in planning sessions, or when they have experienced victories firsthand, they will be among the first to orient a new executive director to the alliance. Prior to the point of achieving such widespread organizational interest, key people such as the board president or senior managers need to be sure to pass on the oral tradition of the alliance. Finally, other alliance members will need to assume responsibility for conducting at least an informal orientation with new executive directors.

Lack of Demonstrable Benefits. Board members will be particularly quick to pull the plug on an alliance that does not seem to be offering any clear-cut benefits. And, if after a reasonable time, the alliance is not fulfilling its promise, that is what should happen. But before individual boards withdraw or the membership as a whole decides to disband, it should be determined why the alliance isn't working.

Tip: Consider a Mega-Board Meeting

At a point in the early stages of alliance development, it is a good idea to consider some type of meeting involving all participants' boards of directors. A full board meeting will probably be unwieldy, so the meeting may have to be done on a representative basis (two representatives from each board, for example). It also needs to be facilitated very carefully, lest it become counterproductive (a single unfortunate remark in the mega-board meeting of mixed religious faith health care institutions set their alliance development process back a full six months). Still, the advantages of people seeing and hearing each other as leaders of their respective organizations are hard to match any other way.

If it is not working because planners misread the possible benefits or because structural obstacles to collaboration were uncovered late in the process, then termination makes sense. However, a more likely explanation is that the process itself is flawed. When members try to provide the alliance's staff support work themselves, the result can be a drifting, unfocused process. Before concluding that the alliance has no value, be sure that the process of making it work is not the culprit.

Stage 6: Workplan by Areas

Task-oriented alliances have it easy when it comes to planning the work. By selecting a single focus point for their efforts, they efficiently narrow the choices available to them. Knowing where they start from and what they want to accomplish, they can fill in the blanks with sensible steps. If they don't know what those steps should be, they can consult an expert.

Process alliances, however, do not have the benefit of a roadmap style of operating. Even though they can and should identify areas on which to focus, half of their work consists of going through a process of mutual discovery and applying the lessons they learn on the fly. It is as though they have to build the bus to take them on a journey while it is driving down the road.

Most managers in a start-up operation devise a plan for future action. Often it is called a business plan, and lenders and investors will usually insist on seeing a business plan before putting any money into the venture. Typically a business plan will contain an overall statement of the new organization's purpose and mission, research into potential markets, a plan for introducing the product or service, and some financial projections. Being aware of this practice, alliance members—or their own boards of directors—will often expect a business plan from the alliance. It is an understandable conclusion, but an impossible demand.

Process alliances are really a series of small business undertakings, each of which could legitimately have its own plan (assuming the task is complicated enough to warrant it—even if it isn't, the principle still holds). The ambiguity comes from the fact that often the specific tasks are not identified until well after the whole process has begun, and then they usually relate to something already accomplished.

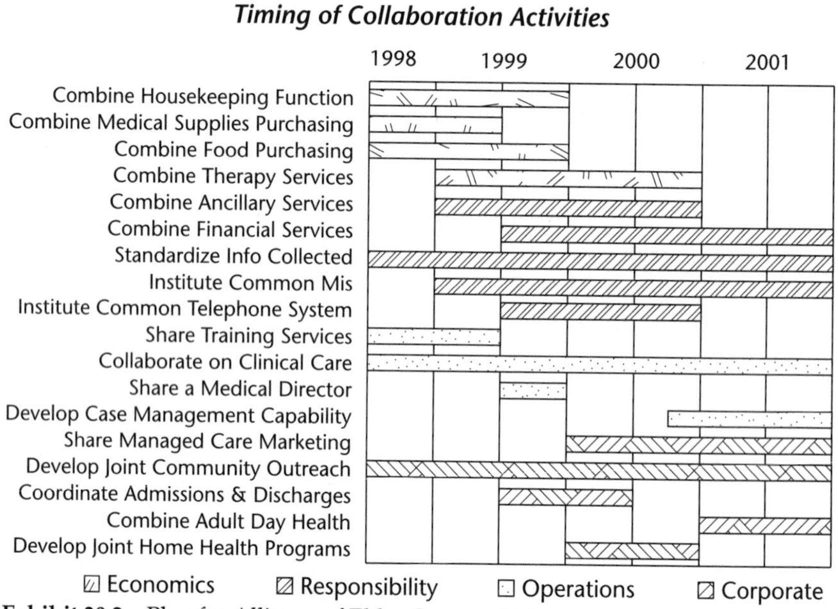

Exhibit 20.2 Plan for Alliance of Elder Care Facilities

Still, in spite of all these uncertainties, it is possible to outline a multiyear workplan for an alliance. Using the C.O.R.E. model will help determine what comes first and to what extent individual tasks should be pursued. Exhibit 20.2 illustrates a simplified plan for a hypothetical alliance of a group of elder-care facilities. The narrative interprets the plan.

Notice that, consistent with the time continuum implicit in the C.O.R.E. model, the alliance plans to pay early attention to economic collaboration. In this case, planners have identified four areas of focus and feel that three of them can be done right away. The fact that combining therapy services is planned for later implies that they believe it will be more difficult than the first three.

Of the responsibility areas for collaboration, the alliance will plan to concentrate on standardizing their information systems first. Considering the complexity of this area, it is no accident that standardizing the information they collect and manage is expected to be a multiyear effort. Operations people will usually find it easiest to integrate training activities early, which is why that is one of the first operations-related tasks to be attempted.

Developing a case management capability, while expected to be a major benefit to the alliance, simply cannot be done until much later in the process. Integrating around such a sensitive function will need a foundation of trust and organizational comfort in working together that will take years to build. Also, from a purely practical perspective, developing a case management system (meaning an administrative system capable of assessing consumers' needs and placing them in the most appropriate setting) needs to be preceded by a lot of work in information systems management and in determining clinical standards.

Finally, this alliance has decided to begin corporate level collaboration by developing joint community outreach or marketing programs, and to continue this effort throughout the life of the alliance. By contrast, it plans to leave potentially complicated projects requiring good working familiarity with each other to a later stage. While it may look like the Planning Committee isn't working hard for the first year or two, what is really happening is that it is overseeing and coordinating collaboration on all the other levels. After a year or two of working together on projects ranging from buying food supplies to sharing clinical training programs, the trust and familiarity levels will be adequate to permit corporate collaboration.

A final word on the chart. What is not shown here—and is extremely important—is serendipity. It won't take long before people at all levels of the member organizations will catch on to the power of the alliance. One idea will lead to another and an-

Tip: Joint Marketing on the Cheap

How does a self-defined alliance, existing only in the minds of its planners, go about introducing itself to the public? One such group came up with a quick and inexpensive idea at its very first meeting. A related community group was having a special event and selling ads in the program book. For a fraction of the cost of a full ad, each member of the budding alliance contributed its share of a single ad, which was signed with all the member organizations' names—instant joint marketing.

other. Paths that seemed to make sense at the beginning fade in comparison to more exciting and valuable projects that were conceived only because of some other success (or failure). Whole new directions and opportunities open up, while others close down or seem less appealing based on experience. As long as participants are prepared to incorporate these happy discoveries, the true workplan will be essentially a framework for opportunism. This is the kind of thing that management thinkers in the 1990s referred to as "learning organizations," and experiencing it is a treat for anyone connected with the project. The fact that it is accomplished by a network of organizations collaborating voluntarily makes it that much sweeter.

Stage 7: Formalized Operational Structure

Many alliances will never need to create a formalized operational structure. They will stick to lower-C.O.R.E.-level collaboration, or perhaps they will fade away over time. On the other hand, some will grow to the point where they need to form at least one legally sanctioned vehicle, and others may spin off initiatives which themselves will need to incorporate (this has been true mainly in the for-profit sector to date). The guiding principle for alliance structure should be the same as for mergers: let form follow function. This means that members will need to pay careful attention to their shared objectives because these will tell them how to shape the organization.

Groups of formerly independent executive directors collaborating via a process alliance for the first time are likely to respond emotionally to the question about formalizing a structure for the process. Some will prefer a legal entity from the beginning, while others may want to keep things informal as long as possible. In the beginning, this is a stylistic matter for the Governance–Planning Committee to resolve. At a certain point, however, the question stops being one of style and becomes one of substance.

For example, some alliances will be able to operate within the existing corporate structure and operations of one or more member organizations. These sponsoring nonprofits initially may donate or lease office space and provide supplies and equipment and maybe even staff time. It is the same model frequently used for small trade associations, where a large member of the association acts as an administrative parent of the association itself. As long as the sponsoring agency is comfortable with this type of arrangement and the members are satisfied with the services, there will be no problem.

It is probably more likely that alliances will persist in keeping matters informal too long rather than the reverse. Even if a few members want to incorporate or set up a formal partnership right at the beginning, there is a good chance that it won't happen. Formalizing a structure takes time, thought, competent legal advice, and at least a bit of start-up capital. Unless there is a strong reason for the members to come up with all of those things, it is easier to manage alliance affairs on the back of an envelope.

The things that will push an alliance away from this informal style tend to be economic forces or legal requirements so strong that a single entity cannot respond satisfactorily. As in mergers, they tend to be powerful enough considerations that they can greatly influence the choice of structure even in the absence of any other forces.

Capital Investment. Having to put a sizable sum of money into an alliance can be a catalyst for developing a legally recognized structure. This is similar to the initial investors in a start-up enterprise. The organization will need to purchase equipment, hire staff or consultants, make deposits on supplies and services, pay incidental fees, do research, and so on. Or, the alliance objective may simply call for acquiring a single piece of equipment, marketing study, or some other one-time-only purchase. Members will insist on having a recordkeeping system capable of keeping track of

Tip: Prepare to Make an Investment

It will be virtually impossible for an alliance to make broad and effective improvements in operations over a long period of time without each member making a capital contribution. How much? The answer to that question will depend on the alliance's goals, objectives, and strategies. Expect it to be more than petty cash. And don't expect to get it back soon.

their money and being able to show the linkage between what they are putting in and what they are getting back (even if it is not expected to occur for a few years).

Liability. As in mergers, liability may be a factor. If members expect to engage in activity that puts them at risk collectively or individually—and it is hard to imagine any activity of consequence that does *not* put organizations at some risk today—they will need to settle on a structure accordingly. Factors influencing liability are often driving forces behind choice of corporate or other vehicle. Partnerships, as described earlier, inherently determine the nature of participants' liability. Corporations will have more or less liability depending on local laws. One of the reasons for formalizing a structure is not so much to escape liability—if that were even possible—as much as it is to make the nature of the liability clear and predictable.

Market Advantage. Finally, participants may find that they gain important credibility in the market by forming a single joint vehicle. For health care nonprofits, the ability to negotiate as a block with payers could be vital. Aside from the administrative ease of committing a variety of organizations with a single signature, the designation of a vehicle sends symbolic messages of continuity and commitment to the long haul. Alliance members could find that the advantages of this move far outweigh the complexity and additional cost.

Note: For-Profits for Nonprofits (and vice versa)?

As more nonprofits explore various types of alliances, we may well encounter a paradox. Nonprofits may be well advised to establish for-profit alliance vehicles, while for-profits may want to establish nonprofits (though not public charities). Nonprofits may find it useful to have a for-profit outlet for their collective entrepreneurialism. For-profits, on the other hand, have all the incentives toward entrepreneurialism that they want. What they may need in an alliance is trust and accountability.

About the Disk

INTRODUCTION

Word Processing Files

(*Note:* Comparative tables are designed to permit unlimited entry of data; tables expand onto additional pages automatically.)

attques.doc (Companion file: attques.xls) It is the nature of nonprofit organizations that staff and board member attitudes are important. Although one cannot expect all parties to favor a particular merger—or even agree that a merger is desirable—it will help planners to be aware of the exact nature of support or resistance from these two key groups. Use this questionnaire and the companion summary worksheet to help determine the degree of acceptance or resistance to a proposed merger. Note that the top questions are about hopes, the bottom questions about fears. The companion worksheet provides an easy way to capture the data, which can then be manipulated, as desired, to produce insights into the perceptions of the two constituencies.

bylawcom.doc It will be essential to know the bylaws of each merger partner, if only to avoid unpleasant surprises such as learning of minimum meeting notice periods too late to be able to meet a deadline. This chart provides a handy form for summarizing key bylaw provisions. It should be completed early in the process and reviewed periodically to make sure that all requirements are being met. *Caution:* bylaws are frequently in the process of being rewritten. Be sure to use the version most recently approved by the board, not the draft version with the proposed changes.

duedil.doc One of the built-in problems with a due diligence process is that it tends to produce a great deal of paper which managers are tempted to either skim or ignore. This presentation grid allows planners to document the essential findings of a due diligence process.

hrcomp.doc Use this form to compare human resource policies such as fringe benefits, vacation and sick time policies, and many other fundamental human resource policies.

matrixa.doc Use this simple grid to document the various services offered by the agencies considering an alliance.

matrixm.doc This form will prompt merger partners to be diligent about identifying all of their programs. It can be expanded as necessary to accommodate more services. At this point, the definition of "service" is rightfully whatever definition that each agency has been using. Therefore, it may be misleading to make any comparisons between the two since they may not be using the same terminology.

merglnc.doc In the early stages of a merger, board members and staff participants in the planning effort will appreciate this form which assembles pivotal pieces of information in a single, easy-to-read manner.

Spreadsheet Files

(*Note:* Once data has been entered into them, spreadsheet files should be used to analyze and manipulate the data for whatever purposes planners may desire.)

bidsuma.xls This worksheet will help summarize purchasing activity for an alliance as it currently exists. Use it in the early stages of analyzing purchasing activity.

fintools.xlw One of the first questions that prospective merger partners must deal with is the financial compatibility of the two organizations. This worksheet helps present and analyze key financial performance indicators and lays the material side-by-side for easy comparisons.

salcomp.xls Since spending on personnel is usually the single largest routine expense of most nonprofits, it is important to know the differences between the organizations before making many major decisions. This worksheet offers a convenient way to summarize that information.

Salary Comparison. Use this form to document the key information *by salaried position type ("exempt")** for each agency in a merger.

Hourly Wage Comparison. Use this form to document the key information *by wage-earning position type ("nonexempt")* for each agency in a merger.

sitinven.xls Space allocation and usage will almost always be an issue in any merger between agencies of moderate size or larger. For the very largest merger partners, keeping track of dozens of different locations can be a major challenge. Use this worksheet to maintain a record of various physical sites involved in a merger. While designed to focus on physically separate sites, this worksheet can also be used to track programs: simply change the word "site" to "program" wherever it appears.

vendors.xlw This worksheet will help collaborating organizations to make a purchasing process more efficient. The first three worksheets are designed for use in a sequential process of research, analysis, and procurement. The fourth worksheet is for those groups wishing to analyze purchasing without necessarily going through a full bidder selection process. The worksheet is designed for alliances, but can easily be adapted for a merger process. It is recommended that one worksheet be used for each

---

*Exempt and nonexempt refer to whether an employee is subject to the provisions of the federal Fair Labor Standards Act, which covers such items as overtime payments. The most critical difference is that exempt employees do not have to be paid overtime. Note that exempt or nonexempt status is determined by federal policy, not agency choice.

type of purchasing such as office supplies or dairy products rather than for a long list of unrelated products.

In all cases, these files deal only with aspects of purchasing activity which can be quantified. They do not include intangibles such as delivery times, vendor consulting, credit policies, or other aspects of purchasing. An effective analysis will include all of these considerations.

Current Purchasing Summary. This worksheet will give a snapshot of current purchasing activity.

RFP Summary. Use this worksheet to document projected purchasing amounts, which may or may not be the same as the summary of all current purchasing. Then, print the worksheet and use it as part of a Request for Proposals (RFP) document to be sent to interested bidders. This can be done either by printing the document and asking vendors to fill it in by hand, or by sending each vendor a copy of the computer file. The latter method will allow vendor results to be cut and pasted, saving planners' some data inputting time.

RFP Analysis. This worksheet will summarize all responses to the RFP, by product and by vendor. Note that it will be important to be precise about the specifications submitted by vendors so that the horizontal comparisons will be valid.

Alternate Vendor Analysis. Alternately, some groups may just be interested in documenting current purchasing activity without going through a full RFP. This may be helpful in a merger or in an alliance that just wishes to compare notes among participants. This worksheet will produce a snapshot of current purchasing, comparing vendors by products.

Slideshow

slidesho.ppt This PowerPoint presentation was created as a self-education tool for board members and senior executives. It is intended to be viewed early in the process of considering a merger, and can be used either with or without a presenter. It should be printed as overheads or slides or used on a properly equipped computer linked to a projector. Key interpretations of each slide are in italics.

SYSTEM REQUIREMENTS

- IBM PC or compatible computer
- 3.5″ floppy disk drive
- Windows 3.1 or higher
- To use the files with a .DOC extension, you will need a word processing program capable of reading Microsoft Word for Windows 6.0 files.
- To use the files with an .XLS or .XLW extension, you will need a spreadsheet program capable of reading Microsoft Excel 5.0 files.
- To use the file with a .PPT extension, you will need Microsoft PowerPoint (version 4.0 or higher) presentation software.

HOW TO INSTALL THE FILES ONTO YOUR COMPUTER

If you would like to copy all the files from the disk to your hard drive, run the installation program provided on the disk. Running the installation program will copy the files to your hard drive in the default directory C:\MCLAUGH. To run the installation program, do the following:

1. Insert the enclosed disk into the floppy disk drive of your computer.
2. Windows 3.1 or NT 3.51: From the Program Manager, choose File, Run.
   Windows 95 or NT 4.0: From the Start Menu, choose Run.
3. Type **A:\SETUP** and press Enter.
4. The opening screen of the installation program will appear. Press Enter to continue.
5. The default destination directory is C:\MCLAUGH. If you wish to change the default destination, you may do so now. Follow the instructions on the screen.

6. The installation program will copy all files to your hard drive in the C:\MCLAUGH or user-designated directory.

USING THE FILES

Loading Files

To use the word processing files, launch your word processing program (e.g., Word or WordPerfect). Select File, Open from the pull-down menu. Select the appropriate drive and directory. If you installed the files to the default directory, the files will be located in the C:\MCLAUGH directory. A list of files should appear. If you do not see a list of files in the directory, you need to select WORD DOCUMENT (*.DOC) under Files of Type. Double click on the file you want to open.

To use the spreadsheet files, launch your spreadsheet program (e.g., Excel or Lotus). Select File, Open from the pull-down menu. Select the appropriate drive and directory. If you installed the files to the default directory, the files will be located in the C:\MCLAUGH directory. A list of files should appear. If you do not see a list of files in the directory, you need to select EXCEL (*.XLS, XLW) under Files of Type. Double click on the file you want to open.

To use the PowerPoint slideshow file, launch PowerPoint. Select File, Open from the pull-down menu. Select the appropriate drive and directory. If you installed the files to the default directory, the file will be located in the C:\MCLAUGH directory. Double click on the SLIDESHO.PPT file.

Printing Files

If you want to print the files, select File, Print from the pull-down menu.

Saving Files

When you have finished editing a file, you should save it under a new file name before exiting your program.

USER ASSISTANCE

If you need basic assistance with installation or if you have a damaged disk, please call Wiley technical support at (212) 850-6753, weekdays between 9 AM and 4 PM Eastern Standard Time. You can also email Wiley technical support at techhelp@wiley.com.

To place additional orders or to request information about other Wiley products, please call (800) 225-5945.

Index

CUSTOMER NOTE: IF THIS BOOK IS ACCOMPANIED BY SOFTWARE, PLEASE READ THE FOLLOWING BEFORE OPENING THE PACKAGE.

This software contains files to help you utilize the models described in the accompanying book. By opening the package, you are agreeing to be bound by the following agreement:

This software product is protected by copyright and all rights are reserved by the author, John Wiley & Sons, Inc., or their licensors. You are licensed to use this software on a single computer. Copying the software to another medium or format for use on a single computer does not violate the U.S. Copyright Law. Copying the software for any other purpose is a violation of the U.S. Copyright Law.

This software product is sold as is without warranty of any kind, either express or implied, including but not limited to the implied warranty of merchantability and fitness for a particular purpose. Neither Wiley nor its dealers or distributors assumes any liability for any alleged or actual damages arising from the use of or the inability to use this software. (Some states do not allow the exclusion of implied warranties, so the exclusion may not apply to you.)